Exploring Advice

Exploring Advice

# What You Need to Know About Good Financial Advice, a Quality Financial Plan and the Role of a Fiduciary

Kevin Knull, CFP®, and 39 Contributors

ISBN-13: 9781530710775
ISBN-10: 1530710774
Library of Congress Control Number: 2016905025
CreateSpace Independent Publishing Platform
North Charleston, South Carolina

**To my wife, Kirsten,
and my children, Hunter, Chase, and Scarlett,
who lovingly tolerate and support
my need to explore.**

A very special thanks goes out to my partners at PIEtech[SM,] Inc., Bob Curtis and Tony Leal, for having the vision, courage, and tenacity to stick with their unwavering goal of helping clients and advisors *Plan* better, *Invest* smarter, and *Enjoy* life more. PIEtech's resources, thought leadership and amazing culture helped make this project possible.

# Contents

**Kevin Knull, CFP®**
President

PIEtech℠, Inc.

One

# A Different Kind of Exploration

Have you ever felt the overwhelming desire to take the least traveled path in the hopes that you can see something new and different? Or perhaps to explore a subject so deeply as to learn something new or even find a better way? When you blaze a new trail, you almost always run into unexpected obstacles, and sometimes you even run into a dead end that forces you to retrace your steps to find your way back. But sometimes, if you are very lucky, that less-traveled trail rewards you with the experience of seeing something from a different point of view than everyone else. Occasionally, that path rewards you with a more enjoyable and efficient route. And once in a while, that new route changes everything. Whether as an officer in the U.S. Coast Guard searching for what was just over the horizon, a hiker heading off of the beaten path, or a fly fisherman seeking a fish that's never been caught miles up a remote stream in the wilderness, the need to explore and find a better way consumes me. But this book represents a different kind of exploration — it represents my goal to help improve the financial industry. I invite you to join me as I continue my journey — exploring advice.

## The search for a definition

A few years ago while speaking on a panel at an industry meeting, I was asked to describe the future of financial advice. Before responding, I thought it was important to first ask the audience three questions:

1) What is the definition of advice; better yet, what is the definition of good advice?
2) What is the definition of a quality financial plan?
3) What does it mean to be a fiduciary?

The audience, comprised of financial planning and wealth management firm leaders, was unable to answer these questions … and I have wrestled with them since.

As I posed these questions to others, they too struggled with the answers. Our industry has been delivering advice and financial plans for decades, yet the answers to the questions above remain ambiguous. Consumers today are under more pressure than ever to take an active role in securing their financial future, and there exists a very real distrust of the industry given the malfeasance of a few over the past decade. If the financial services industry is unable to define good advice or a quality financial plan, then it's probably unfair to assume that consumers know whether they are receiving good advice or what should be included in a quality financial plan. Do consumers understand when a financial advisor is required to act in their best interest, or do they already assume that is always the case? How will they know that the advice recommended and delivered is truly in their best interest?

The last question is central to the discussion about the protection of consumers and the changes from the U.S. Department of Labor (DOL) in regards to best interest standards. It is time we define good advice and a quality financial plan for the benefit of our clients, firms and our industry.

## What you will get from this book

Rather than writing an entire book of my own opinions, this book brings together the experience and knowledge of some of the most sought after thought leaders in our industry. They share their original, uninfluenced thoughts, stories and advice. You will also see how the quantitative research and data from financial advisors and plans highlight similarities and disparities around the three questions mentioned previously.

The first few chapters are my own observations based on thousands of client meetings, in-depth research, volumes of data and hundreds of conversations with advisors, regulators, attorneys, etc. These early chapters reveal what I personally perceive to be good advice and what it means to be a fiduciary, outline the key components that ought to be considered in a quality financial plan and identify some best practices to utilize while building a plan.

The quantitative data contained herein includes input from over 1,600 financial professionals across all types of business models, compensation structures and credentials. The consensus among advisors about the necessary elements of a quality financial plan are explored and then compared to the data from more than one million actual financial plans created by financial advisors.

The next set of chapters is unique in that they contain the insights from some of the most influential people in the financial services industry. You will have the opportunity to learn from chief executive officers and the heads of financial planning and wealth management from wire houses, regional and independent broker-dealers, and global and regional banks. You can explore the minds of principals of registered investment advisory firms and the thoughts of key individuals from law firms, technology providers, the media, academia, consultants to the financial services industry and even a former U.S. Securities and Exchange (SEC) Commissioner. Each contributor adds depth and a different perspective to these topics with which our industry is struggling.

In an effort to genuinely maintain the purity of each person's voice, thoughts and vision, I have dedicated a chapter to each of the contributors in which they share their uninfluenced and unedited opinions — and sometimes their firm's point of view regarding what you need to know about good advice. They outline how to approach a quality financial plan and explain the relationship that is essential between a financial advisor and a client in order to be successful. They also share their thoughts on what it means to be a fiduciary, what the future holds for financial planning and talk about the catalysts for change and what to watch for. Some answer all three questions, some focus on one question, and some even focus on an aspect of a question. All, however, were given the exact same three questions to answer.

This book is intended to be a real representation of the industry's perspective and may be the first time, in one place, you will see direct competitors willingly giving their uninfluenced opinions side-by-side. These topics — good financial advice, what constitutes a quality financial plan and what it means to be a fiduciary, are critical to conducting business in the financial services industry today and in the future, and each contributor was impassioned to share their opinion in their words.

You may find the contributors' positions insightful, challenging, disturbing or perhaps even offensive. The thoughts portrayed by each are his or hers alone and do not necessarily reflect my position, my firm, or that of the other contributors on the topic(s). Regardless, the point of this book is to start the conversation and to equip you with information to consider different ways of addressing these questions.

After reviewing the contributors' chapters and analyzing the data, although varied at how each arrived at their own conclusion, I found it comforting and satisfying that while the contributors come from different business models and different parts of the industry, the recurring themes throughout are similar. It's fascinating that so many contributors and survey respondents arrived at a similar place, but the journey each took as they explored the questions was completely different.

This book is not about investment advice, strategies or financial products. It is my vision that the insight presented will help formulate or further develop your approach to the topics at large and how you think about the advisor-client relationship. It is my hope that by exploring the definition of good financial advice, the elements of a quality financial plan and the role of a fiduciary in today's world, we can collectively improve the quality of advice rendered to investors.

**Kevin Knull, CFP®**
President

PIEtech℠, Inc.

Two

# What Is Good Advice and What Is the Role of a Fiduciary?

What is the definition of advice? This is a difficult question, but the better question would be to ask, what is the definition of 'good' advice? Financial professionals are paid by clients to render, ostensibly, "good" financial advice. I doubt anyone would want to pay for bad advice. As an industry, we do not get graded on whether our advice is good or bad. Most of the time, an advisor only learns the client considered his or her advice "bad" when it is discovered that the client has moved on to another advisor — or worse yet, filed a complaint. If there were a clear definition of good advice, what it really means to be a fiduciary, or performance measures to track the quality of their advice, perhaps advisors would be better able to define their offering and clients would have a better understanding of an advisor's value.

The U.S. Department of Labor (DOL) has stepped in to help yield change by fueling a new paradigm for good financial advice. While the new rules don't eliminate the risk of bad advice, they are designed to help provide guidance and set expectations around the advisor-client relationship. Most advisors and firms assert that they are currently and have always acted in their client's best interests, but many agree that a full and holistic understanding of every client's situation will be necessary in order to comply with the new rules.

For advisors, these changes should yield an improved quality of service as they disclose and eliminate conflicts of interest and, due to these new regulations, must act in an enhanced fiduciary capacity for all clients who have IRA and ERISA governed retirement accounts under the purview of the advisor.

## The new standard for good financial advice

In April 2016, the U.S. Department of Labor (DOL) issued two new rules that will forever change how financial services firms must conduct business. The first rule sets new requirements for a fiduciary standard by extending the fiduciary/best interest requirements formerly limited to Employee Retirement Income Security Act (ERISA) plans to all individual retirement accounts (IRAs). The second rule sets legal limitations for fiduciary actions by making it impermissible for advisors and brokers to receive variable compensation, such as commissions, 12(b)-1 fees, and ticket charges, unless they are covered under the Best Interest Contract Exemption (BICE). For a thorough explanation of these rules, please see Marcia Wagner's chapter later in this book.

In the first rule, the fiduciary requirement is defined: [An advisor must give advice that is in the] Retirement Investor's Best Interest (i.e., prudent advice that is based on the investment objectives, risk tolerance, financial circumstances, and needs of the Retirement Investor, without regard to financial or other interests of the Adviser, Financial Institution, or their Affiliates, Related Entities or other parties).

My interpretation of the new regulations is simply this — **"good advice" is advice rendered in the client's best interests — and one must fully "understand the client" in order to comply.**

This new definition of a fiduciary in IRA and ERISA accounts will force some advisors, for the first time, to answer the question "what is good advice" and genuinely think about "what it means to act as a fiduciary." The new rules requiring "good advice" may have some advisors evaluating their business models because it may no longer be possible to operate as they have in the past. Advisors can no longer "sell" a single product without considering the client's total financial circumstances and fully understanding the client going forward — and this is a very significant change for our industry.

## "Know Your Customer" rule morphs into "Understand Your Client"

Before the recent DOL rules were released, registered representatives operated under Financial Industry Regulatory Authority (FINRA) Rule 2090 — the "Know Your Customer" (KYC) rule — which represented a suitability standard that did not require an advisor to ensure recommendations were in the client's best interest. Essentially, the KYC rule was created to prevent "bad" advice with respect to a particular product, that is, to prevent a product recommendation that was likely to have one or more undesirable outcomes for the client. The KYC rule was created to help prevent brokers and advisors from selling inappropriate products to their clients which might result in long surrender charge periods, illiquidity, inappropriate risk exposures, high fees, or other undesirable and inappropriate outcomes given the client's situation. The KYC rule allowed an advisor to look at a product in a vacuum, because there was no requirement to evaluate how that product interacted with all of the other investments. In most cases, the advisor didn't have to do much more than document total net worth and have the client complete a brief risk tolerance questionnaire of 8-15 questions. The new DOL regulations effectively shift from the "Know Your Customer" standard to a new, "Understand Your Client" requirement, if I may coin a phrase. Why? Because without truly understanding your client, it will be very difficult to ensure that your recommendations are in their best interest. "Understand Your Client" is my summation of the path to success when operating under the new DOL rules.

I believe that the most significant takeaway of the new fiduciary rule that cannot be ignored is that **the Best Interest standard places the burden of proof on the advisor.**

In the months leading up to and following the release of the DOL's fiduciary rule, I spoke with hundreds of financial firms and found that most were focusing on the most obvious, but perhaps less important, aspects of the rule. Financial advisors and firms must act in a retirement investor's best interest, yet may be so focused on creating a BICE contract and a fee comparison that they are missing the most important fact. The DOL rules aren't really about fees or conflicts of interests — the rules are really all about the client. Said differently, they are about ensuring that the client's best interests are served. Period. Yes, fees and disclosure of conflicts of interest are important, but the rules are really attempting to make sure the client's best interests are met regardless of the business model.

## How do you deliver good advice?

For advisors, the question we are left pondering is — how do we know we are actually delivering good advice? The DOL rule essentially states you must understand a client's overall financial circumstances, needs, risks, goals, etc., but how do you do that? How do you extract from a client the necessary information needed to be able to provide good advice and act in their best interest as a fiduciary? While there will certainly be more ways than one to accomplish this, I believe that creating a quality financial plan will likely be the easiest, most prudent, and valuable method of doing so. More specifically, if you create a quality financial plan you will be able to extract most of (but perhaps not all) the necessary information to fully understand the client. As an alternative, firms may be able to meet the new requirements through a very thorough discovery process, but the evaluation of how all of the data interacts is ultimately going to be very difficult without a plan or robust evaluation tool.

When we asked more than 1,600 financial advisors whether they could fulfill the role of a fiduciary without a quality financial plan — 48 percent said "no" and 11 percent said they "didn't know." But good advice, acting as a fiduciary and a quality financial plan should go hand in hand.

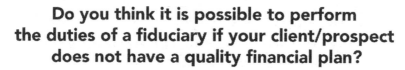

**Do you think it is possible to perform the duties of a fiduciary if your client/prospect does not have a quality financial plan?**

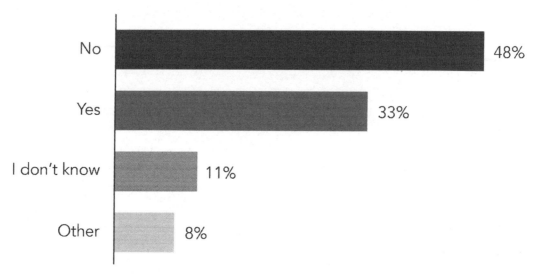

*Advisors believe that a quality financial plan plays a critical role in performing the duties of a fiduciary.*

# Learn from the physicians

Most advisors could learn a thing or two from the medical profession. Physicians have long been perfecting the practice of gathering information from patients. They, collectively, have determined that "good" advice cannot be rendered without the most complete assessment possible. In the medical world, the standardized solution to understanding the patient is to ensure a patient completes a "medical history" and symptom questionnaire, a cursory examination by a nurse, a thorough examination by a physician, and then further diagnostic tests the physician deems appropriate to gather more information.

I recently sought the help of a physician for something that was causing me pain. Prior to the appointment, I received an email which required me to complete an online medical history and symptom questionnaire. The instructions were quite clear, "If you do not complete this questionnaire prior to your arrival we will reschedule your appointment." I didn't have a choice — I was hurting and wanted to get better, so I did as instructed and completed the form. When I arrived at the physician's office, this electronic process streamlined my visit and I never even had the chance to sit down in the waiting room. The nurse took me into the exam room, took my vitals, reviewed my answers to the questionnaire, and proceeded to ask all the same questions again with a slightly different approach. This resulted in the discovery of a few more relevant pieces of information. When I met with the physician, his additional questions surfaced another key point of information that was materially relevant to my situation. Why do they keep asking the same questions in slightly different ways? Because in the medical profession if you leave out a detail, such as the medications the patient is currently taking, a new prescription could interact with the others and potentially kill the patient. It's pretty serious stuff.

Similarly, in the financial services profession, the conversation between an advisor and a client yields critical information not discoverable on any form. Some telltale signs are the way a client shifts in his or her seat when you discuss family life expectancy or the way a spouse holds his or her breath when discussing market volatility. Human empathy, experience, dialogue, and body language allow advisors to explore the real areas of concern to their clients. And that cannot be done by anything other than a human — at least, not yet. Stay tuned as artificial intelligence continues to improve.

Let's fast forward to sometime after April 10, 2017 when the fiduciary rule goes into effect. You, an advisor, or another advisor from your firm is among the first unlucky advisors to be called before an arbitration panel following a market correction. A former client has filed a lawsuit alleging that your recommendations were not in their best interest. Much like the prescription analogy above, a critical piece of information, such as identifying that the client had been diagnosed with a terminal illness immediately prior to being allocated into a portfolio of products, could have resulted in a completely different portfolio had the advisor asked a question about any current medical conditions. Check your risk tolerance questionnaires — you will probably find that a question about current health conditions doesn't exist on yours, or on anyone's risk tolerance questionnaire. It is likely that knowing about the client's illness would have caused you to adjust how you thought about investing that client, and I doubt seriously the panel (or jury) is going to side against the dying patient. She wouldn't know that her health would have a bearing on how you would invest her, and no reasonable prudent person would expect her to know. You are the professional and should have known to ask the question.

Under the new DOL rules, the client does not have the burden of proof. The burden of proof now falls on the advisor. What does that mean? It means that the advisor needs to demonstrate that he or she understood the client's needs and objectives and acted in the client's best interests. That understanding must happen *before* advice is rendered to the retirement investor on or after April 10th, 2017.

Even if a financial plan was outside of the scope of your engagement with the client, missing just one important fact can completely convert your "good" advice into "bad" advice. The above example shows how key information might very likely alter the advice rendered, especially as it relates to time horizon, liquidity needs, etc. You can't expect clients to volunteer information — they may not connect the dots to realize how a key piece of information may alter advice provided.

The allocation or recommendation might have been appropriate for the client's market risk tolerance, but failure to collect enough data to "understand" the client's situation exposes the client, the advisor, and the firm to additional risk. A financial plan may not be necessary to discover this sort of information or to render investment advice, but the well-developed process necessary to develop a quality financial plan would likely have uncovered this issue and might have been a more prudent approach.

## The "human value" of a financial advisor

The example of the visit to the doctor calls to mind the various robo-advisor solutions available today. Robo-advisors face the same problem of being able to identify required, relevant information from their clients. How will robo-advisors discover this level of information without a human applying both the art and science of the discovery process? I believe the human advisor will continue to be the key to obtaining the pertinent information so as to operate in the client's best interest. My proof? Vanguard is now offering personalized advice to its clients, Financial Engines recently purchased The Mutual Fund Store franchise to add human advisors to their offering, and most of the robo-advisors have begun shifting to a business to business (B-to-B) model.

I believe that good financial advisors and planners will continue to be necessary until artificial intelligence can actually *care* about the client.

## The biggest mistake our industry ever made

The biggest mistake our industry ever made was to charge on the investments and then give everything else away for free. Whether an advisor is paid through commissions or through fees based on assets under management (AUM), neither model clearly communicates the value of the services the financial advisor provides to the client. The robo-advisor space has capitalized on our industry's failure to communicate the value of the advisor, and by charging 25 basis points permanently commoditized asset management. The truth is, asset management may never have been worth much more than 25 basis points, but the real issue is that investors are now comparing 25 basis points in fees to the 125 basis points a typical fee-only or fee-based advisor might charge. That is not a fair comparison. The client should take into account all of the other services being rendered in a full-service traditional advisor relationship. Consider this table.

## A Comparison of Robo Advisor and
## Traditional Advisor Service & Fee Models – An Example

| Robo Advisor | | Traditional Advisor | | Service |
|---|---|---|---|---|
| Yes | 0.25% | Yes | 0.25% | Initial investment allocation and quarterly rebalancing |
| No | N/A | Yes | 0.20% | Initial financial plan |
| No | N/A | Yes | 0.10% | Semi-annual financial plan update |
| No | N/A | Yes | 0.25% | Managing client behavior & expectations |
| No | N/A | Yes | 0.10% | Operational (Ensuring RMDs, ensuring IRA contributions, etc.) |
| No | N/A | Yes | 0.10% | Insurance analysis / improvement |
| No | N/A | Yes | 0.15% | Estate planning |
| No | N/A | Yes | 0.10% | Personalized investment research and due diligence |
| Total | 0.25% | | 1.25% | |

Each of the above services has real value. For example, client advice on debt management may provide greater value for most clients than finding a slightly better performing portfolio. Perhaps the reason the industry didn't specifically list out each advice item was because it creates additional accountability, or more likely this is just the result of business models developing as they did over time. Perhaps there is some other reason. Regardless, going forward it is going to become increasingly necessary to illustrate the value of the services rendered in order to compete within the new regulatory/fiduciary environment in which we now operate.

## A Hippocratic-style Oath for the financial services industry

Although the DOL has issued the new rules, the industry has a lot of work to do to "internalize" and even "formalize" what it means to act in a client's best interest in everyday practice. The best interest requirement of the fiduciary rule is similar to the "first do no harm" rule under which physicians practice. The modern Hippocratic Oath, originally written in 1964 by Louis Lasagna, Academic Dean of the School of Medicine at Tufts University, would probably be a very good rule of thumb for the financial services industry. It reads as follows …

> "I will apply, for the benefit of the sick, all measures which are required, avoiding those twin traps of overtreatment and therapeutic nihilism…I will not be ashamed to say "I know not"…I will prevent disease whenever I can, for prevention is preferable to cure…I will remember that there is art to medicine as well as science, and that warmth, sympathy, and understanding may outweigh the surgeon's knife or the chemist's drug…I will remember that I remain a member of society, with special obligations to all my fellow human beings, those sound of mind and body as well as the infirm."

Until now, we've had multiple business models that permitted some advisors and firms to put their own business interests ahead of the clients' best interests. The new rules change the game. If advisors were to adhere to a similar oath in the financial services industry, I believe that it would help to act in a client's best interest and as a fiduciary — every day.

## There is "no safe harbor"

One of the most unfortunate items missing from the DOL's fiduciary rule is a clear roadmap for financial professionals to ensure recommendations are in the best interests of the client. There is no "safe harbor" or bare minimum requirements necessary to meet the best interest standard. The elegance of the "principles-based" DOL rules is that it leaves the interpretation of the rule to the courts. This makes sense if you think about it — had the DOL issued a "rules-based" regulation, then some firms would only strive to meet the absolute bare minimum. The DOL has established a best interest require-ment, not a minimum interest requirement, "OK" interest requirement, or even "better" interest requirement. They don't say one should act according to the "best interest-*ish*" standards. The ambiguity of the rule, however, creates a real challenge for advisors.

## The bottom line

In a post-DOL world, advisors must be able to answer one very important question, **"How will you defend that your recommendations were in the best interests of your client?"** Perhaps even more specifically, "How will you prove you engaged the client in a dialogue that allowed you to understand their mental, emotional, physical, and financial state with enough clarity that you could make the appropriate recommen-dations?" Most reading this will likely be saying, "Yikes! I don't have an answer." If you don't have immediate answers to the above questions, you may want to study the next chapter.

And please note, while the DOL rules do not specifically mention the words "finan-cial planning," the rules repeatedly mention, albeit generally, all of the elements that would comprise a financial plan. Client goals, needs, objectives, overall financial circum-stances, risks, etc., are all components of a quality financial plan.

## Acting in a client's best interests is "just common sense"

The DOL rule is a step toward protecting investors from those advisors that prefer to put their own interests first. Contrary to what is published in newspapers, magazines, and on the internet, I believe the vast majority of financial advisors provide good advice, care about their clients, and only want to do what is in their best interests. After years of maintaining a relationship, most advisors become dear friends with their clients, and often the advisor has more intimate knowledge of a client's situation than even their own children. Unfortunately, the unscrupulous few have spoiled it for the whole lot, and here we are with new guidelines.

John "Jack" Bogle, the founder of Vanguard, and without question one of the single most influential industry thought leaders of our time, said it perfectly, "Acting in the cli-ent's best interests is just common sense." I can't say it better than that. That is the role of the fiduciary in today's world.

**Kevin Knull, CFP®**
President

PIEtech℠, Inc.

Three

# What Is a Quality Financial Plan?

As the industry shifts from a transactional culture to one of advice and planning, most financial advisors will create financial plans for their clients — but the quality of these plans is going to vary widely. Even if the DOL had set the requirement for every fiduciary to ensure their clients have updated financial plans in place before advice is rendered, we would still be faced with the question, "What is a quality financial plan?" The next two chapters will explore this question, both quantitatively and qualitatively.

## A quality financial plan is not...

A quality financial plan is not a 200-page static, printed report, nor does it necessarily have to be comprehensive and contemplate every single possible outcome or scenario. If we as an industry were to require everyone to have a comprehensive financial plan before providing advice, investors would be waiting a long time for good advice. Despite the many variables that should be contemplated in a financial plan, I have found some dominating themes that I believe are essential to creating a quality financial plan. These themes are echoed and validated by the many advisors and thought-leading contributors to this book and are key to an advisor's ability to provide clients with quality financial plans.

# A quality financial plan is....

In my opinion, a "quality" financial plan is goals-based, collaborative, dynamic, current, incremental, engaging, addresses the issues relevant to the individual client or couple, and dare I say it......is fun! Let's face it, there's nothing better than finding ways to get greater enjoyment out of one's retirement, right? Above all else, a quality financial plan must include the key components necessary to be able to render "good" advice.

Since there exists no formal definition of what constitutes a quality financial plan, we set out to "crowdsource" the definition. In March of 2016, our firm conducted an extensive survey of all types of advisors titled, "What is a Quality Financial Plan?" With contributions from 1,653 seasoned financial professionals from all types of business models, credentials, and compensation structures, we received an overwhelming consistency across the data set.[1]

Regardless of the type of advisor, there were no statistical differences between the respondents' answers regardless of education, compensation structure, firm type, licenses, or business model. Of those that participated, most held a CFP®, CFA®, MBA, or PhD designation or degree. Seventy-four percent held insurance licenses or had someone in their office who possessed an insurance license. The most common pricing model was fee based (a combination of fees and commissions) and less than 7 percent modeled a flat fee, hourly or salary model. The median tenure of the respondents was 16 years (average 17 years).

---

1 There is likely a survey bias in the data. Despite the fact that there were 1,653 respondents, it is likely those that participated were interested in financial planning and therefore were more likely to complete the survey. Only 25 percent of the survey respondents were MoneyGuidePro® subscribers, and 25 firms invited financial advisors to participate in the survey.

## Attributes of 1,653 survey participants

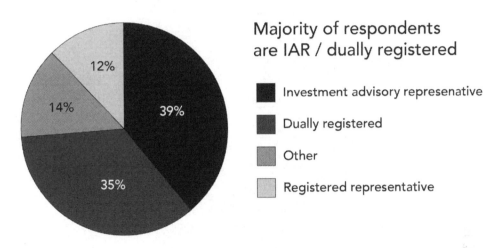

### Majority of respondents are IAR / dually registered

- ■ Investment advisory represenative
- ■ Dually registered
- ▨ Other
- ▨ Registered representative

## Attributes of 1,653 survey participants

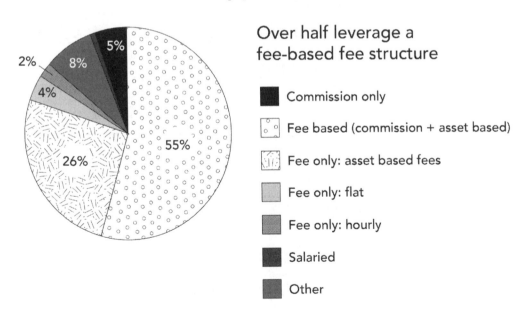

### Over half leverage a fee-based fee structure

- ■ Commission only
- ▫ Fee based (commission + asset based)
- ▨ Fee only: asset based fees
- ▨ Fee only: flat
- ▨ Fee only: hourly
- ■ Salaried
- ▨ Other

## Attributes of 1,653 survey participants

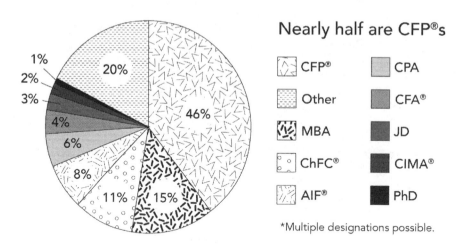

Nearly half are CFP®s

| | |
|---|---|
| CFP® | CPA |
| Other | CFA® |
| MBA | JD |
| ChFC® | CIMA® |
| AIF® | PhD |

*Multiple designations possible.

The conclusions are drawn from the findings of the survey mentioned and then compared to the data contained in a random sampling of 1 million financial plans created by financial advisors. What I found fascinating is that despite advisors' overwhelming consensus of the key elements that should be included in a quality financial plan, many of today's financial advisors overlook (or even ignore) many of those elements when providing financial plans to their clients. Please take the time to look at each section, and pay close attention to the overwhelming agreement among advisors as to what should be included in a quality financial plan.

## The quantitative "stuff" — start with the client's expectations

A quality financial plan should always start with a discussion of a client's expectations. Expectations tend to describe the intangible, qualitative desires of the client. They might indicate a desire to have an active lifestyle or quiet lifestyle, time to travel, a need to help others, time with friends or family, start a new business, or even to work when they want to. Most of these behavioral-type expectations tend to lead to the discovery of tangible goals — goals that might be missed if the topic isn't discussed. For example, if a couple wants to help others but then doesn't have a bequest goal, knowing the client has the expectation might cause the advisor to ask further questions. Ninety-nine percent of advisors consider it necessary to explore expectations when delivering a quality financial plan.

## Advisor opinion – expectations

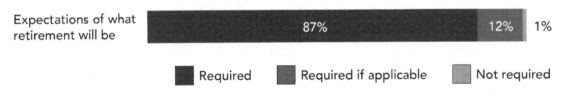

*Ninety-nine percent of advisors consider it necessary to explore a client's expectations of retirement when delivering a quality financial plan.*

## Include client concerns

For most people, financial advice is one of those things that you don't really worry about until there is a pain point. An investor may be approaching retirement, selling a business, going through a divorce, have lost a spouse — it usually takes one of these life events or something similar for an individual to engage the help of a financial advisor. We can certainly argue that everyone needs and deserves a quality financial plan, but in reality, most will procrastinate until often their choices are limited. Rather than waiting for an event to occur, try asking the client, "What are your greatest concerns in retirement?" This is not unlike the physician asking, "Where does it hurt?" In my personal experience delivering thousands of client seminars and client meetings, this is the question that elicits the most information.

The most common concerns expressed by clients, according to the data, were:

**Money**

☐ No longer having a paycheck

☐ Running out of money

☐ Suffering investment losses

☐ Leaving money to others

**Health**

☐ Cost of health or LTC

☐ Current/future health issues

☐ Early death

☐ Living too long

☐ Getting Alzheimer's

**Personal & Family**

☐ Parents needing care

☐ Too much time together

☐ Being bored

Once again, 99 percent of advisors stated concerns should be explored when creating a quality financial plan.

## Advisor opinion – concerns

General concerns or "worries" about retirement: 85% Required | 14% Required if applicable | 1% Not required

*Ninety-nine percent of advisors believe that a client's concerns about retirement need to be explored when creating a quality financial plan.*

## Explore the client's goals

Goals are the foundation of any quality financial plan and can be separated into three types: needs, wants, and wishes. "Needs" goals can be described as the goals required to subsist in retirement such as food, shelter, clothing, utilities, taxes, health care, home maintenance, and transportation. It is important to split these out, particularly because many of them inflate at different rates. For example, if health care expenses are inflating at an average rate of 6.5 percent, then bundling this expense with another goal and inflating it at the consumer price index (CPI) would result in a gross underestimation of the costs that are going to be experienced in retirement.

Wants are discretionary goals such as travel, home improvement projects, fun money, club memberships, large celebrations, education for children/grandchildren, and other goals that typically represent those things that a person might consider the "fun" part of retirement. These goals can be reduced if times get tough, but for many they are less negotiable than one might think. Often people will choose to save more or retire later in order to realize these types of goals.

Wishes are just that — the aspirational types of goals that might include leaving an inheritance, gifting money to one's alma mater, or perhaps buying that long desired beach house.

The most common goals represented in financial plans are:

### Needs

☐ Basic retirement needs (food, clothing, shelter, taxes, utilities, home maintenance)

☐ Health care costs in retirement (Medicare Part B/D, Medigap, out-of-pocket expenses)

☐ Transportation costs

### Wants

☐ Travel goals

☐ Second vehicle goals

☐ Education goals

☐ Major purchase goals

☐ Home improvement goals

### Wishes

☐ Major purchase goal

☐ Leave bequest goal

☐ Charitable goals

Ninety-six percent of survey respondents stated that **all** of the above goals should be discussed and/or incorporated in a quality financial plan. Additional goals listed were a desire to fund long term care, eliminate debt, address special needs, plan for business succession goals, etc.

## Advisor opinion – goals

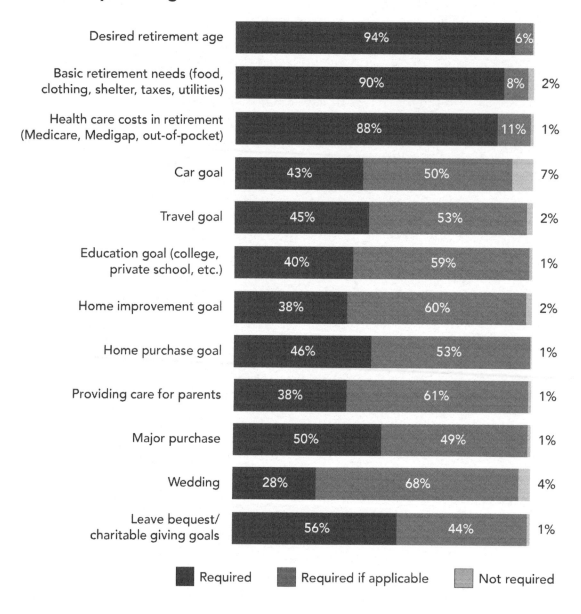

| Goal | Required | Required if applicable | Not required |
|---|---|---|---|
| Desired retirement age | 94% | | 6% |
| Basic retirement needs (food, clothing, shelter, taxes, utilities) | 90% | 8% | 2% |
| Health care costs in retirement (Medicare, Medigap, out-of-pocket) | 88% | 11% | 1% |
| Car goal | 43% | 50% | 7% |
| Travel goal | 45% | 53% | 2% |
| Education goal (college, private school, etc.) | 40% | 59% | 1% |
| Home improvement goal | 38% | 60% | 2% |
| Home purchase goal | 46% | 53% | 1% |
| Providing care for parents | 38% | 61% | 1% |
| Major purchase | 50% | 49% | 1% |
| Wedding | 28% | 68% | 4% |
| Leave bequest/ charitable giving goals | 56% | 44% | 1% |

*Most advisors agree that a detailed exploration of goals is necessary in a quality plan. At the very least, they agree that the above goals should be explored with a client.*

## The sad fact about goals

In reality, most financial advisors fail to include the goals desired by the client, presumably because they don't see the value of identifying individual goals in the process. Despite the previous chart indicating that 12 goals should be explored with a client, **today's average advisor-driven plan contains only 2.7 goals.**[2] Typically this means that the advisor puts in a total amount for the "needs" goals and a total amount for the discretionary or "wants" goals. This represents missed opportunities for both the advisor and client, and likely means that many plans are significantly underestimating the amount of money a client requires in retirement. So why the discrepancy between the two? My guess is that too many financial plans are still created without the involvement of the client, meaning the detailed goal conversations are just not happening. My proof of this? When given the opportunity to enter goals themselves, clients enter an average of 7.5 goals.

### Clients enter more goals than advisors

Advisor-driven plans average
**2.7 goals** per plan

VS.

Client-driven plans average
**7.5 goals** per plan

*When given the opportunity, clients include almost three times the number of goals that advisors typically include in a financial plan. More goals can both improve the directional accuracy of a plan and create new opportunities for the advisor to engage the client.*

## Get into the personal information

At some point you have to explore some of the ugly stuff. No one wants to talk about personal health conditions, life expectancy, or even their income. As soon as an advisor begins asking these questions it becomes a bit intrusive — but you can't skip them if you are going to create a quality financial plan. According to the research, advisors clearly believe that personal information is essential in creating a quality plan, including the following:

---

2 2016 MoneyGuidePro® aggregated data analysis of 1 million financial plans.

## What Is a Quality Financial Plan?

☐ Ages/dates of birth     ☐ Employment income     ☐ Personal health condition

☐ Marital status     ☐ Other income     ☐ State of residence

☐ Dependent info     ☐ Life expectancy     ☐ Smoking preference

## Advisor opinion – personal information

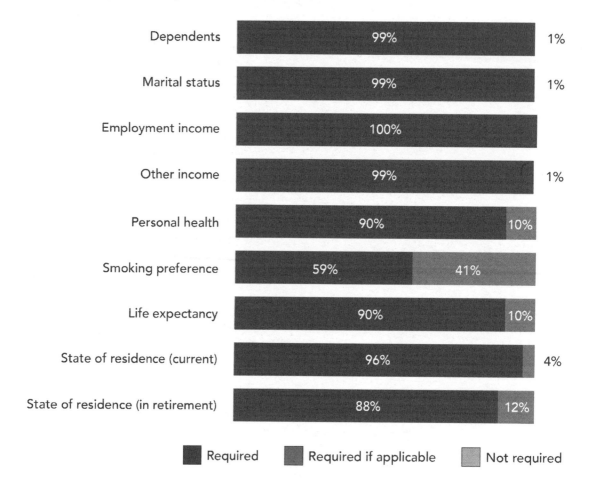

*While the majority of advisors agree that basic personal information is necessary, surprisingly personal health and smoking preference are often overlooked when building a quality financial plan.*

What is odd is that 41 percent of advisors stated that smoking preference is not required information. The first question every consumer is asked when applying for life insurance is, "Do you smoke?" It's also a key factor in evaluating longevity risk and causes a meaningful reduction in life expectancy — a critical component to planning.

Additionally, it is interesting that 10 percent of advisors said both personal health and life expectancy are not required. Skipping these variables could lead to an incomplete plan in terms of product recommendations and investment allocation (based on time horizon).

## Identify all of the client's resources

Nearly all advisors agree that a complete list of a client's assets should be included in a quality plan. This is not surprising as firms and advisors are currently compensated primarily based on how these resources are invested. For most advisors, it is a race to get this information so that they can size or quantify the complexity of the client's situation (and evaluate how much time he or she can spend on the client's case). Examples of resources that should be included according to survey data:

**Retirement Income**

☐ Sources of retirement income

☐ Social security optimization

☐ Pension options

☐ Annuity income

**Assets**

☐ Emergency account

☐ Taxable accounts

☐ Tax deferred accounts

☐ Other assets

☐ Willingness to save more

**Employer Based Accounts**

☐ Retirement accounts

☐ Deferred compensation

☐ Stock options

☐ Restricted stock

## Advisor opinion – resources

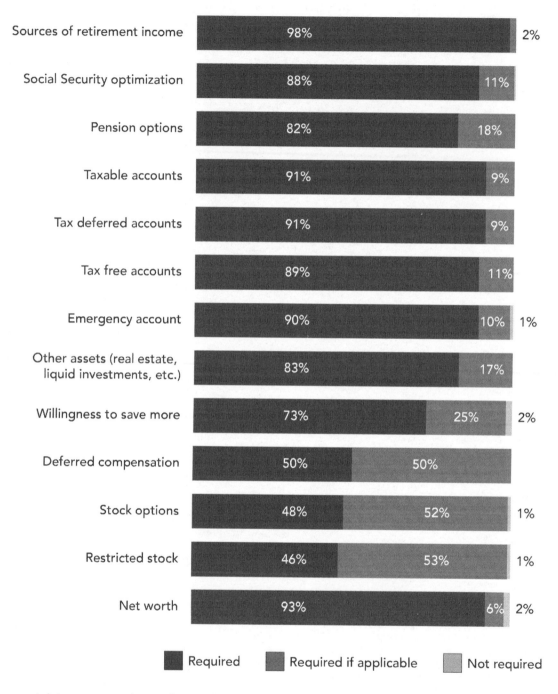

| | Required | Required if applicable | Not required |
|---|---|---|---|
| Sources of retirement income | 98% | | 2% |
| Social Security optimization | 88% | 11% | |
| Pension options | 82% | 18% | |
| Taxable accounts | 91% | 9% | |
| Tax deferred accounts | 91% | 9% | |
| Tax free accounts | 89% | 11% | |
| Emergency account | 90% | 10% | 1% |
| Other assets (real estate, liquid investments, etc.) | 83% | 17% | |
| Willingness to save more | 73% | 25% | 2% |
| Deferred compensation | 50% | 50% | |
| Stock options | 48% | 52% | 1% |
| Restricted stock | 46% | 53% | 1% |
| Net worth | 93% | 6% | 2% |

■ Required    ■ Required if applicable    ■ Not required

*Advisors agree that a thorough discussion of a client's resources is necessary to have an understanding of their full financial circumstances.*

Despite advisors' opinions regarding resources, what's included in financial plans often falls short. For example, less than 12 percent of financial plans included the recommendation of a Social Security filing strategy. While this could potentially be out of scope or may be addressed outside of the financial plan, a filing strategy may still be important to include when making investment recommendations in the best interest of the client. Not only does Social Security increase by a guaranteed 8 percent for each year income is deferred for those born in 1943 or later, but a recommendation to take Social Security early will impact the total fees paid by the client over time due to having a greater amount of money invested with the advisor versus deferring the income from Social Security. An advisor should include a filing strategy in their plans.

## Identify the liabilities

A quality financial plan must include liabilities. Over the last 30 years, Americans have taken on increasing amounts of debt, and **older Americans are not eliminating debt** before retirement. **In fact, 8 in 10 baby boomers still have debt in retirement** while 47 percent continue to pay off homes.[3] Education and car debt are also prevalent among all generations at 21 percent and 37 percent of people holding liabilities, respectively. Examples of liabilities that should be included according to the survey data:

☐ Mortgage                ☐ Home equity line of credit    ☐ Student debt

☐ Credit card debt        ☐ Vehicle loan                  ☐ Alimony

☐ Taxes owed              ☐ Business debts                ☐ Other recurring debt

While nearly all advisors in our study agreed that debt should be included in a quality plan, this practice is often overlooked. Failure to include a client's liabilities severely impacts both the directional accuracy of the financial plan and the appropriateness of the investment recommendations. Question — should a client be invested the same way if he or she owes nothing versus owes a few million dollars? Probably not. Perhaps the reason liabilities are absent from plans is that current compensation structures do

---

3 The Pew Charitable Trust: The Complex Story of American Debt, 2015.

not specifically address a fee for the management of debt. This may be a shortcoming of the current business models.

## Advisor opinion – liabilities

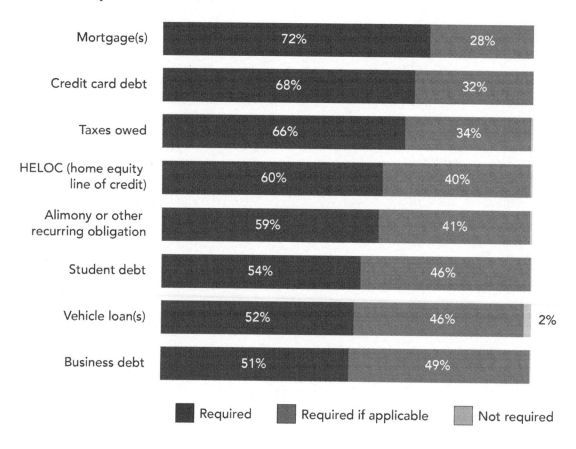

*The majority of advisors believe that a thorough understanding of clients' liabilities is important for building a quality financial plan.*

## Consider the risks — and communicate the risks to the client

I don't believe most clients truly understand the myriad of risks that could impact the probability of success of their plans for retirement. It is important that the most significant risk exposures be explored in a plan. A robust evaluation of risk not only includes market risk, meaning the tolerance a client has for losing money in a down market, but also longevity, liquidity, health, and inflationary risks. Unfortunately, nearly all risk tolerance questionnaires today are focused on market risk. In a quality financial plan it is important to explore the impact of these risks. The survey showed that examples of risks that should be evaluated in a quality plan include:

**Market Risks**

☐ Client market risk tolerance

☐ Spouse market risk tolerance

☐ Household market risk tolerance

☐ Concentrated stock risk

**Other Risks**

☐ Inflationary risk

☐ Property/casualty risk

☐ Liquidity risk

**Health Based Risks**

☐ Disability risk

☐ Life insurance needs

☐ Long term care needs

☐ Health care exposures

☐ Longevity risk

Few advisors address all of this information, and **25 percent said a property and casualty discussion is not required** with clients. This is alarming as 70 percent of Americans and 80 percent of Baby Boomers own their home.[4] They also tend to have higher incomes and are more likely to work with an advisor. It is also unnerving that disability insurance is not discussed with all clients especially for single-income earning couples. Of the 41 percent of single-income-earning couples, less than 4 percent of those had disability insurance addressed. This may be a result of these individuals having disability insurance offered by their employers, but even so it should still be addressed in the plan. Prior to retirement, a severe injury could create an unrecoverable situation for many, and probably represents one of the most likely potential catastrophic risks to a successful financial plan. In retirement, the same is true for illness and longevity risk. Other than life insurance centric firms, fewer than 10 percent of financial plans include a life insurance needs analysis, and only 22 percent include life insurance. Talking about risks is never fun or easy, but advisors have a responsibility to prepare families for the unexpected.

---

4 Gallup study: Own or Rent, 2015

## Advisor opinion – risk exposures

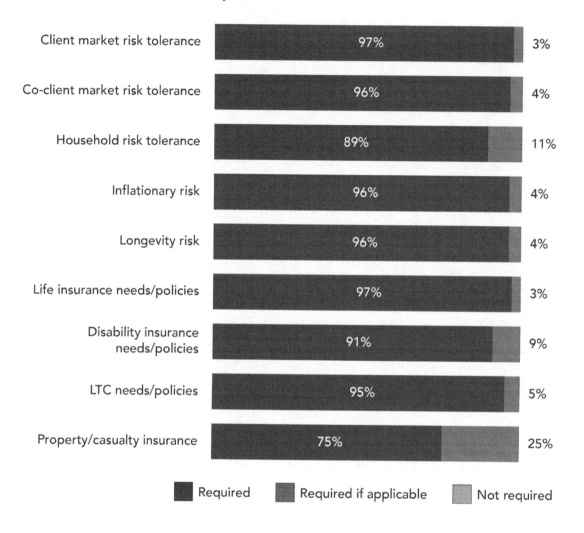

| | Required | Required if applicable | Not required |
|---|---|---|---|
| Client market risk tolerance | 97% | | 3% |
| Co-client market risk tolerance | 96% | | 4% |
| Household risk tolerance | 89% | | 11% |
| Inflationary risk | 96% | | 4% |
| Longevity risk | 96% | | 4% |
| Life insurance needs/policies | 97% | | 3% |
| Disability insurance needs/policies | 91% | | 9% |
| LTC needs/policies | 95% | | 5% |
| Property/casualty insurance | 75% | | 25% |

*Surprisingly, risk categories that can be financially devastating to households (e.g., disability, long term care need) are not deemed required for all client plans.*

## Explore different scenarios and discuss the results

Quality financial plans do not have to be delivered via printed reports. They should be engaging, interactive, and up-to-date when the client wishes to see the current state of the plan. This is, and will continue to be, a challenge for advisors. As mentioned before, a client wants to know whether he or she is able to fund all of their goals in retirement, as well as how something outside of their control could impact their plan. Advisors agree a quality financial plan should illustrate:

☐ Likelihood of funding basic needs (Monte Carlo)

☐ Likelihood of funding all goals (Monte Carlo)

☐ Impact of unexpected market losses

☐ Impact of premature death

☐ Impact of lower returns

☐ Impact of long term care need

☐ Impact of living too long

☐ Impact of sequence of returns

☐ Impact of concentrated stock risk

☐ Impact of reduction in Social Security benefits while still in retirement

☐ Impact of reduction in pension

☐ Impact of unexpected health costs

## Advisor opinion – impacts to plan

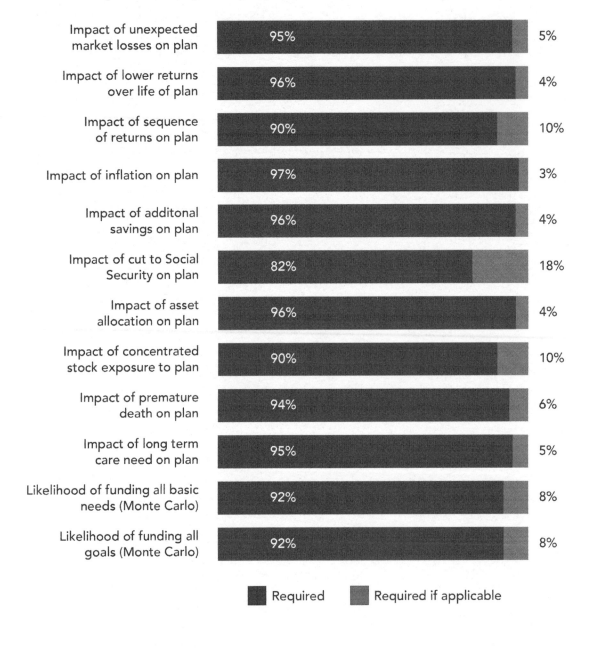

| | Required | Required if applicable |
|---|---|---|
| Impact of unexpected market losses on plan | 95% | 5% |
| Impact of lower returns over life of plan | 96% | 4% |
| Impact of sequence of returns on plan | 90% | 10% |
| Impact of inflation on plan | 97% | 3% |
| Impact of additonal savings on plan | 96% | 4% |
| Impact of cut to Social Security on plan | 82% | 18% |
| Impact of asset allocation on plan | 96% | 4% |
| Impact of concentrated stock exposure to plan | 90% | 10% |
| Impact of premature death on plan | 94% | 6% |
| Impact of long term care need on plan | 95% | 5% |
| Likelihood of funding all basic needs (Monte Carlo) | 92% | 8% |
| Likelihood of funding all goals (Monte Carlo) | 92% | 8% |

*Advisors are inconsistent in their inclusion of elements outside of their or their clients' control.*

Advisors overwhelmingly agreed that the impacts should be explored when delivering a quality financial plan. The bottom line? A simple calculation of the growth of an account value over the next thirty years at a certain rate of return is not going to be enough.

## Estate planning and all the other stuff

Last but not least, a quality financial plan should explore estate tax liability (if any), beneficiary designations, tax planning, gifting strategies, and ensure the client has a current will, durable power of attorney, and advanced medical directives in place. Often overlooked is the requirement to ensure assets are titled properly and beneficiary designations are correct. All of these can be explored incrementally, but must be done at some point to avoid ugly outcomes. If we were to explore all of the estate planning permutations of a plan, we would have had to add another three hundred pages to this book.

## Come up with your own definition

This is not a complete list, but it is a start. Each advisor and firm should carefully evaluate their own definition of a quality financial plan, socialize it, and create a standardized process to both better help their clients and protect their firms from unnecessary risk exposures.

Determining the definition of a quality financial plan is similar to determining the difference between advice and good advice. A friend of mine once said that having any plan is better than having no plan at all. I disagree. A plan that is not a quality plan, on its own, may very well be more detrimental than not having a plan. For example, a plan that doesn't include the cost of health care might just cause an individual to retire far sooner than they might have without a plan at all. Once the client realizes the mistake, it may be too late and that individual may no longer be employable. Oops.

**Kevin Knull, CFP®**
President

PIEtech℠, Inc.

Four

# The "Secret Sauce" to Creating a Quality Financial Plan

So now that we have a general baseline of the elements that should be included in a quality financial plan, let's explore the best practices that can help make this possible. The DOL has essentially brought financial planning to center stage while bringing the class action bar to our industry, so firms and advisors need to figure out how to create and deliver quality financial plans quickly, efficiently and ensure that their recommendations are justified. The following are my best suggestions for firms to excel in this process.

## Don't believe everything you think

The above is one of my favorite sayings, but unfortunately, most mislead themselves into thinking something is true that may not be. Many advisors will argue that a client doesn't want to take the time to have a financial plan created, or may even suggest that clients don't care. I maintain that this is fundamentally untrue. Show me an individual who doesn't want to know whether they can achieve their goals in retirement. I don't think there are many. The only reasonable way to competently answer whether the client can meet their goals is to build a quality financial plan. Below are some additional obstacles, as stated by advisors. Most advisors' perceptions are likely indicative of the client's lack of understanding or perhaps even the advisor's failure to communicate the value of a plan.

## Advisor-perceived obstacles to financial planning

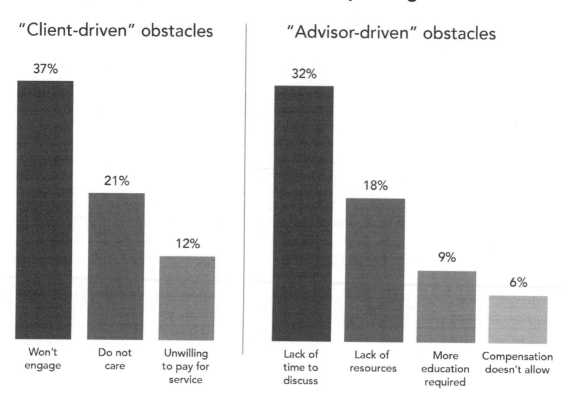

*The perceived lack of client interest and the advisor's ability to scale financial planning have negatively impacted the delivery of advice.*

As a point of note, during our consumer testing, we found most investors can build a quality financial plan from start to finish in about 90 minutes without any financial knowledge — provided that they have the right tool and instruction to do so. A knowledgeable advisor ought to be able to create a quality financial plan in a fraction of the time. Wouldn't a reasonably prudent person argue that 90 minutes or less seems an appropriate amount of time to spend before investing a client's portfolio?

## Ask the right questions, and then listen

The financial planning process usually begins with what many of our contributors call "the discovery process." Discovery is perhaps the most important part of creating a quality financial plan and will become increasingly more important to our industry as we navigate and eventually have to defend our actions in the post-DOL landscape. It enables a financial advisor to gain a full understanding of a client's specific situation including their wants, needs and wishes. As we all know, what one client considers a comfortable retirement may not be comfortable to someone else.

While listening is essential, alone it will not lead to a quality financial plan. You must ask the right questions. Many start this process with a questionnaire but these forms only go so far. By engaging the client in conversation and asking thoughtful personal questions, you can learn about the client's current marital situation, who they need to provide for in the future or the state in which they would like to retire. You will learn and determine if their goal is to travel to exotic locations or to stay with friends and family during the holidays, or if they intend to travel alone, with a spouse, children or grandchildren. Even if you have asked a client to be specific, as mentioned earlier, he or she may not be specific enough if not prompted appropriately.

The more specifics you can extract, the better able you will be to develop a personalized, quality financial plan. By asking for specifics you are also doing much more to engage the client than simply asking him or her to fill out a form — something the client can do with a robo-advisor.

## Create a goals-based financial plan

Financial planning was born from the accounting profession, but it has completely shifted from a cash flow approach to a goals-based approach because clients care more about their goals and whether they can achieve them than anything else. Financial planning boils down to two goal-related questions: First, "Can I fund all of my goals without running out of money?" And second, "What do I need to do to protect against the things outside of my control that might prevent me from reaching my goals?"

Engaging in a goals discussion with a couple can be an incredibly powerful experience, but most advisors shy away from digging deeply into the conversation. They make the tragic mistake of jumping straight to an asset discussion, which is usually the least interesting to the client. Clients today don't care as much about the investment strategy, they simply want to find the best way to achieve their goals. If they think you understand and can help them reach their goals, they will trust you to worry about the investment strategy.

For some, the first meeting with a financial advisor could be likened to an invasive surgical procedure. It is not uncommon for couples to have their first goal exploration conversation in front of the advisor. This is not ideal for two reasons — first, this is a highly personal conversation between a couple, and second, most advisors aren't really interested in the couple's goals in retirement. After all, these are the clients' goals, not the advisor's goals. You should also know that the typical husband and wife need to discuss (and perhaps even argue about) their goals. My wife and I can't even agree on paint colors — just imagine how hard this conversation is for the couple approaching retirement.

One way to circumvent this is for the advisor to begin a conversation about goals, then excuse himself or herself for a few minutes as the couple discusses which goals are relevant and whose are most important. Rarely will both agree on the goals, their priority or the amount that should be spent on each. If this is uncomfortable for you as the professional, consider asking the clients to explore this conversation before they arrive at the office and instead give them access to a tool for the discovery process that includes goals. Whatever you decide, please don't skip the conversation as it is the secret "sauce" to ensuring success with a client. No component of a quality financial plan is more important than the client's goals and objectives.

## Don't be afraid to give the client the bad news

You also need to advise the client on which goals are achievable under certain financial scenarios and which are not. A client may want to travel overseas each year and with enough assets and limited liabilities that may be possible. But you need to be honest with a client with more limited financial means — this may mean a trip overseas once every few years or several annual domestic trips. To be successful, help the client set realistic goals based on his or her financial situation (income, job stability, assets, liabilities, risk tolerance) and then devise a financial plan to meet those goals. One of my favorite questions to make this point when discussing a financial plan with a client is this — "If you are going to run out of money in retirement, would you rather I tell you today or after it happens?" Given the lack of retirement readiness of many Americans today, there are going to be a lot of difficult conversations in the future.

## Make the process fun

For most, this will probably be the most challenging (or most dismissed) statement I will make in this book. Financial planning can be fun. It's true. If your clients liken a financial planning discussion to a root canal, you can be assured they will not remain engaged in your process. Bob Curtis, my partner and the visionary behind our firm's financial planning software, coined the phrase "funtirement" years ago. Why? Because retirement should be fun and it looks nothing like your parent's definition of retirement. And just because a client doesn't have millions of dollars doesn't mean they can't have fun in retirement — they just need to have realistic goals that match their resources.

If you would like to experience a completely different kind of client meeting, schedule an entire meeting in which you barely speak. Just listen. Let the couple list and describe all the things they would like to do in retirement. Ask them to be specific. It will be the client's favorite meeting they ever have with you.

## Engage your client

A plan that is created but not accepted by the client is of little value. A plan that is created and not implemented is useless. Engaging a client from the beginning can be the biggest asset to the success of implementing a plan. If the process is interactive and the client is engaged throughout each phase, clients are more likely to be open, honest, actively involved and vested in the plan which makes them more accountable and more likely to implement it.

Clients want to be involved, to some extent, in the planning process. As investors, clients want to engage, learn and stay involved in the process if given the opportunity.

The best firms today make the planning process collaborative and interactive by using the big television screen in their conference room, or better yet, via a tablet such as an iPad. Keep in mind, your clients are getting older, just like us, and they may not want to admit that they cannot see the eight-point font you've used in your report or have shown on the monitor. Allow your clients to interact with you, and focus your attention on the person speaking the least. The odds are that if you don't, he or she will leave you as soon as the "controller" in the relationship passes away. Hand the iPad to this individual and let him or her manipulate the plan.

## Make the plan incremental

Financial planning can be overwhelming to some and may be more effective if approached in phases. Asking a client, on the spot, to think about their entire life in one meeting can be a very overwhelming task and most clients haven't thought that far in the future or just don't want to. Therefore, creating a financial planning process that is incremental and done in more digestible pieces can be less intimidating.

The implementation of everything addressed in a financial plan does not need to be completed all at once. Financial planning and investing can be handled in the same manner that a physician triages a patient. Once you've identified the outstanding issues as a result of a financial plan, then you and your clients can determine what should be tackled now and what can be postponed for the future. What is critical, though, is that the client leaves the meeting understanding that if any outstanding issues remain, then it is possible that those issues may have a significant adverse impact should the risks become reality.

Some of you reading this are saying, "This is impossible. It is going to take too much time." But believe it or not, even clients who have absolutely no financial experience can build a basic quality financial plan in less than 90 minutes.

## Make the plan dynamic

The days of static, rarely altered financial plans are a thing of the past. Today's world is complicated and so are most people's lives. Life happens when you're making other plans and often things don't happen in the traditional order they used to. Plans need to be flexible and, as I mentioned, advisors need to regularly check in with clients to see if they are still on track to meet their goals. Did something happen that requires an overhaul or a shift in strategy?

Additionally, people receive pay increases, get married, divorced, have children, get better jobs, lose jobs, have unexpected health costs, have unexpected investment gains or losses or have other life/financial changes that mean differences in the assets, liabilities and other considerations upon which the initial financial plan was built. As the plan's foundation changes, so should the plan. Additional children could mean additional life insurance is warranted. A job change could mean changes in retirement contributions. Plans should be reviewed when any of these significant changes occur.

A quality financial plan should be dynamic and be available at any time online. Why? Because the moment a plan is printed it is obsolete. With so much information online, in real-time, clients want their advisors to be able to provide up-to-date information on the status/performance of their financial plan and any assets they have with you. The plan should be current whenever the client wants to see the status of the plan — that means it needs to be online and connected. Markets move, goals change, life expectancies shorten, expenses increase, children are born, and so on and so on. A quality financial plan should change as do our clients' lives, and with the modern integration of technology systems this has become easier than ever before.

Investors want to know, "Can I achieve all of my goals without running out of money? What happens if I retire today? Can we buy that little convertible? What if we were to contribute more to their 401(k)'s? What if we changed our allocation?" All of these can be answered at a moment's notice if their plan is kept up-to-date, dynamically.

What about the ugly stuff? What if there is a market correction? What if their concentrated stock position loses half its value? What if Social Security benefits are cut or someone requires long-term medical care? Again, these are the things that wake people up at night, and all can be answered with a current, up-to-date plan.

## Address their fears

No one wakes up in the morning and shouts, "I can't wait to open an investment account!" It is far more likely a client will wake up in the middle of the night in a panic wondering: "Now that the market has fallen, will we still be able to retire in June and achieve the goals we've been dreaming about?" Or perhaps, "Now that my pension has been cut in half, will we be able to remain retired or will we have to go back to work?" Based on the current environment, the most likely question on everyone's mind is, "What would happen to us and our portfolio if there was another significant market decline?"

All of us have things that "keep us up at night" and when we are thinking about planning our financial future, there are usually several. A quality financial plan not only covers a client's retirement goals, but covers the client's goals as they pertain to life's unexpected events. Many of our contributors have referred to these unexpected life curve balls as the "what ifs."

It is our job as advisors to work with clients to identify and get them thinking about these potential and usually very unpleasant scenarios — things like a job loss, a sudden accident or an untimely death. Then, we need to work with them to develop a plan for each scenario no matter how unpleasant the process may be. When people are in distress it is not the best time to think about what to do. Planning in advance for the most challenging things life can throw our way usually brings a sense of comfort during an otherwise heightened emotional event/time in a client's life.

Our consumer testing has shown us that clients find real comfort in being able to spend time on their own manipulating their financial plan to see the effect of these unexpected scenarios. Some clients will test their plan regularly. An advisor should consider making this functionality available to clients so that they can remain calm in periods of adversity. Typically it is a lack of information and fear that causes clients to do irrational things.

Part and parcel of this is understanding a client's true risk tolerance. A client may initially indicate he or she is willing to risk losses, but further questioning might reveal the client would rather earn less on an investment than risk a loss. And the client's risk tolerance likely changes as he or she nears retirement and foresees the end of wage income. So we need to work with clients to develop plans to handle unexpected (sudden job loss) as well as expected (planned retirement) scenarios.

## Monitor the plan

Last but not least, make sure you keep your clients on track. It is our job as advisors to make sure they are doing just that. We need to check in regularly, not just on birthdays and at tax time. Some of our contributors have likened this task to being more of a coach — a financial coach, if you will. Cheer your clients on when they have met a goal or make them work harder when they fall off course. But most importantly of all, make them accountable to the plan that you developed together.

## Parting thought

We have an enormous opportunity right now to improve the quality of advice and add greater value for our clients. We must find new and innovative ways to scale the delivery of quality financial plans and this will likely require engaging clients and prospects in the process. Financial planning has finally, finally come into its own, and the firms that are able to embrace the shift from a sales culture to one comprised of goals-based planning and good advice will thrive in the future. And clients will be better for it.

Now that you have my thoughts, research, and plan data, I invite you to read the following chapters from the contributors comprised of their uncensored, unedited thoughts and advice. And I wish you the best as you explore your own path to good advice, a quality financial plan and the role of a fiduciary.

**Luis A. Aguilar**
**Former Commissioner**

**U.S. Securities and Exchange Commission**

Five

# A Client's True Partner

## About the Author

Luis A. Aguilar served as Commissioner at the U.S. Securities and Exchange Commission (SEC) from July 2008 through December of 2015. As the eighth longest-serving Commissioner in SEC history, Aguilar is one of three Commissioners to have been nominated by two U.S. Presidents from two different political parties. Aguilar's distinguished business and legal career prior to his appointment includes serving as general counsel at Invesco, Managing Director for Invesco Latin America and President of one of Invesco's broker-dealers, as well as, tenures at some of the country's most prestigious law firms. He is known for working to modernize the SEC's rules and focusing on cybersecurity.

—〰—

## Financial advice and the benefits of the fiduciary standard

Demographically, the Baby Boomer Generation represents the largest percentage of the American population. Aging Baby Boomers have also accumulated substantial assets, either through inheritance, home equity, or a lifetime of saving for retirement, that are ripe for abuse, as noted by Kimberly Blanton in *The Rise of Financial Fraud: Scams Never Change but Disguises Do.*[i] Unfortunately, the generations that follow may be at greater risk of having less assets.

According to the Pew Research Center's *The Rising Age Gap in Economic Well-Being*,[ii] households headed by older adults have made dramatic gains relative to those headed by younger adults over the past quarter of a century. For example, in 2009, households headed by adults ages 65 and older possessed 42 percent more median net worth than households headed by their same-aged counterparts in 1984. During this same period, the wealth of households headed by adults younger than 35 had 68 percent less wealth than households of their same-aged counterparts.[iii]

These facts underscore the importance of high-quality investment advice — both for Boomers looking to manage their significant wealth and for the next generations which are still in the wealth-accumulation stages of life and face an increasingly complicated financial landscape. Moreover, as the United States soon enters what many consider will be the greatest wealth transfer in our nation's history, many complex issues arise that call for good financial advice from a professional.

As Americans, both wealthy and those with aspirations for a prosperous and secure future, consider what to do, I've been asked to address three questions: 1) What is good financial advice?; 2) What is a quality financial plan?; and 3) What does it truly mean to act as a fiduciary to a client both today and in the future? Or more specifically, can a financial advisor or professional perform the duties of a fiduciary if one's client does not have a quality financial plan?

Much can be written in response to each of these questions. While they seem simple and straight-forward on the surface, the answers are not. As with many things, the devil is in the detail. For example, what is good financial advice? Can it be limited to just a client's investment portfolio or do other aspects of an individual's specific situation have to be taken into account such as insurance needs (home, life, disability), real estate holdings, tax planning, etc.? How holistic must the advice be before it can be considered good?

Other factors that underlie these questions may pertain to the expertise and qualifications of the person providing the advice or the "advice-giver." How equipped is he or she to provide good advice or create a quality financial plan? Are they properly qualified? And, what does that mean? Financial professionals can use a host of designations that can make them appear well qualified — such as Chartered Advisor, Accredited Financial Counselor, Board Certified in Securities, Chartered Senior Financial Planner and many, many more. But what does each designation mean? And, which is appropriate for a particular individual's needs? Also, many advisors may not have a professional designation but may be very good at what they do. Determining the right advisor with the right qualifications can be daunting.

Financial planning as a value proposition may depend on what a client is looking for and what he or she is willing to pay, both of which often depend on the client's level of financial knowledge and experience — for example, a client's experience or knowledge dealing with investment strategy and portfolio development, including asset allocation decisions. Moreover, many complex situations may require the collaboration and inclusion of other qualified advisors like attorneys and accountants for legal and tax advice. The possible variables are too many to address here.

The point is that some clients may be better equipped than others to select the right financial advisor. For most, I think the task is a difficult and complicated decision. Even after an initial decision is made, prudence demands that the relationship receive periodic attention to ensure the hired advisor remains the right advisor as an individual's situation changes over time.

Fortunately, there are several resources like the Campaign for Investors[iv] that can help a client work through the many difficult issues when it comes to selecting an advisor and ensuring that the relationship is still productive over time.

Clearly, it can be a difficult decision to find the right advisor that can deliver quality services. For me, a starting point to answering all the questions above is to begin by focusing on the person providing the advice — the advice-giver. Whose interest does he or she have at heart? If an advisor doesn't have the client's best interest at the forefront of the relationship, then I have to question the quality of the advice or financial plan.

With many American families needing to rely heavily on advisors for their financial well-being, it is important to make sure that clients receive the best advice. For my money, the best way to do that is for all advice-givers to abide by a fiduciary standard that requires them to always put a client's interest first. And I do mean "always."

During my tenure as the eighth-longest serving Commissioner at the U.S. Securities and Exchange Commission (SEC), I advocated for the vitality and durability of the advisory profession and for the importance of advisors to be client-focused and to always put their client's interest first.

Today's financial landscape provides an ever-evolving spectrum of investment options that challenge even the most sophisticated and experienced investors. It's no wonder that investors desire the help of trained professionals — and that the need for that help has fueled enormous growth in the number of individuals calling themselves investment and/or financial advisors.

Putting a client's interest first should be a non-controversial, common sense idea that is universally embraced. It is to be expected that advisory clients would demand they be put first if they understood that their advisors were putting themselves first and their clients second. Certainly, registered investment advisers (RIAs) have long adhered to a fiduciary standard — and both advisors and their clients have successfully prospered under the standard.

## All investment advice-givers should be fiduciaries

The concept of a fiduciary standard has been around for centuries and clearly influenced the drafting of the Investment Advisers Act of 1940. The Advisers Act and its companion legislation, the Investment Company Act of 1940, resulted from a comprehensive congressionally mandated study conducted by the SEC that examined investment companies, investment counsels and investment advisory services following the market crash that led to the Great Depression.

Ultimately, the report concluded that the activities of investment advisers "patently present various problems which usually accompany the handling of large liquid funds of the public.:"[v] The report stressed the need to improve the professionalism of the industry, both by eliminating fraudsters and other scam artists and by emphasizing the importance of unbiased advice, which was seen as the most important factor in distinguishing the advisory profession from investment bankers and broker-dealers.[vi] As the report made clear, the general objective "was to protect the public and investors against malpractices by persons paid for advising others about securities."[vii]

The report stressed that a significant problem in the industry was the existence, either consciously or unconsciously, of a prejudice by advisers in favor of their own financial interests. Reading through the SEC report, the overriding concern was that if the advice to a client resulted in a financial benefit to the advice-giver — over and above the fee — then the resulting advice might be tainted. Even more importantly, as subsequently noted in a 1968 Supreme Court decision, the SEC staff rejected an early market discipline argument by recognizing that "a significant part of the problem was not the existence of a deliberate intent to obtain a financial advantage, but rather the existence subconsciously of a prejudice in favor of one's own financial interests."[viii] Consequently, the Court underscored that the Advisers Act required advice-givers, as fiduciaries, to bear the burden of providing disinterested advice and being able to prove it.

As stated by the Supreme Court, the Advisers Act reflects a "congressional intent to eliminate, or at least to expose, all conflicts of interest which might incline an investment adviser — consciously or unconsciously — to render advice which was not disinterested."[ix] Moreover, Congress and the Court placed the burden for providing disinterested advice and eliminating or disclosing conflicts squarely where it belonged, in the hands of the advice-giver. This places the obligation in the hands of those responsible for upholding their fiduciary duties rather than unfairly and unrealistically burdening investors to become mind readers and discern conflicts and incentives — an often impossible task, particularly with today's more complex investment products, such as structured products, many of the complicated exchange traded funds (ETFs) and the like.

## The fiduciary standard — a fundamental investor protection

Financial advisors that are subject to a fiduciary standard owe their clients an "affirmative duty of 'utmost good faith, and full and fair disclosure of all material facts,' as well as an affirmative obligation to 'employ reasonable care to avoid misleading'" their clients.[x] Accordingly, they are required to serve the interests of their clients with undivided loyalty. An adviser that has a material conflict of interest must either refrain from acting upon that conflict, or it must fully disclose all material facts relating to that conflict, and obtain the informed consent of its clients, before acting.[xi]

The fiduciary standard has served advisory clients well for many years, but it isn't always the standard that is required of many advice-givers. That is particularly true as to representatives of broker-dealers that often provide personalized investment advice to individuals but that need to only meet the so-called "suitability standard" — a standard that doesn't require that the investment advice be in the client's best interest and that allows for the broker-dealer to recommend lower quality investments and/or higher priced products — even when better alternatives are readily available.

There are many benefits to making sure that a financial adviser is required to act in his or her client's best interest. This is particularly important in an era of growing complexity in the "financial industry ecosystem," whether it involves the securities sold and traded in the capital markets, the insurance and annuities market, tax issues, etc. The duties of care, loyalty and utmost good faith that underpin the fiduciary standard will invariably lead the adviser to choose the products and services that are in the client's best interest.

For that simple reason — putting the client first — one of the first things a client should determine is whose interest the advice-giver has at heart. Any financial advice or financial plan that doesn't put the client first is questionable on its face. If the advice-giver is not required to act in the client's best interest, the prospective client should think twice. No amount of an advice-giver's expertise can make up for them putting his or her interest ahead of the client's. Only a real fiduciary can serve as a true partner to a client.

i.    Center for Retirement Research at Boston College (February 2012), page 3, http://fsp.bc.edu/wp-content/uploads/2012/02/Scams-RFTF.pdf

ii.   Pew Research Center, (November 7, 2011), http://www.pewsocialtrends.org/2011/11/07/the-rising-age-gap-in-economic-well-being/?src=prc-headline

iii.  *Ibid*

iv.   www.campaignforinvestors.org

v.    Transamerica Mortgage Advisors, Inc. v. Lewis, 444 U.S. 11, 17 (1979).

vi.   *Ibid*

vii.  SEC v. Capital Gains Research Bureau, Inc., 375 U. S. 180, 194 (1963).

viii. In the Matter of Kidder Peabody & Co., Inc., Advisers Act Release No. 232 (Oct. 16, 1968).

ix.   *Ibid*

x.    Suitability of Investment Advice Provided by Investment Advisers; Custodial Account Statements for Certain Advisory Clients, Advisers Act Release No. 1406 (March 16, 1994) ("Investment advisers are fiduciaries who owe their clients a series of duties, one of which is the duty to provide only suitable investment advice. This duty is enforceable under the antifraud provisions of the Advisers Act, section 206, and the Commission has sanctioned advisers for violating this duty." (Footnotes omitted).

xi.   See In the Matter of Alfred C. Rizzo, Advisers Act Release No. 897 (Jan. 11, 1984).

**Bill Bachrach, CSP, CPAE**
Chairman and Chief Executive Officer

Bachrach & Associates, Inc.

Six

# Advice: A Recommendation of Action

## About the Author

Bill Bachrach is a financial services industry thought leader, keynote speaker, author and trainer. Books authored by Bill include his latest eBook: *The Confident Advisor: How to Thrive in the New World of DOL Fiduciary Standard, Digital Advisors, and the 5 Other Critical Industry Disruptions*, along with previous industry best-sellers: *Values-Based Financial Planning: The Art of Creating and Inspiring Financial Strategy, Values-Based Selling: The Art of Building High-Trust Client Relationships, High-Trust Leadership: A proven system for developing an organization of high-performance financial professionals* and *It's All About Them.*

## About the Company

Bachrach & Associates, Inc. provides professional training and coaching for top financial advisors and those who aspire to be. They developed Advisor Roadmap™, an affordable and scalable virtual training platform for advisors who want to improve their skill and confidence at implementing values and goals-based financial planning, for both transitioning existing clients to full-service planning and to win new clients.

—⟳—

## What is advice?

According to Wikipedia, advice is a recommendation of *action*. Perfect. Without action there is no benefit. If the client doesn't act on the advice, then the advice is useless. That is why the significant number of incomplete and unimplemented financial plans is such a disaster for clients, advisors, and firms. Perhaps one of the reasons so many financial planners are only moderately successful is that they make suggestions instead of confidently giving advice. Advice is a recommendation of action. **Action = Results**.

## The best client value promise

Planning, advice, and accountability are the three hallmarks of the best client value promise. **Planning** is a process, not a document or binder. The value for the client comes from the **advice** generated from the planning process. The ongoing relationship between advisor and client sits on a foundation of **accountability** to implement the advice and stay the course when emotions, usually fear, are causing clients to want out.

The best advisors help clients prepare for the future and help them have more confidence, in the present, about the future. The best advisors facilitate conversations about clients' core values, help them define their goals, dreams and aspirations, benchmark their current financial reality, and create a game plan to mitigate risks and achieve goals. The best advisors also hold clients accountable to implement the advice of the plan and continue to hold the clients accountable to do what needs to be done to achieve their most important goals and fulfill their most deeply held values … especially when that's emotionally challenging.

Additionally, the best advisors hold the technical subject matter experts accountable to produce the work product / deliverables so the clients continuously receive the best advice possible to stay on track to achieve their goals. As a result, the clients are more confident about having a secure, free, fulfilled, and happy future. Because life is dynamic, adjustments are made as needed, maintaining the client's confidence about having a secure, free, fulfilled, and happy future.

## Success is always within our control

This client value promise is effective because it's based on the universal principle that financial success is never a function of what's out of our control. Success is always the result of making good fundamental choices to be financially successful in any market, economic, political or world event climate. Not everyone went bankrupt during the Great Depression and many who did rebounded. The market recovered after the economic crisis of 2008-2009, right? Other than those people who actually lost their jobs, for all the anxiety and stress experienced during that period, if one had simply ignored the noise and stuck to their plans, it was uneventful.

During progressively longer lifetimes, humans live through many market, economic, political, and world event ups and downs. Some of these events are enormous, like world wars, genocides and massive global economic crises. Yet no external event is the determining factor of financial success or failure. The determining factor was, is today, and will always be the personal choices made before, during, and after these events.

## Can you predict the future?

Smart advisors and clients don't try to predict future events. They prepare strong financial foundations and build robust personal economies that position them to move through negative events without catastrophic consequences. They plan for their clients to always be in the game to enjoy the benefits of a world that is growing and improving. The day-to-day ride is sometimes bumpy, but the trajectory of our world overall is consistently up. Cable news and political posturing is not an accurate depiction of everything that's happening in the world. They just represent the worst events, with the most negative spin possible, because that's what boosts ratings, sells advertising, and gets votes.

## Help people make better choices

The most rewarding aspect of our business is when we help people make better choices at some of the most crucial moments in their lives and in world history. We help them develop the financial habits that put them in a position to weather any storm in the nation or the world. We help them ignore all the distractions and stay focused on building their own, strong personal economic foundation, and enjoy life.

You are so much more valuable when you help people develop a **plan**, give them good **advice** based on the plan, and hold them **accountable** to implement the advice, especially when that's emotionally difficult. That's why managing money is being delegated to machines. Machines can manage money, but they can't lead people. What's much more important is leading people to make good choices. Your future in this business depends on your skill and confidence to do that.

The most successful firms will be those companies and firms that embrace outsourcing and technology to achieve scale in servicing and advising clients, focus on goals-based planning while keeping in mind a client's aversion to loss of assets, and remain close to the client by discovering the right mix of technology-based and in-person communications. Advisors should consider outsourcing some – or all – aspects of investment management for their clients. Money management is time-consuming; it keeps advisers riveted to their computer screens instead of engaging with their clients.

– Jeff Cerulli; Cerulli & Associates

## Retain clients

The "Advisor as Portfolio Manager" value proposition, based on trying to predict and beat the market, is a dying approach. You can try to hang on to it if you like; however, the truly comprehensive, values- and goals-based, full-service financial professionals are much more likely to retain their best clients and win new clients from advisors who are slow to adapt to the new world. Perhaps some old dogs will take solace that a few stock brokers survived the last seismic industry shift to professionally managed money, but who really wants to hang their hat on that rationale?

## The value-delivered-to-the-client metric

At the pre-conference dinner the night before my keynote speech for a group of top advisors (27 advisors with $5.5B of AUM and a client minimum of $1M) the CEO, let's call him Bob, introduced me to the firm's "top advisor," Mark. After shaking hands, I said, "Congratulations, Mark, on being the top advisor here." He said, "Thank you very much." Then I asked, " Mark, you are the top advisor… how do you *measure* that?" In the ensuing awkward silence, I imagined they were thinking, "This is our keynote speaker and he doesn't know what 'top advisor' means? Where did we find this moron?" Mark finally said, "Well, Bill, I have the highest production, I bring in the most assets and I have the most AUM at the company. That's why I'm the top advisor." Bob nodded in agreement. To which I replied, "That's fantastic, Mark, congratulations on your success." I looked at the CEO and asked, "Bob, I'm really glad to meet Mark and I'd also like to meet your top advisor *as measured by value delivered to the client*, who would that be?" There was another long, awkward pause before Bob said, "Uh… we don't measure that." "Hmmmm," I said, "well as a client, do you think I would be more interested to meet the top advisor based on *production* or the top advisor based on the *value delivered to the client*?" To his credit, Mark asked, "Can I sit with you at dinner and talk to you more about this?"

And we wonder why the government and regulators feel a need to impose the fiduciary standard.

## "Rescue" clients from other advisors and institutions

Creating the best client experience and delivering truly great planning and advice drives higher production and referrals. Higher production and referrals drive retention. Nothing succeeds like success. Being a truly better planner, giving truly better advice puts advisors in a position to "rescue" clients from the production-focused, asset-gathering advisor who still dominates the industry. Let's not soft-peddle the objective. You want your existing clients to consolidate *all* of their business with you, effectively firing *all* of their other advisors and institutions. Your goal is to give your clients zero reason to interact with any other financial advisor or financial institution. Every time your client interacts with another financial advisor or institution that relationship is at risk.

Your *future* clients are people with money who are currently doing business with other advisors and institutions. In order to motivate them to change, you have to have the *people* skills to engage them in a positive and compelling way, hire you, and then fire their other advisors and institutions. This is your job. Instead of mass marketing where you *hope* to show up when the "money is in motion," *you have the power to move people who were not in motion...until they met you.* As the leader of a financial services business today, your job is to train a cadre of advisors who have the people skills and the technical resources to make that happen. Seize the day!

True, comprehensive values- and goals-based financial planning has always been a good idea. Now it's the only practical option to succeed in a post-DOL Fiduciary Standard world and to successfully compete with the best human advisors, the ever-improving robo-advisors, and the big financial institutions that can give away money management as a "loss leader."

How will you differentiate yourself when everyone finally jumps on the financial planning bandwagon? By actually being great at it. In a business where everyone has the same tools, the same technology, and the same products, what's the key to success? Great execution.

Everyone deserves a *quality* financial plan and financial planning software isn't supposed to be a sales tool. It's supposed to be the foundation for delivering maximum value for the clients. And because money follows value, advisors who do *real* financial planning also do more business. Will you choose to be *great*?

More than rich, more than famous, more than even being happy... I wanted to be great.

– Bruce Springsteen

**Bill Benjamin**
Chief Executive Officer

U.S. Bancorp Investments

Seven

# A Noble Profession

## About the Author
As CEO for U.S. Bancorp Investments, Bill leads a national team of wealth management professionals specializing in investment management, financial planning and insurance services. Bill's 25 years of wealth management and sales experience span key roles at Piper Jaffray, UBS and IBM.

## About the Company
U.S. Bancorp Investments provides investment products and services, including comprehensive wealth management strategies, and aims to help clients reach their retirement goals. As a division of U.S. Bancorp's Wealth Management Group and an affiliate of U.S. Bank, it is part of a rich history of serving customers since 1863.

—⟋⟋⟋—

## Helping clients achieve their life priorities

Advisors play a critical role in helping clients develop and execute plans that guide them on a journey to achieve their life goals, priorities and a dignified retirement. Based on a full understanding of a client, educating the client, developing a plan and setting realistic expectations, the advisor can help clients navigate life events, adjust as appropriate and add value in meaningful ways throughout life.

## Simplicity

Steve Jobs was well-known for his management style and never-ending quest for perfection, but I believe the greatest contributions to his and Apple's success were due to his focus, first, on the client experience (before the technology solution) and the "incredible benefits" Apple solutions could deliver to the client; and second, his maniacal focus on simplicity.

Just look at any Apple product - easy, right? Hardly, it's quite the contrary. All Apple products are highly sophisticated and extremely robust, but the delivery and usability are just plain simple. The key to being a successful financial advisor is the same — put the client's interest and experience first, thoroughly understand the client's situation and life priorities, and simplify the delivery of solutions that help clients achieve their goals.

A big part of what we need to accomplish when offering financial advice is to make it simple, yet robust and valuable. It needs to be simple for the advisor to deliver and simple for the client to understand and execute. This doesn't mean we need to dumb it down. Like Apple, it has to be robust, meaningful and helpful. If we make it complicated, it won't get done. We have to be maniacally focused on simplicity and value.

## We have a retirement income crisis in America

I believe we are facing a retirement crisis in America and we need to solve it before it gets worse, especially given the 77 million Baby Boomers entering or soon to be entering retirement. The 2013 "National Institute on Retirement Security" report states that the retirement savings deficit in America is between $6.8 and $14 trillion. The research further states that the median retirement account balance for all working age households (age 25-64) is $3,000, and is only $12,000 for near-retirement households (age 55-64) — not enough for a dignified retirement.

The Social Security Act was signed by Franklin Delano Roosevelt in 1935. According to the U.S. Social Security Administration, in 1945, there were 41.9 workers for every Social Security beneficiary. In 2013, there were only 2.8 and this ratio is expected to get smaller as more Baby Boomers enter retirement. This trend has created stress on the Social Security system. Since 2010, Social Security expenditures have exceeded primary income. Here is part of our challenge: Social Security is relied on by millions of Americans for retirement income. According to Social Security Quick Facts, the estimated average monthly Social Security benefit payable to retired workers in June 2016 equaled $1,348. Unfortunately, 64 percent of Americans rely on Social Security for more than 50 percent of their retirement income and 36 percent of Americans rely on it for 90 percent of their retirement income.

As we age, our need for medical help increases significantly. I read a statistic from the 2014 HealthView Retirement Health Care Cost Index® that said medical costs in retirement equal approximately 90 percent of our Social Security benefit. That fact alone shows the need to deliver advice that helps clients achieve a dignified retirement.

Increasing financial literacy in the U.S. is an important step in solving the retirement income crisis. Every American is responsible and accountable for his or her retirement. I believe that most people, if equipped with the right information, will make the right decisions. We have a significant opportunity to enhance financial literacy in the United States. We should start that education in elementary school and deliver it consistently in multiple forums throughout a person's life.

People deserve to understand how they can get from where they are today to where they want to be, or to know what is possible given their circumstances. This is the foundation of financial planning. But beyond understanding the planning process, Americans deserve to know and understand the various components that go into a quality financial plan.

That's why we must think of planning as a process, not an event. It's a lifelong process. We have an aging population. For those 50 years or older, the average savings is about $44,000, and that's biased by the wealthy. The median is below $10,000 and when you look a bit closer you will find that too many people age 50+ have saved zero dollars for retirement.

As an industry, I believe we have a moral obligation. As a country, we have to solve the retirement income crisis. If we don't, we may end up with unintended consequences that negatively impact mainstream Americans who don't have the financial literacy to make informed decisions and achieve dignified retirements.

A critical step forward would be for everyone involved in financial services to conduct themselves at all times with the client's best interest at the center of their thinking and actions, thoroughly understand a client's situation, life priorities and help develop and execute a plan that guides the client to achieving his or her goals.

## What's important to the client?

Good financial advice starts with the client. It starts with understanding his or her current situation, life priorities, goals, dreams and aspirations. It starts with questions that are more like a discussion — a verbal stroll through what's important to the client. We need to know our clients before making recommendations.

As the client's advisor, it is critical to help the client articulate his or her priorities. A lot of people have aspirational thoughts, but more often than not they haven't answered the questions, "What are my priorities and how do I achieve them? What are the things I need to know to put me in the best position to achieve my goals? What are the potential issues and how do I protect myself and/or my family?"

Clients want and deserve a dignified retirement, but too many haven't started to think about where they are now, where they want to be in 10, 15, 20 years and what steps they can take to put them in a better position to get there.

Having that conversation is the all-important first step in the process of providing quality financial advice.

It's also a required step in building trust. You're not going to have that conversation with me if you don't trust me. Having a conversation where you see that I'm genuine and sincere, that I really care about you and your success, is important. Part of good financial advice is genuinely caring about other people and having the desire to help them accomplish their life priorities.

The second part of quality financial advice is understanding that clients don't spend their days thinking about capital markets, asset allocation, risk management, cash flow and other financial matters. We need to help clients understand risk, timeframes, goals and ways they can, within their comfort zone, accomplish their goals or the need to adjust to realistic goals given their situation. A conversation about family and health is one part of the financial advice equation. Talk to me about your family history. Tell me about your parents, grandparents and siblings. Are you married? How long did your parents and your spouse's parents live? Did they have any health issues? How might you think about that relative to the work we are doing to create your financial plan?

## What is the client not thinking about?

The next step is to get the client to think about things he or she might not have been thinking about. Again, small and simple things make a big difference.

Let me give you an example. I was having lunch with a friend, let's call him Joe. He's very successful and has financial relationships with multiple firms. I asked him: "If you were to walk out of here today and get hit by the proverbial bus, is your family prepared? Is there one place they can go to find everything, organized and in order? Have you pulled it all together? Do you have a plan in place that's going to help them in their time of mourning?"

Looking concerned, Joe said, "You know, I don't. I think everyone's going to be well-off, but you're right. I need to simplify and organize all my information."

Another example is long term care. Seventy percent of elder Americans (65+) end up in a long term care situation. The average long term care stay is somewhere between two to three years. The average cost today for a semi-private room is $80,000 a year. We need to help clients think about the potential impact of a long term care event on their plans. It's not forcing a client into something; it's getting clients to start to think about things they might not have been thinking about that could have a negative impact on their goals.

## Now we can start to think about a strategy

Once that conversation has happened, all scenarios have been thoroughly talked through and trust has been built, we can look at developing a strategy.

Here the analogy of a financial advisor as a personal trainer makes sense. I'll get a better workout with a personal trainer because he or she is going to push me harder than I might push myself, but not before understanding my goals or health-related limitations.

Getting good financial advice is like having that personal trainer. He or she is going to do things in ways that are aligned with what you're trying to accomplish. What's more, he or she is going to help you think about how to get from where you are to where you want to be.

Through experience and knowledge, the financial advisor will educate and guide the client to get from the current state to the desired future state. Good financial advice is putting together the pieces of the plan to give the client the path and peace of mind.

## Financial planning that can adjust to changes

Sometimes life throws a curve ball. Something happens that's out of your control. You see a friend go through a situation that's devastating both personally and financially, and you say, "I don't want to go through that. How do I protect against that? I see what that did to my friend."

Unexpected things happen in life and that is why the planning process has to be a living process. It's not a one-time event. Together, the advisor and the client engage in reviews to ensure they stay on track. As life happens, we might have to help the client adjust. Maybe they adjust and are now able to do things faster with more confidence. Maybe the initial goal is to retire at 65, but based on their reality, they're going to have to work until 67. By reviewing our client's plans, we can help them make adjustments that help, given their circumstances.

Good financial advice is bringing those things together in a very trusting, caring and passionate way, always putting the client's best interest at the center of everything we do.

## The value of putting the client first

To clients: Client-advisor mutual trust is critical. Trust leads to open, honest and transparent conversations. If you don't trust your advisor, you owe it to yourself to find someone you can trust and then to be completely open and honest with him or her. I believe this is the only way your advisor will have a complete picture of your current situation, your life priorities and be able to put a plan in place for you.

To advisors: Always put the client's interests first. Any one person who stretches the envelope on that dynamic does a disservice to himself or herself, the client, the firm and the industry. Then be the best you can be. Put your energy into helping your clients achieve their life priorities. This is the business of helping people, and you play an important role in the client's life.

It's simple: If you focus on doing the right thing for the client, put his or her best interests first at all times and are fully transparent, the client should feel comfortable with you, your advice and the plan.

We should ensure we discuss anything the client has on his or her mind and should be fully transparent about anything, including the economics of the advice.

If a client came to me and said, "I have $1 million to invest. Will you invest it for me?" My reaction would be: "I'd be happy to help, but first I need to know more about you, your goals, timeframe, risk tolerance, life priorities, etc."

If all I did was put the client's money into an investment vehicle how could I be a fiduciary to that client? It doesn't feel right to me if I don't understand the client's whole situation.

Now, if the client chose not to give me the requested information and said: "All I want from you is to invest this money." Then as a financial advisor/fiduciary, I have to make a decision — and must ask myself the following:

- Is this a relationship I believe I can engage in and create value?
- Do I truly feel I'm putting that client in the best position to succeed?

I think those are the questions we have to talk about and answer as an industry. We owe it to clients to help them get from where they are to where they want to be.

Clients own their retirement and their plans, but they need help understanding what that means and how to do it. An advisor can put them in a better position for success, but can't guarantee success. Client behavior plays a significant role. Markets change. People's lives change. Still, we owe it to clients to put them in a better position for success.

We are in a great industry because we get to help clients in meaningful, heartfelt ways. I have read letters from clients in which they express how much they respect and care for their advisor because their advisor helped them achieve something meaningful in their life that they didn't think they could achieve. Some of these letters bring tears to your eyes and show why we are in a noble profession. Every client deserves a great advisor.

—◦◦◦—

**Marty Bicknell**
Chief Executive Officer

**Mariner Wealth Advisors**

Eight

# The Sleep at Night Rule

## About the Author

As the founder and chief executive officer of Mariner, the parent company of Mariner Wealth Advisors and Montage, Marty Bicknell is a recognized leader in the field of financial problem-solving for companies, closely-held family businesses, executives and entrepreneurs. At A.G. Edwards, Marty spent 15 years as a leader providing customized wealth management solutions.

## About the Company

Mariner Holdings is an asset management holding company that provides wealth management services through its subsidiaries, including Mariner Wealth Advisors and Montage. Founded in 2006, the company is based in Kansas and has offices across the country to serve families, individuals, business owners and institutional clients.

—⟋𝕞⟍—

## The process of understanding

We tend to think about good financial advice in subjective terms based on past experiences with advisors, how our expectations were shaped and whether or not they were met.

For example, a client meets with an advisor for the first time and brings an existing portfolio. The advisor takes the client through a process to determine if the portfolio is too aggressive or too passive. If so, the advisor will help the client reallocate assets so he or she has a more diversified portfolio. In all likelihood, this would be a good experience for that client because that was all he or she wanted to achieve.

But consider the client that comes in with the expectation that an advisor is going to review his or her tax situation, estate planning documents and investments to make sure the client is properly protected from a risk management perspective. If all the advisor did was advise the client on reallocating a portfolio rather than addressing the tax and estate needs, the client probably wouldn't have a good experience.

The key to ensuring a good experience is to take the client through what I like to call "the process of understanding." The advisor needs to gain a true understanding of what the client wants to achieve. The advisor accomplishes this by asking questions and finding out what is important to the client and then clarifying or outlining the client's goals. After the advisor has completed the process of understanding, he or she can develop a customized, comprehensive plan that focuses on giving the client the confidence needed to feel like he or she can reach those goals.

At Mariner Wealth Advisors, we call that the Sleep at Night Rule. For us, the Sleep at Night Rule is confidence and clarity in the client's mind that the advisor understands the client's personal financial goals and objectives.

## Consider the client's perspective

I believe advisors should approach every situation, no matter how difficult, from the perspective of what is best for the client. If advisors do that, then everything else works out.

I tend to focus a lot of my attention on full wealth planning rather than investment advice. I see investments as commodities, a means to an end. They are components of wealth advice, or good financial advice, but there are many other factors that need to be taken into consideration when creating a holistic wealth plan. Advisors need to spend their time in front of clients and have a passion to fully understand their client's goals, while also considering the client's experiences.

Frankly, being a financial advisor is a lot like being a therapist. An advisor helps the client determine his or her wealth goals and what wealth has already been accumulated. Often, advisors simply need to ask great questions and be more of a listener to uncover critical information.

During this process, I find a lot of clients have decent ideas of what they would like to accomplish, but they have a very hard time articulating their goals and thinking through all the different scenarios they may encounter in their lifetime. Again, it's not just about the allocation of a portfolio.

## Avoid the Lone Ranger

When a client thinks of good financial advice, it should not be the Lone Ranger approach in which one advisor attempts to be all things to all people. There should be a solid team behind the advisor that includes support staff and experts in areas like accounting, taxes, estate planning and insurance.

## What a financial plan isn't

A financial plan is not a product nor is it one-size-fits-all.

Instead, it's a never-ending process. It's not something in a binder that gets placed on a shelf never to be touched again. It's really about making sure the client understands that it truly is an on-going, ever-changing journey.

Consider the different steps needed to create a dynamic, quality financial plan: There is the discovery process, data collection, developing the plan, implementation and monitoring. Each of those phases has a start and finish but the entire process continues, changes and evolves as the client moves through life's stages.

Even though wealth goals should be planned over a client's life span, some advisors make the mistake of taking a short-term focus, possibly on investment returns or on certain products that can best be distributed among a group of clients.

## Navigating change

Interestingly, both advisors and clients often make too much of the precision and accuracy that need to happen in the planning process. While it's really important there's clarity, no advisor — whether a financial advisor, tax advisor or an attorney — has a crystal ball. But what advisors do have is confidence in making long-term projections. Still, things change … in the market … with tax codes … in the lives of our clients. Any projection is a guide, like a map or a GPS application. It's there to help direct a client toward the goal, but there will be times the navigation needs to change.

## Put the client first

As an investment advisor, you are a fiduciary to your clients. According to the U.S. Securities and Exchange Commission (SEC), this means you have a fundamental obligation to act in the best interests of your clients and to provide investment advice in your clients' best interests. You owe your clients a duty of undivided loyalty and utmost good faith. You should not engage in any activity in conflict with the interest of any client, and you should take steps reasonably necessary to fulfill your obligations.

In addition, you must employ reasonable care to avoid misleading clients and you must provide full and fair disclosure of all material facts (what a reasonable investor would consider to be important) to your clients and prospective clients. You must eliminate, or at least disclose, all conflicts of interest that might incline you — consciously or unconsciously — to render advice that is not disinterested. If you do not avoid a conflict of interest that could impact the impartiality of your advice, you must make full and frank disclosure of the conflict. Lastly, you cannot use your clients' assets for your own benefit or the benefit of other clients, at least without client consent.

There are people in our nation's capital who would like to move everybody, including those who are not registered, to the fiduciary standard. I don't think the fiduciary standard as it stands today can apply to all the different constituents. If officials combine the suitability and fiduciary standards, it will mean that the intents of both will have to move to the middle. If that happens, I think the end consumer loses.

For me, a fiduciary must always be an advocate for the client at every stage of the relationship. By contrast, the suitability standard relates only to the time of recommendation. Anything in between is bad news for the client.

The U.S. Department of Labor (DOL) has recently released a new ruling redefining who qualifies as a fiduciary, but the government ought to consider the different business models that exist and what would be accomplished from a regulatory oversight standpoint with each. Again, because there are different business models, it can't be a one-size-fits-all answer.

What has and will continue to come out of Washington on what it means to be a fiduciary won't likely have a big impact on the way we at Mariner deliver advice.

The future of financial advice is changing because of technology, the aging of advisors and a kind of youth movement that are occurring simultaneously – from both a client and an advice-giving perspective.

Even in the future, the quality of the advisor, and whether he or she is doing a very good job for their clients, will be a constant.

The client who finds the right advisor, with the right capacity to understand his or her situation, will be well-served. That means not just allocating capital, managing money and giving investment advice, which are certainly important, but also providing wealth advice.

I'm not sure everybody understands the difference, but it's an important one. And it is the job of advisors to help clients understand the difference.

**Catherine Bonneau**
Chief Executive Officer

**Cetera Investment Services**

Nine

# Advisors as Financial Coaches

## About the Author
Catherine Bonneau joined Cetera Investment Services in January 2006 as COO and currently serves as president and CEO. Her field tenure of over 30 years has been centered in retail financial services with an emphasis on the high net worth market. Catherine has held senior positions at ING Trust USA, BankBoston (now Bank of America), Bank of New York and Citibank.

## About the Company
Cetera Investment Services LLC, member FINRA/SIPC, provides investment, advisory and insurance solutions exclusively through its relationship with over 400 Financial Institutions and more than 1,800 advisors.

―――ᘓ―――

## Relevance and financial education

For more than 30 years, I have witnessed a great deal of change in the industry but one constant has been my belief in financial planning. Historically, what made the strategy illusive was the amount of effort for the reward. Financial advice only has value if it is relevant and customized for the person with whom an advisor is working. Also, good financial advice isn't a one-and-done process; the advice needs to consider the client's current situation, which includes financial goals, health, family status and similar items that will change over time. The advice also has to incorporate non-personal factors such as capital markets assumptions, tax rates and economic outlook. As the personal is balanced with the economic, the advice needs to change as the client's needs evolve.

For example, a client's status, family situation and financial goals will be weighted very differently in his or her 30's than in his or her 50's. Financial advice is meant to chart a course and create a direction for the client that will help maximize his or her resources for the best possible outcomes.

It's somewhat amazing that despite all financial news covering interest rates, inflation, wage trends and market performance that most consumers have no idea how these factors affect their specific financial goals and their ability to reach them. Consumers don't connect with the majority of what is shown in the media about the markets or the economy, thereby leaving advisors to act as translators to help consumers understand the markets or basic fundamental financial principles.

Many people view preparing for retirement as something that should be done, but do not have the formal education, skill or experience to know how to go about it. Relatively little media exposes them to matters that would help inform them on the components that are necessary to make and implement a good financial plan.

At its best, good advice helps fill the financial literacy void and erase the misperceptions consumers have about financial savings, such as the importance of the time value of money, a regular savings plan in order to sustain themselves in retirement or the need to have the financial ability to decide where to invest.

## Avoiding potholes

Creating a financial plan or getting financial advice is not just about investing. In fact, I think the scales have gone too far to the side of investing and not enough to other equally important personal elements of financial planning.

These key elements can have a greater impact on the overall outcome of success for an individual than the actual investment program. An example would be if someone wanted to send money to a family member in need and took those funds from his or her IRA instead of a savings account. Withdrawing the funds from the wrong bucket could potentially harm the person's financial well-being in a way that will make it virtually impossible for the investment returns to recover.

This is the kind of problem that can occur without good advice from a financial coach. Without this guidance, clients run the risk of making decisions that can harm their financial futures. It's the result of not understanding all available options, such as what account they should withdraw money from, how to maximize their tax benefits or knowing the benefits of different investment strategies. Half of heads of households between the ages of 30 and 39 with at least $100,000 in investable assets agree or strongly agree that they are willing to pay for advice, compared to 47 percent for households across all age groups, according to The Cerulli Report: Retail Investor Practices and Platforms, 2015. Someone who provides good financial advice is like someone who spots potholes and helps people steer away from them. Much of what an advisor covers is rarely, if ever, intuitive. Helping clients develop a contrarian stance to buy when others are selling is invaluable. Financial acumen is something that is learned through formal education or self-taught, both of which take plenty of initiative. Advisors identify the risks, steer clients away from them and smooth the road ahead for a better chance at a good journey and financial success.

## Keeping track

Another enormous problem that advisors can help clients with is the tracking of their financial holdings. People forget to regularly check the status of accounts, which then can easily be forgotten. This is mainly because the reporting and statements have different reporting cycles, so it's becoming harder for people to remember or to track where all their resources are located. Organization is why I'm a big believer in continuously taking a holistic view by bringing everything together. I urge clients to check their accounts regularly, but most only still tend to do so when it's necessary, such as when applying for a mortgage. To complete mortgage applications, people need to gather a large amount of documentation regarding their resources, assets and liabilities, so they are forced to pull everything together.

Short of that kind of need, people do not make the effort to pull things together and can forget about assets. Keeping track becomes increasingly challenging if you heed the statistics on the number of employers that millennials will have over the course of their careers. With 15 to 20 employers in a millennial career, according to the Multiple Generations@Work survey by Future Workplace (2012), this group runs the risk of scattering their wealth in many places, making it difficult to assemble all of their finances when they are seeking financial advice, particularly about retirement.

Another key component of sound financial plans is insurance. It is not well understood and as such, it is not something that people actively seek out. Like the adage goes: insurance isn't bought, it's sold. People tend to think about insurance protection around life events like the purchase of a home or the birth of a child, but it is far more versatile. The absence of adequate insurance coverage can be catastrophic. Moreover, people don't think about it as a tool for creating a legacy or as a type of wealth accumulation strategy that can greatly help their financial plans.

Because the contracts are complex and not easily understood by consumers, the need for education cannot be underestimated. Yet again, a good advisor needs to work with the consumer to determine the goals for obtaining insurance and creating a strategy for coverage. The advisor needs to determine how much and what type of insurance is appropriate, as well as how much risk the consumer is looking to mitigate by obtaining insurance. I think it's very challenging to get insurance protection on your own.

## A good coach

Good financial advice comes from a good financial life coach. Setting goals and reaching them can easily be accomplished when you have a coach who helps you stay on track. Having a good personal financial coach means having someone who offers good financial advice and makes certain you stay true to your plan and what you want to achieve.

It's very much like having someone help you with a diet and exercise plan. That coach keeps you working toward your goals and makes adjustments as needed but keeps you moving forward.

It is not a financial coach's role to set objectives and hold you to them. A good coach recognizes that your goals will change over time, as everyone's tend to do. When I was 30 my goals changed from earlier, when I turned 40 they changed again and then again at 50. How those goals are modified over time and what resources are available to fund those goals also evolves over time. It's a time continuum that your coach helps you think about, such as modifying things over the course of one's life to make sure goals remain relevant and the action steps to achieve them stay appropriate.

## Robo-advice versus robo-investing

It's my opinion that the term "robo-advice" is terribly misleading. Most of the tools that hold themselves out to be robo-advisors are really robo-investing systems. They will ask some basic questions to gauge a person's risk appetite to get at an acceptable model for one's risk tolerance. That's not advice. That's going right at the heart of the investment process. All of the focus is on investment, not actual advice. All of the other factors I've talked about — financial literacy, sticking to your goals, insurance protection and the right distribution strategies — are not currently addressed by the robo-investing utilities I have surveyed in the market.

These robos set things at a point in time. You complete the risk questionnaires at a given point, with X amount of dollars. Now that robo utility really doesn't know if that's your last dime or if it's a small portion of your overall money without a broader view or thinking about how you will feel about risk over time.

For the most part, robo-investing utilities are only getting at the best way to manage the identified resources, as well as the best way to implement an investment strategy for said resources. That's not to say that we won't get there, with robo-investing information as a start, but at the moment I really only see this as robo-investing and not robo-advice.

## Planning is a creative process

Developing an effective financial plan needs to be a creative process that occurs between the client and the advisor. During the planning process, the client brings his or her resources, goals, aspirations, desired outcomes and what he or she wants to accomplish based on the available resources. All of this is considered within the scope of the financial plan in collaboration with an advisor.

A good advisor helps the client see potential gaps or blind spots in his or her goals and resources. A parent may be incredibly passionate about funding his or her child's education, putting all his or her chips on the table for the child's future. A good financial advisor will say, "But you also have to protect yourself in order to achieve that. You have to be concerned for your longevity and your own retirement."

If that client waits until after that child is educated, he or she may have insufficient time to provide for his or her own financial well-being in retirement. The advisor serves as a check and balance for a client's resources as it relates to his or her goals. For the advisor to be a source of trusted advice, he or she needs to have access to the tools and the knowledge of things that can affect a client's financial well-being, such as the tax code or strategies and product solutions that can help fulfill the client's goals.

If a financial plan doesn't have an ongoing review process built in to measure the progress toward goals that are specific, measurable, achievable, relevant and time bound, it is not worth the paper it's printed on. If an advisor and client don't check back to see the progress or lack thereof, both will have wasted their time in developing the plan. Remember, even if the client's goals don't change, the markets do.

Additionally, there'll be changes in the regulatory landscape or the tax code that may affect the plan's outcome. A financial plan that is incredibly detailed and weighty, but is never touched again, might as well be a cinder block. It has to be a living document that is continually revisited, ideally, by both the client and the advisor.

## It should be human nature

I'm not sure clients really understand what it means for their advisors to be fiduciaries. I think it is human nature to want to trust each other. Looking to put definitions around human nature is very hard. At its core, the term "fiduciary" means you are trustworthy. You will treat others as you would want them to treat you.

If you can look in the mirror and say, "Yes, this is how I would want to be treated and this is how I would want my loved ones to be treated," then the fiduciary concept is nothing to worry about. It is a standard and a code to live by. One way I like to describe it is the "Grandmother Test." Is it something I would do for my grandmother and, then, be able to tell her about it without any anxiety or sense of shame? After all, she's my grandma.

Simply stated, it's a matter of integrity. When there isn't constant integrity or trust in the system, plenty of regulations and rules will be developed to try to ensure one is acting from the position of integrity and professionalism.

That seems to be what's giving the industry some cause for pause. It's not that people aren't acting with integrity. It's that their integrity is almost being impugned by new rules that may undermine what they would do in treating others as they would want to be treated. It's those unintended consequences that are challenging the industry as a whole.

A likely case in point: People say I was acting in good faith. I believed it was in the best interest of my client at that point in time. The client and I made the best possible choices based on what the client had and what was available in the marketplace at the time. But these choices will be subject to future scrutiny and events that will change with the passage of time.

At its core, the fiduciary standard is about acting in a client's best interest by putting the interest of the client ahead of all other considerations. This does not necessarily mean providing services or securities at the lowest price. As a result, acting in the client's best interest is often open to interpretation, especially after the fact, and can be complicated because of multiple standards that may apply.

Financial advisors may be subject to multiple fiduciary standards. The Advisers Act of 1940 and the U.S. Department of Labor (DOL) rules all have fiduciary requirements that can vary based on the type of account and advice that is being provided. The U.S. Securities and Exchange Commission (SEC) is currently discussing additional fiduciary rules.

There can be no specific answer as to what is in the best interest of every client because the needs of every client vary. However, that is what makes personalized advice from financial advisors so important. They are in a unique position to understand not only a client's financial needs, but also the goals and dreams of clients that may not be directly related to their investments. While there are no guarantees, those advisors that provide the most thoughtful and personalized advice to clients and provide advice that is in the best interest of clients are the least likely to be questioned about their advice at a later time.

## Excited about the future

I'm more excited about financial planning now than I ever have been. Earlier in my career, financial planning was ponderous. It was cash flow-based and loaded with analytical details, the majority of which never got implemented. It was an effort that, at the end, both clients and professionals wondered why they even bothered.

Technology is the reason I am so excited. It makes everything that goes into a financial plan very visible to the client and increases the ease for the advisor as well. Very soon, as soon as a client checks Instagram and their Twitter feed, he or she will be able to see how the plan is doing, what progress is being made and what adjustments need to be made to the course.

My children are twenty-something. They love constant checking and validation. I think millennials coming on as clients of financial advisors are going to be strong adopters of planning, making smart use of technology and the information available online.

That said, as an industry, we still face the challenge of improving everyone's technology skills to where they are confident rather than threatened. The key is to recognize that technology, as a tool, is one thing; it makes the validation, checking and updating of information much easier. But the collaborative and creative process that occurs in the beginning between clients and their advisor that helps create good financial plans is quite another.

The blend of human intelligence and computing power will be with us for quite some time. Maybe I'm old school, but I do not see artificial intelligence eliminating the human advisor from the financial planning and management processes any time soon.

## Brent R. Brodeski, MBA, CPA, CFP®, CFA®, AIFA®
### Chief Executive Officer

### Savant Capital Management

Ten

# Growing and Sharing the Pie

## About the Author

Brent Brodeski brings more than 25 years of experience to his role as CEO of Savant Capital Management. Brent is the co-founder and past president of the industry association Zero Alpha Group (ZAG) and the co-founder of boutique industry group Alliance for RIAs (aRIA). Brent is regularly featured in local, industry and national media.

## About the Company

Established 30 years ago, Savant Capital Management is an independent, fee-only wealth management firm with a focus on providing integrated investment management, financial planning and tax and family office services to individuals, trust funds, retirement plans and non-profit organizations. Headquartered in Illinois, Savant has 13 offices across three states and clients nationwide.

—ɯ—

## The triangle – creating value

Financial advisors are in the business of building ideal futures for clients, their teams and the communities they serve. The big question is: How does an advisor do that? How do they simultaneously deliver top financial advice to clients, provide great career opportunities to their team and ensure they benefit from an enjoyable and profitable career?

In simplest terms, it's not a win-lose matter. Rather, it's about growing the pie as big as possible, creating maximum value, and, then, sharing the pie. Do that and everyone's going to end up with their fair share.

For example: Imagine a triangle, where one point is the client, the next is the advisor, and the third is the advisory firm. Look at the space in the middle of the triangle as the value created. If you don't have all three constituents, there's no value.

That's not to say you can't get clients and have a business. You'll have clients who come in, realize they're getting duped and leave. For that matter, capable advisors won't stay around either. And, by extension, the advisory firm may be unprofitable and eventually hit a wall from a growth perspective. Bottom line, lack of alignment between all three constituents means it is far harder to create value and all three parties lose.

I call it a balance; the advisor needs to trust the firm and the firm needs to trust that the clients want it to be successful. There's a leap of faith that all three parties need to make that can yield a win-win-win type of outcome.

You have to care about having a relationship with all parts of the triangle lasting over time. Other approaches tend to produce smaller pies.

## Clarifying client vision

Before developing a financial plan, you need to think about the clients' goals. They don't really care about the tools advisors use, or the investments, the plan or the taxes. What clients really care about is how to get to their ideal futures. It's not about the money. The money is just the tool to get there.

When thinking about how to maximize the value, advisors should start by helping the clients clarify values and priorities.

Interestingly, clients don't often have answers to these questions because they are busy living their lives. But the advisor is in the unique position of being able to help clients figure out their goals and make recommendations on how to help them achieve those goals. The advisor can help clients clarify what success looks like and what their ideal futures can be.

## Getting to the destination

Developing a financial plan, choosing investments and declaring a tax strategy are the easy parts. I look at them as gasoline; you need to fill the tank if you want to get to a desired destination. Make no mistake, investments are important, but in more ways than not, they're simply what can be used to help get a client to their destination.

But the advisor who helps the client determine what success looks like will then be able to step back and say: "This is the structure, the comprehensive financial plan and the recommended investments." They may not guarantee success, but they will get the client much closer to his or her ideal goal. Helping clients get to where they want to be is the primary job of a good advisor.

## Delivering 'peace of mind'

Clients may tell an advisor they want simplicity, ease, clarity, confidence and focus. But when looked at together, what the client is really saying is he or she has a strong desire for "peace of mind." A good advisor helps clients implement customized financial plans, solid investment strategies and tax-efficient benefits. If an advisor does that, he or she is certain to deliver "peace of mind," which manifests itself as the best outcome possible for the client, his or her family and his or her heirs. That's what it's really all about.

In our view, advisors are far too focused on the investment decision. The problem is that a solid investment portfolio alone does not create "peace of mind." Not to diminish the importance of a sound portfolio and good retirement projections, but an advisor's true focus when creating a quality financial plan is to align the assets and the strategies with the values and priorities of the client.

Next is the need to understand the value being created. Let's say a client is on a trip to his or her ideal future. The client may want to take a snooze for a couple of hours and then wake up that much closer to the destination. During that nap, the client needs to know that the driver — the advisor — is in control and the client doesn't have to worry about getting into an accident along the way, or, if there's a detour, the advisor will work around it.

I call that "invisible value." The advisor makes everything more manageable and easily understood. The advisor does this by showing the client he or she is in a good place and will be able to do the things he or she cares about. That is value that cannot be assigned a number or show up on an investment statement. It's about helping turn aspirations into reality.

If a client gets to a good place, he or she will tell their friends: "I'm able to retire now because my advisor really helped me along the way." Or, "We just took this great family vacation because my advisor pointed out that I could afford to go and, wow, it was great spending time with my grandchildren."

That's a different type of endorsement than, "My advisor recommended a great portfolio that had a low standard deviation and high expected returns." That's boring. But, "My advisor enabled me to be successful" is a more meaningful type of endorsement, one that creates value for the relationship.

## A common alignment

First and foremost, an advisor needs to be a fiduciary. The advisor puts the client and the firm's interests first. A fiduciary, in my view, is someone who stands in another person's shoes, looks through the other person's eyes and says, "If this was my money or my family's, this is the way I would handle it."

That's a great theory, but it only works if the way the advisor and the firm are paid are aligned to create the best outcome for the client. Absent that, the conflict of interest means the investments, the structures and the products may be great for the firm or the advisor, but not so great for the client.

How many times have we heard about products being sold that are good for the advisor or the firm, but not for the client? Or situations where there were kickbacks and revenue sharing to promote one product over another? Maybe it was disclosed, maybe not. Those situations can't possibly represent a common alignment.

## Compensating supportive behavior

Let's look at compensation. The compensation system needs to find a balance between stunting growth and creating value. It has to encourage both a focus on proactive business development and the optimal delegation of client service work. If you're a top advisor and you're really good at getting clients and managing relationships, you need capable people to whom you can hand off a lot of the day-to-day detail work.

A good advisor needs to encourage mentorship within his or her firm. A healthy growing organization has gray hairs and capable understudies who will one day be the gray hairs. The gray hairs need to embrace the next generation of smart young talent.

A senior advisor should be doing what he or she does best, which is get clients, advance relationships and convey wisdom. The next generation should be able to do meaningful work and gain experience working on the gray hair's larger clients.

The associated compensation needs to take into account the encouragement of relationship building between the generations. If a firm can grow its own talent, it can scale with far greater ease. If the compensation system is not structured properly, it tends to encourage competition between generation one and generation two, when what you really want is collaboration between them so that the mentor and mentee both win.

A well-designed compensation system also needs to encourage a culture of teamwork. Pure "eat what you kill" cultures or structures inhibit teamwork and scalability. They also don't create an enterprise focused on making the pie as big as possible. It focuses on high payouts for specific individuals.

Growth, good service, mentorship, teamwork and making sure services are priced properly, when taken together and done the right way, means the pie gets bigger. The advisor makes more, the supporting team gets to do what it is good at and likes to do, and the client gets a great outcome.

## The fiduciary and the platform

The non-fiduciary model is essentially one that says, "We don't care how you get it, go get it." The fiduciary model, one that aligns the interests of all involved, requires a robust platform that enables advisors to be very efficient and effective. It allows them to truly help clients.

When I talk about a platform, I mean a support platform. With that in place, advisors can take their time to develop their businesses and relationships, and to mentor the next generation. I think the optimal model enables senior advisors to focus on mentoring the new generation while developing, advising and servicing client relationships 80+ percent of the time. The advisor, the next gen and the client all win. For most advisors this is an awesome model.

If you enable advisors to do what they're really good at, they're going to drive more revenue, have more fun and create a lot more value for clients.

# The bionic advisor

There was a TV show a number of years ago where Steve Austin was "The Six Million Dollar Man." He wasn't a robot, he was human, but had technology that supplemented his human qualities so he could do superhuman things like run faster, see farther and use superhuman strength. Firms should have a platform that turns its advisors into Steve Austins — into bionic advisors.

Another program that is relevant is "24." The storyline is based on the premise that characters never have time to prepare or follow up — they're just on, in real time, always going. Looking out 20 years, that's what I expect to see for advisors.

The more traditional model for advisory is the client meets with an advisor. The advisor collects some data; the data is reviewed, put into a model and evaluated. After that, the advisor shows the outcomes to the client. This can occur over the course of several meetings. It's a long, arduous and expensive process; not efficient for the advisor or the client. It just takes too long.

I recommend a platform that leverages the concept of the two shows I referenced — providing advisors with bionic tools that enable them to do everything in real time. We create processes and packages that add value in terms of workshops, assessments and technology. The client meets with the advisor about the plan and hits the ground running. When the client walks away from each meeting, value has been created.

Of course, this won't work for every advisor. Even as technology is developed and deployed to help make better decisions faster, there are many advisors who want to maintain the status quo; to keep doing what they're doing the way they have been doing it for however long. The problem with that attitude is they won't be able to make the pie bigger. And by not embracing change, stagnation inevitably enters the equation.

# It's about growth

We've looked at the client and the advisor, now let's turn our attention to the firm; the last component of the triangle.

Growth is imperative for a firm. Profits are important. But growth is equally or possibly more important. Growth allows the firm to invest in people, technology, and the processes - those bionic tools that enable advisors to, in real time, create value for clients.

If you're not growing, it's impossible to attract and retain top new talent and develop them into the next generation of gray hairs and mentors. That new talent allows for efficiency. They create the profits. If the firm is set up with the gray hairs doing all the work and keeping all the money for themselves, the company can't re-invest in itself. If you're not creating the next generation and bionic tool kits to create more value for clients, you're not growing the pie.

Hiring smart also addresses succession planning. Having understudies means clients will continue to be well served when the gray hairs go off into the sunset in pursuit of their own ideal futures.

I recall a Harvard professor speaking on the growth of professional services firms, citing 15 percent annual growth as the target. That target allows for a level of growth that supports attracting and retaining good talent, putting in place strong tools and helping firms achieve scale in a manageable manner.

Another requirement is collaboration. A firm can't have a bunch of cowboys and grow at 15 percent per year. It needs to be an organization in which people are encouraged to focus on their strengths, their unique abilities and support each other.

The platform, the incentive structure that is in alignment with the interests of the client, the advisor and the firm, plus a commitment to grow the pie for everyone's benefit must all be in place. There must also be a continuous assessment by the firm that those components are working optimally for top-notch performance over time.

It is my experience and unwavering belief that if people have skin in the game, a firm will operate better and produce better results. If employees are just transactional functionaries, get W-2 forms and show up 9 to 5, the business won't be all that it can be — for the employees or their clients.

Truly successful businesses are the ones that empower their teams to participate in the upside. There are lots of ways to do this. One is to make key employees owners. Another is to create bonus plans that tie payouts back to the firm's success. There are several other options, but what way is chosen matters less than getting employees from being on the sideline into the heart of the game. Your team members need skin in the game!

You also need a sustainable culture that people can genuinely relate to. The wheels fall off, as it were, when interests are not aligned. And, of course, the pie shrinks.

## Plan for your future and that of your practice

Many advisors have poured their hearts and souls into building their businesses — early mornings, late nights and long weekends. Advisors do it to develop a successful practice that serves their clients' best interests by safeguarding and growing their hard-earned wealth. But the question that rarely gets asked is, "Who's helping to look out for *your* best interests?" After all, when all is said and done, your happiness and your success are inexorably linked to achieving an "ideal future."

Sure, you're good at what you do and your clients trust you without a hint of hesitation. But let's not overlook the fact that this is a relationship business. Yes, there are training, tools and experience developed over time. But I believe it's as important for the financial professional to take stock of his or her advisory practice and day-to-day role within the firm.

As you think about the best path forward for you, your clients and your firm, I suggest you think about the following:

- Do you still enjoy your daily routine? Are you focused on clients or are you weighed down by administrative tasks like compliance, HR matters and dealing with technology?
- Do you have the time, energy, interest, capital and know-how to bring you and/ or your business to the next level?
- Do you have a plan to extract the equity you worked so hard to build when it's time to step away?

Your clients have trusted you for years, perhaps decades. You wouldn't want to leave them high and dry, so to speak. How can you effectively manage a transition when you are ready to retire?

It's as much your responsibility as it is a matter of fairness and transparency to your clients that you have taken the necessary steps to ensure they will receive the same caliber of planning and advice. This assurance allows you to move on to enjoy the most satisfying part of a good financial plan — knowing that you have helped your clients achieve retirements they can thoroughly enjoy.

In that regard, merging with a larger firm, with the capabilities to handle all your clients' needs, does not signal failure on your part. It says, "I'm thinking of that triangle." At the same time you're also thinking about you. And there's nothing wrong with that.

## Looking ahead

There have been many recent discussions about new regulations or ways to define the meaning of the term fiduciary, particularly in regards to the new rule from the U.S. Department of Labor (DOL) regarding the best interests of clients. I look at all this and see something that doesn't serve much purpose.

I'd rather think about disruption. Uber comes along and disrupts the taxi business; Apple's iPhone disrupted cameras as well as all sorts of other industries, like music. Blockbuster was disrupted and destroyed by Netflix. I could go on and on.

When you look at an industry that gets disrupted, it actually grows. There is more music played today than ever before. There are more photos taken. There are more people using Uber.

When disruption inevitably comes along in the financial advice business, our industry will get bigger — albeit with many new entrants. However, what won't ever change is the need for good financial advice.

Yes, we will see consolidation in our industry as sole or smaller practices prepare for the day their work ends and as the bigger players become more effective at institutionalizing the creation of the value process, by leveraging people, process and technology.

But on the positive side, we will also see organizations that represent a true alignment of the interests of their clients, their teams and the firms. And that is the triangle concept on a larger, more efficient scale — in which all parties benefit. I look forward to and welcome this new reality. While disruption will challenge our industry and those resistant to change, clients will be better served and disruption will provide new and profitable opportunities for the most innovative and forward-thinking advisory firms focused on value creation.

**Joel P. Bruckenstein, CFP®**
President

Technology Tools for Today (T3)

Eleven

# Planning: A Meeting of the Minds

## About the Author
FinTech consultant, author and journalist Joel P. Bruckenstein, CFP®, is the Publisher of the T3 Tech Hub (T3newsletter.com). He is a frequent contributor to financial planning publications and was the Senior Technology Editor at MorningstarAdvisor.com for six years. Joel, a practicing financial planner for many years, brings together the needs of financial services together with technology tools in the Annual T3 Enterprise Conferences.

## About the Company
Technology Tools for Today (T3) publishes the T3 Tech Hub and hosts two conferences per year, both of which bring together technology and the challenges of financial services. The annual conferences provide financial advisors and executives an opportunity to learn about new technology and influence future technological developments.

―――ⁿⁿ―――

## A meeting of the minds

The first thing one needs to understand is that financial planning is a process, not a one-time occurrence. It's really important to understand that at the beginning.

The most important thing that has to happen is a meeting of the minds. The potential client and the planner should discuss the scope of the engagement. Once the scope has been set, the planner needs to gather some information.

The following are the steps of the financial planning process:

1) The planner must gather whatever information is necessary to understand the client's goals. That information is essential to creating a plan that helps the client achieve his or her goals.
2) Then the planner does some analysis and strategizing with the client to look at various options.
3) Recommendations are made.
4) The plan is implemented.
5) The planner monitors the plan.

## Process equals planner

A consumer needs to determine if the planner has a planning process. If not, the person is probably not a real planner. If the planner doesn't talk to the client immediately about the scope of the engagement, what he or she is going to do or help the client analyze his or her needs, then the person offering the "advice" is not a planner.

There are a lot of people out there today that put the title "financial advisor" on their business cards. I've seen insurance agents do it. I've actually seen mortgage brokers do it. I've even seen loan officers at car dealerships do it. Clearly none of these people are offering comprehensive financial planning.

## Client's interest first

The cornerstone of good advice is to be as objective as possible. As a planner, you must put the client's interests first. If you're not recommending the best course of action and the best products and services based on the client's needs — as opposed to what's good for your pocketbook — then you're not providing good advice.

In my opinion, good advice is always putting the clients' interest first and making sure that you're addressing their needs and not your own.

In any relationship there's always a chance for some conflicts of interest. It's important for anybody holding himself or herself out as a financial planner to disclose what those potential conflicts might be and what, if anything, the planner is doing to address those issues.

To some extent disclosures work, but there may be cases where there are certain things the planner can't disclose away. There are some financial institutions that give pages and pages of disclosure. Obviously, nobody reads them. Financial disclosures have unclear language that a layperson can't understand. Disclosures need to be short, sweet and in plain English.

## Finding a planner

If a consumer is looking for a financial planner, a good place to start is with industry organizations and credentialing groups. They should look for somebody who is either a Certified Financial Planner (CFP®) or Personal Financial Specialist (PFS). The latter is the financial planning designation of the American Institute of Certified Public Accountants (AICPA). At the very least, the credentials show some level of competency. The National Association of Personal Financial Planners (NAPFA) is another good source of referrals and consumer information.

Referrals obviously are one way to start. If the consumer knows someone who is satisfied with their planner, that might be a relationship with potential. Today there are electronic means of conducting due diligence before meeting with somebody. Consumers should go to the firm's website. If the planner is a Registered Investment Advisor (RIA), consumers can review the firm's Form ADV Part 2. Many people make that form available now on the web.

Another good place to look is LinkedIn. If an advisor or planner has a complete LinkedIn profile, it reads very much like a resume. The consumer can see the person's job history, professional designations and whether or not he or she is registered with the Financial Industry Regulatory Authority (FINRA) and more. BrokerCheck has a database that lets a potential client check someone's work history and if there are any complaints. There are a number of organizations, like the National Association of Personal Financial Advisors (NAPFA), that offer a checklist of questions a consumer should ask when interviewing a potential financial advisor.

If somebody starts to make recommendations before knowing the potential client and understanding his or her situation, that's a red flag for sure. If somebody is affiliated with a firm, whether it's a broker-dealer or an insurance company, and all that's being recommended are investments from their company, that's a red flag.

Consumers should look to understand how the planner is compensated. Is it a flat fee? Is it a fee-based on assets under management (AUM)? Is it by commissions? Compensation needs to be spelled out.

They should see if they can get something in writing that states the planner is going to act as a fiduciary and will put the client's interests first at all times. Consumers probably will want to know whether or not they accept referral fees from others. In addition, they'll want to know what kind of clients he or she has.

The client should ask if they are a typical client for the advisory firm or an outlier. If the firm has a lot of people just like them, it's more likely to be a satisfactory relationship.

If the client has a lot of their assets tied up in company benefit plans, whether it's a 401(k) plan or deferred compensation, is that firm or individual advisor conversant in those plans or is it something new? It's better to have a firm or individual advisor already familiar with those types of plans.

Another thing I think is becoming more and more prevalent in the industry is the succession plan. If I'm engaging an advisor, I'll want to know what happens if something happens to him or her. Is there somebody else in the firm who can carry on or am I going to be left holding the bag?

A lot of firms are trying to use state-of-the-art technology to automate the financial planning process as much as possible and make it efficient to keep costs down while also providing a better experience for the end client.

## Technology matters

If an advisor is doing calculations on an abacus or an old hand-held calculator, it wouldn't give me a lot of confidence that he or she is with a state-of-the-art firm. The consumer can get a feel for an individual planner or firm's technology aptitude by looking at the planner's website or seeing if he or she has a presence on social media such as LinkedIn. A visit to the planner's office offers a helpful view of the technology capabilities as well as how the planner processes paperwork. Will the client have the option of electronic signatures for paperwork or is everything manual? Does the planner use faxes or allow the client to log onto a website to access information? Reams of paper and use of fax machines are not confidence builders today.

Professional designations show the planner is continuing his or her professional education to maintain those certifications. Interestingly, not every organization requires continuing education in technology. I would want to know from anybody I am doing business with what he or she is doing to stay current with technology. I would make sure the best software is being used to give me the best experience, to provide me with proper service. Additionally, given how our society is increasingly mobile, I will want to know if the firm's site and other portals are mobile-friendly.

The reality is if a business isn't being run efficiently, it's not going to be successful and you're going to have to look for a new planner.

If a firm has policies or a history of policies that aren't consumer-friendly, I'd be concerned. Further, I would ask: "Can you assure me that you're going to follow 'client-first' practices or that there is no pressure being put on you to do things that are not in my best interest?" The answer you hear will likely be influenced by compensation models and disclosure. If somebody is willing to put into writing that he or she will put your interests first, then you have something to hang your hat on.

## Better technology, better planning

We need to realize that as technology improves there will be new tools that enable us to better serve clients. Right now, for risk tolerance, we ask people questions and develop their portfolio based on the answers.

I think people are trying to give the right answers, but there may be subconscious or emotional undertones that advisors are not picking up on particularly when they first meet clients. They're relying on what clients tell them.

Clients may not even be aware of some of the subconscious issues they have. There is technology emerging that can help us better understand what clients' emotions or inner feelings are as well as their "real" needs that will enable us to do better planning.

There is plenty of financial planning software available today. However, very few programs do a good job. I would say it's very difficult for the end client to judge whether his or her advisor is using good software and whether it's comprehensive.

The consumer should ask a few questions to get a clearer view of the tools being used. Here's another red flag: When the planner says his or her firm has "the proprietary system that nobody has," that's something to worry about.

If a commercial software is being used by thousands or tens of thousands of advisors across the country, the odds are good that any problems with the system have been uncovered somewhere before. Whereas if it's a proprietary system, those problems are likely to still exist.

A client's financial planning report should cover all of the aspects of his or her finances that were laid out at the beginning of the planning process. If it's just an investment plan, then it's not a comprehensive financial plan. It needs to include:

- Various aspects of risk
- Life insurance
- Disability insurance
- Long term care insurance
- Retirement planning
- Education planning (if indicated)
- Tax aspects
- Estate planning
- Social Security planning
- Employee stock options

A comprehensive financial plan needs to cover everything discussed initially and must be thorough. Just as important as the elements mentioned earlier, the client must understand and be able to act on it. Otherwise, it's not a good plan.

## Recent regulatory developments

Despite the recent adoption of the Fiduciary Rule by the U.S. Department of Labor (DOL), a significant minority of industry participants still oppose the decision. I've heard many folks say: "If we don't have a commission-based system we can't afford to service those smaller accounts." My answer to that is: "The problem is not a regulatory problem; it is a technology problem. Many industry participants either have the technology to efficiently service smaller clients under the new standard, or they are creating that capability. The fault is not in the regulation; it is in the inefficient, antiquated systems that have existed for too long within many financial services firms."

Again, I think technology is the answer to servicing smaller accounts efficiently. Technology has disrupted just about every other industry that I can think of. Now it is our turn. The lesson that we can learn from other industries is that those who stubbornly stick to traditional industry practices are often marginalized by those who adopt technology.

## What's next?

Historically, personal financial planning has put more emphasis on assets and less on the liability side of the balance sheet. We've put more emphasis on accumulation and less on decumulation. Going forward there will be more emphasis on better management of liabilities as well as assets. In addition, the more challenging aspect of financial planning is managing the decumulation phase.

No one has come up with the silver bullet to address that yet and as such, I think there'll be continuing research to devise more effective methods.

**Mercer Bullard**
Founder and President, Fund Democracy, Inc.

Butler, Snow, O'Mara, Stevens, and Cannada Lecturer
University of Mississippi School of Law

Twelve

# The Fiduciary Standard: A Predicate for Prudent Advice

## About the Author

Mercer Bullard, president and founder of Fund Democracy and a securities law professor at the University Of Mississippi School Of Law, has over 25 years of regulatory experience. Prior to founding Fund Democracy, Mercer was an Assistant Chief Counsel in the SEC's Division of Investment Management. His legal experience spans private roles and public posts, including as an attorney in the investment management practice of Wilmer, Cutler & Pickering and as a clerk for Judge Will Garwood, U.S. Court of Appeals, Fifth Circuit.

## About the Company

Fund Democracy, founded in January 2000, serves as an advocate and information source for mutual fund shareholders and their advisors and has testified before Congress on more than 20 occasions. It provides a voice for mutual fund shareholders by publishing articles that target mutual fund practices, policies and rules that are harmful to fund shareholders and by lobbying policymakers on investment-related regulatory issues.

—⟋⟍—

# The fiduciary standard: A predicate for prudent advice

It might not be obvious why prudent advice and effective planning services depend on holding advisors to a fiduciary standard. The fiduciary standard goes to an advisor's standard of conduct, whereas financial advice goes to the quality of the advisor's services. In fact, they are closely related.

A society that does not hold professionals such as doctors and lawyers to a fiduciary standard cannot expect them to provide medical or legal advice that is based solely on the best interest of the patient or client. All modern economies have for centuries applied the fiduciary standard to medical and legal services. The fiduciary standard is no less a necessary predicate for the relatively new profession of financial planning. Fiduciary standards are an inherent element of good advice and effective planning services.

# Information gathering

Good advice is about helping clients achieve financial security, which depends on far more than simply the makeup and size of their investment portfolio. Good advice reflects the advisor's evaluation of the client's overall financial picture and the integration of multiple aspects of the client's financial life. For example, an important aspect of every individual's financial situation is the way in which he or she finances the purchase of a home, often through a mortgage, and the way in which the client protects against risk, typically through insurance.

An advisor can only provide good advice after having gathered a substantial amount of information from the client. In financial planning, it is critical to begin by asking the client questions covering a wide range of topics. What insurance coverage does he or she have? How is the client financing housing? Does he or she have dependents? How does the client expect to live in retirement? What are his or her financial worries?

Good advice starts with a fairly intensive fact-gathering exercise. If a financial planner has not exhaustively interviewed the client and developed a very sound sense of the client's financial situation, future plans, goals and specific concerns, then the planner cannot give the client good advice. There is often a misconception that good advice is an objective standard. It is not. Good advice is highly individualized. Advice that is not tailored to the particular client is not good advice.

## The client's future self

Perhaps the most difficult component of good advice is impressing upon the client the importance of balancing the interests of his or her current and future self. It is difficult for clients to make decisions today in terms of their effect on a quite distant tomorrow. Many clients have difficulty reducing current consumption to save enough to support their expected lifestyle decades into the future. Few clients embrace planning for a future in which death or disability prevents them from providing for their families.

Good advice regarding clients' future selves is the most important advice that an advisor can give. A perfect storm is brewing in advanced economies as a result of rising life expectancy and increasing rates of mental incapacity. Longer lifespans exacerbate longevity risk by increasing the number of years after retirement that assets must generate income. In elderly clients' later years, when their income is most likely to be stretched, they are most likely to have lost the mental capacity to make sound financial decisions or to protect themselves against fraud.

Good advice includes the uncomfortable issue of how and under what circumstances the best decisions will be made if the client is not capable of making them. This is a sensitive area, particularly because experience shows that the persons who are most likely to exploit the elderly are their own family members, while these same family members feel entitled to make decisions for their aging relatives. These considerations may create conflicts and good advice will entail navigating them with extreme caution and heightened care.

## Active versus passive management

The relative merits of active and passive investment management have become a prominent issue in discussions of what constitutes good advice. Commentators often characterize one as good advice and the other as bad advice. Neither is correct. There is no empirical support for the view that it is inherently bad advice to recommend, for example, specific securities for investment based on an evaluation of how they will perform relative to the market of similar securities. Nor can it be said that designing a portfolio to match but never exceed the performance of an asset class is necessarily bad advice. Neither active nor passive management is inherently good or bad advice.

Nonetheless, bad advice regarding the passive versus active management abounds, and it is most prevalent for the latter. Active managers often fail to provide adequate advice regarding the special considerations and risks that are attendant upon active management. This includes fully explaining, for example, that active management does not make sense unless the added value of active management is expected to exceed the additional cost of providing it. The issue here is not whether such a belief can be reasonable, but rather that the explicit nature of this tradeoff is commonly ignored or obfuscated. Advisors generally do not explain that the probability of underperformance is, on average, greater than the probability of outperformance because of the additional fee paid for active management.

This common failing is exacerbated by the related failure to ensure that clients understand the heightened downside risk of active management. Few clients understand that the cost of a dollar of market underperformance exceeds the benefit of a dollar of outperformance. To illustrate, imagine a client with a $1 million portfolio that is expected to produce, assuming a 4 percent drawdown rate and $40,000 in annual income in retirement. If the portfolio rises 40 percent in value, the expected annual income rises to 4 percent of $1.4 million, or $56,000. If the portfolio falls 40 percent in value, expected income falls to 4 percent of $600,000, or $24,000.

These outcomes appear to be evenly balanced, but they are not. The effect on a client's lifestyle will be very different. If the client's income drops from $40,000 to $24,000, the client might be unable to pay medical bills or rent, or put food on the table every day. If income increases from $40,000 to $56,000, the client may be able to eat out more often, or afford a vacation or gifts for grandchildren.

The point here is that, whatever the additional benefits of outperformance are, they will include fewer necessities and more non-necessities than what will be given up if income declines as a result of underperformance. The pain of a decline in income therefore will necessarily exceed the pleasure realized from an equal gain in income.

In my view, active management is bad advice unless the heightened downside risk of active management as to assets that are intended to pay for essentials is fully understood by clients. To be clear, this risk can be rationally assumed. And this risk is neither unvarying nor unique to active management. It can be mitigated by diversification and proper liquidity management. And this risk is shared by passive managers to the extent that they recommend investing in volatile asset classes, the value of which may decline precipitously. Advisors who offer active or passive management services in both cases typically fail to explain the advantages of purchasing an annuity — a fixed income stream provided by an insurance company — to cover a client's minimum income needs, and thereby minimizing underperformance risk.

In summary, the failing of active management is the routine failure to disclose and ensure that clients understand its particular value proposition, the higher probability on average of underperformance and the higher cost of underperformance relative to out-performance. There are comparable disclosure obligations for passive managers, such as the fact that the client will not do better than the market (while some active managers' clients will) and that large losses may occur. However, the scope and frequency of disclosure failures is greater when advisors recommend active management.

## Effective planning

The goal of providing good financial advice is the implementation of an effective financial plan. Like good advice, an effective plan reflects the individual characteristics and financial situation of the client. An effective plan matches the client's individual profile with a course of action.

For example, an effective plan matches the liquidity of a client's assets with the client's potential liquidity needs. A fixed, indexed or variable annuity is often not consistent with an older client's liquidity needs. Neither is investing in college funds for a client's 17-year old child in volatile assets, or deducting a commission equal to 50 percent of a client's initial investment in a long-term investment contract. Yet these have been common practices in the financial services industry, in direct contradiction of what constitutes an effective plan.

A key requirement of an effective financial plan is that it be current and flexible. At its inception, an effective plan reflects the implementation of a strategy based on a client's then-current financial situation. But every client's financial situation is inherently fluid, which means that a plan can be effective only as long as it is regularly updated. A plan that is created and then left unreviewed for years ceases to be an effective plan.

However, ongoing evaluation of a plan increases the client's costs. The cost of an effective plan is highly scalable, that is, the complexity and cost of an effective plan does not rise commensurately with an increase in a client's assets. Importantly, this means that professional advice and planning are most expensive for clients with the least amount of assets. This is mitigated to some extent by many advisors' pricing strategy of providing a free or low-cost initial plan that can be independently implemented by the client.

Nonetheless, the most salient aspect of what makes for an effective financial plan is, unfortunately, being wealthy enough to afford one. Most Americans cannot. Policymakers have set America's retirement system on a path of becoming increasingly self-directed, including for those who are least able to afford financial planning services. As a result, financial planning will become increasingly less effective.

# The fiduciary standard

As has been true of professionals for centuries, a fiduciary standard is a necessary pre-condition for good advice and effective planning services. Doctors are held to a fiduciary standard because the nature of their services requires it. Lawyers are held to a fiduciary standard for the same reason. What both professions have in common with financial advisors is that they establish relationships of trust and confidence with their patients and clients.

Advisors enter into relationships of trust and confidence with their clients and hold themselves out as doing so. Virtually all advisors use titles such as financial planner, financial advisor and wealth manager precisely because they attract clients who seek not the services of a salesman, but instead the professional expertise of a trusted counselor. For centuries, common law countries, which not coincidentally represent the world's most economically advanced countries, have applied a fiduciary standard to professional service providers.

Not only history and experience establish the importance of applying a fiduciary duty to financial advice, the laws of economics also demonstrate the efficiency of the fiduciary standard. A capitalist democracy is based on the premise that free markets should be the dominant model by which resources are allocated. A necessary condition of free markets is the free flow of information, without which efficient markets and competition cannot exist. Free markets also depend on the rule of law, in particular, the enforcement of anti-fraud rules and property rights, including contract rights.

The fiduciary standard furthers each of these free-market goals. The most important element of the fiduciary standard is the duty of disclosure, with particular emphasis on the disclosure of fees. Fee disclosure is essential to genuine competition in the financial services industry, as well to the detection of fraud. Nowhere is fee disclosure more fulsome than in the mutual fund expense ratio. The extraordinary success of the mutual fund industry is partly owed to fee disclosure rules. Some argue that more regulation of an activity necessarily means that there will be less of it. Mutual funds are proof that regulatory disclosure and standardization can promote growth rather than inhibit it.

Another focus of the fiduciary standard is mandatory disclosure of conflicts of interest. Conflicts of interest are particularly insidious in relationships of trust and confidence because in these relationships clients are likely to replace vigilance with trust. When information is concealed and advice is conflicted, it is inevitable that less scrupulous advisors will give advice that is in their own best interest in derogation of the best interest of their clients.

The fiduciary standard also requires that professionals reasonably believe their recommendations are in their clients' best interest. Note that this standard does not establish an objective standard for what is in a client's best interest. As discussed above, good advice and effective planning are complex and highly individualized. The unique character of advice and planning militates for an especially rigorous legal standard because it is easy to claim that bad advice and poor planning is actually justified by a client's particular circumstances or characteristics. And clients are required to bring these claims in an arbitration forum where decisions are virtually never explained. For brokers, arbitration is controlled and operated by a regulator that is, in turn, controlled and operated by the same financial services firms from which claimants seek redress.

Currently, non-fiduciary advice is embedded in the structure of most advisors' compensation. Consider the example of commissions on mutual fund sales. Before making a recommendation, an advisor analyzes the optimal allocation of assets among different asset classes based on the client's particular characteristics and circumstances. The same amount of time and skill is required regardless of the particular allocation that the advisor recommends. However, the advisor will typically be paid twice as much for investments in stock funds than in bond funds and three times more for investments in short-term bonds funds. This compensation structure is flatly inconsistent with the objectivity needed to provide good advice.

Similarly, when developing an implementation plan an advisor will often have funds from many different fund families from which to choose. The time and effort needed to develop this recommendation is the same regardless of which fund family's offering the advisor selects. But the advisor may be paid significantly more as a result of a client's investment in a fund offered by one fund family rather than another. Again, this compensation structure is flatly inconsistent with the objectivity needed to recommend an effective implementation plan.

Payout grids for financial advisors provide a more extreme example of non-fiduciary advice. Some firms pay their advisors a percentage of commissions earned that jumps significantly when a benchmark is reached. One such payout grid retroactively paid an additional 10 percent of advisors' total commissions once their 12-month commission total reached $300,000. Thus, recommending a higher-commission stock fund over a lower-commission bond fund could mean the difference between a $30,000 commission and a $100 commission for the advisor. Such distorted incentives will not produce good advice or an effective implementation plan.

Only a fiduciary standard can provide an effective counter to differential compensation that bears no relationship to differences in services, and to financial incentives that encourage advice that is driven by the advisor's self-interest. These arrangements have long been permitted under the so-called suitability standard. Neither the U.S. Securities and Exchange Commission (SEC) nor the Financial Industry Regulatory Authority (FINRA) has ever brought a case against an advisor on the facts described above. These open and notorious practices will inevitably thrive when clients invest trust and confidence in professionals held only to the morals of the marketplace.

The laws of economics tell us that if advisors are paid more for imprudent advice, more imprudent advice will be provided. Unscrupulous advisors will provide *substantially* more imprudent advice. Even scrupulous advisors will, at the margins, provide less prudent advice than they would provide if their compensation were neutral. Empirical studies consistently show that financial advice is distorted by differential compensation. The fiduciary standard is a necessary predicate of good advice and effective planning services.

**Ryan Caldwell**
Founder and Chief Executive Officer

**MX**

Thirteen

# The New Advocacy Reality

## About the Author

Ryan Caldwell founded MX in 2010. As its CEO, he directs MX's strategic vision and leads its talent. While still in college, Ryan founded and developed multiple Internet and tech businesses and drove them to multi-million dollar exits. His experience spans mergers and acquisitions to consulting with companies from small startups to large Fortune 500 companies throughout the U.S., Singapore and London.

## About the Company

MX provides financial institutions with data-driven money management solutions that focus on user loyalty and driving revenue growth. Founded in 2010, the company's products and solutions include data aggregation and cleansing as well as analytics, marketing and training.

## A foundation of advocacy

Two fundamental and worldwide shifts are driving a societal demand for advocacy at a rate that has accelerated over the last two decades. Businesses and industries that adapt to this new demand will thrive, while those that ignore this demand will struggle, dwindle and eventually fail.

What are these two shifts that make the business need for advocacy so strong? First, consumer choice is rapidly increasing. Second, switching costs for consumers are rapidly decreasing. This is a worldwide phenomenon.

Among the millions of examples of this phenomenon, banking is one of the most striking. It was only a few decades back that if you wanted a loan you would go to one of only a few local banks and apply in person. If you did not match exactly what those few banks wanted, then you were likely out of luck. All the power was in the business's hands. Advocacy was not fully required. Advocacy was nice and helped with branding and provided some lift in a few areas of a company's business, but very unfortunately, predatory and even abusive practices were often a more profitable route. In today's new digital and connected world, anyone with a smartphone can instantly search for loans and get more than 300 million results in under a second.

The shift in the playing field favoring the consumer and the near real-time transparency, reviews, ratings and social media feedback endlessly educate the consumer on which deals and actors took great care of them and which did not. Each consumer has an endless line of other options they can easily find, measure, evaluate and switch to.

With the rise of near effortless and mostly automatic saving and investment platforms like Acorns, Digit, Wealthfront, Betterment, etc., this wave of change is hitting the investment community and is nowhere close to cresting.

Different attitudes in the investment arena will lead to vastly different results. Those who deny or are unaware of the potential impact of technology-driven change feel beautifully well equipped for a world that no longer exists. They face "Kodak moments." To certain others who are innovation laggards, this change is terrifying. It's a wave of change that will tip and sink many ships. However, these changes should be more exciting than terrifying as waves can be ridden, not just feared. The same technology that can steal business and clients away from firms and advisors can quickly, and in large numbers, attract clients and better care for clients than was possible before. If the entire experience of financial advice and guidance is, first and foremost, based on advocacy and then improved and optimized using the newest technology and ways of interacting, a firm and advisor can ride on top of and benefit from this wave.

The financial services industry is still getting used to increased choice and decreased switching costs. Even though digital advancements have made a lot of actions easier, it is still hard to move your mortgage, your auto loan or change to a different financial advisor. But that's rapidly changing. Almost daily, a new Silicon Valley company creates an app that changes things. All of a sudden, with a simple login, the app pulls your demand deposit account (DDA) information and it's transferring money out of your account in a seamless, non-intrusive way. You, the consumer, are never really affected by the withdrawals, but the money in your savings and investment accounts starts to pile up slowly, automatically. The world has never seen this before and the financial industry has surely never provided it, but consumers love it and are quickly adopting it. They benefit from this digital service that helps them painlessly and automatically save.

And then there's the robo-advisors, or what I call automatic investment funds. They have brought a new level of ease, simplicity, transparency and efficiency. The investment advisors have no choice but to find better, newer, more digital ways to serve their clients or accept that they will lose them.

The flip side is also true. New solutions allow financial institutions and advisors to become advocates for their clients while being far more profitable, achieving scale and thriving. They will see that they can reach more clients in a more engaging and powerful way by leveraging newer digital solutions, real-time data feeds and automatically updating and adjusting financial plans. This is what the client wants - a low-friction, always-on, always-updated view of their financial lives and investments available from anywhere on any device. Anything short of that will be quickly replaced by those that implement a digital solution first.

Shockingly, before the digital age, giving advice that didn't get the individual to his or her goal could sometimes work for an advisor. Many advisors thrived in these circumstances. A small number of proactive clients would painfully research how well their returns could have been with other investment choices. They would get frustrated, but they too would often hang on. And the advisor would keep getting whatever fees from their clients. No longer. In an era when a growing number of startups will digitally and painlessly analyze the returns of anyone's clients and clearly inform them of how well they could have done, only advocacy will win. Each day more and more clients are entering a few credentials on a mobile app and seeing in seconds how they are not being optimally cared for, all while they sit on the subway, in a cab (I mean Uber) or at home on their couch. They don't even need to go into someone's office or talk over a round of golf. A co-worker mentions in the elevator how he or she loves this or that new app and how their investments are so much clearer and better off now. Moments later, your client is sitting at his or her desk downloading that app. This will occur at an increasing rate.

This is of no concern to the financial institutions and advisors who adopt advocacy now. They will sit back and relax knowing that each of their clients will download this or that app, only to find that it is really no better than what they are already using with you and that the financial plans they can see on your site and on your app are just as good, real-time and optimized, if not better.

An advisor must be a person who truly feels the burden, who feels the moral imperative of being the client's advocate — helping the client to achieve the goal of being financially strong.

## Advocacy needs data

No doubt you've seen an ad for a carmaker touting an automated braking system that will stop the car if sensors determine there's a risk, like hitting the back of a stopped semi-truck. The carmaker is an advocate for the driver. In this example, advocacy is made possible by data. Many data points are being constantly gathered. What's the rate of speed? How close is the car ahead? How slowly is it moving? Is the brake being activated by the driver? That information and much more is delivered in real time, analyzed in real time and an emergency action is determined in real time. The system determines when to brake and with what level of force, possibly saving the driver's and passengers' lives.

Finance has the exact same problem. Is somebody going to hit a financial wall and, if so, when? Is the client saving too little, spending too wildly or investing in irresponsible ways such that the client is putting himself or herself in a precarious position? Is the client plowing his or her financial life into the back of a stationary semi-truck at 70 miles an hour? The auto industry has figured out a way to alert and proactively protect its consumers. It is inevitable that the financial industry will have to do the same. The advisors who will thrive in the future already know this.

They know that they can't give advice on whether or not someone is at risk of a financial collision unless they have all the data. The advisor has to know the data is accurate, and is available in real time. If it changes a year from now and no alert goes off, there could be the financial equivalent of a disastrous wreck on the road. With current actionable data, an advisor can guide the client to safety.

## DDMM killed PFM

It's my opinion that personal financial management (PFM) no longer exists. It died because it couldn't deliver on its promises. It wasn't sufficiently data driven and wasn't automatic or actionable enough.

We've invented a new approach called data-driven money management (DDMM). The back-end technology that ensures there is up to date, structured and accurate data is the foundation. Without that, nothing built on top would matter. With that foundation, however, a great user interface and experience becomes possible and therefore becomes key.

If a consumer can't interact with his or her finances in an effortless way that is engaging and immediately informative, he or she will disengage. If a client isn't taking the time to link all of his or her accounts to aggregate the data, then the raw data isn't there. By extension, being able to give good financial advice is no longer possible. Therefore, solid aggregation and data cleansing with a great user experience above it is key if good financial advice is the goal.

This is especially true with younger generations, today's newest clients and those soon to be. Of course, they expect good advice, but for them, it even feels frustrating to be given good advice if it is not easy to consume and act on. For most, they have no idea where their finances currently stand. Keep in mind that these are people who grew up in a real-time world. By having the consumer's data and showing them you understand it, then you, as an advisor, are in a position to give advice that will be seen as credible and useful. The data gives the advisor insight into the individual who wants advice and a financial plan. Absorbing, analyzing and sharing it gives you permission to be that person's advisor because they see you acting responsibly — as an advocate.

Finances are oddly intimidating for most people and can cause frustration and headaches even when a client is using a decent interface. Most people don't want to think about their finances. They don't want to feel anxiety. This is especially true among today's younger generations.

The key is to make one's finances clear, simple and engaging. Understand that showing someone his or her net worth is not enough. The client needs to know what that number means. Are they trending up or down? How quickly? Is it controllable? What should the client do and how? When? Old-school tables and charts can't do that. They confuse and cause anxiety. Design graphical interfaces so they're intriguing and your client will come back repeatedly to explore, learn and feel good about what he or she is seeing. Make it easy for the client to understand how each interface affects each other. The client needs to understand how each aspect of their finances affects other aspects.

## Advocacy as a fiduciary

I think it's shocking that anyone could be financially advising somebody and not be a fiduciary. Any of the modern companies like Google and Amazon understand that they have to act as an advocate. If you're acting as an advocate and you're doing so to the proper degree, then you will be properly acting as a fiduciary. I can't emphasize strongly enough that it is wildly irresponsible for a financial advisor to suggest he or she is acting as a fiduciary if the advisor doesn't have accurate data.

When an advisor has accurate data, sees it in real time, and is able to act on that data as it changes, then he or she is able to say, "Alert. You've put yourself on this kind of trajectory. That trajectory was good when your accounts were in this state, but now they're not. You need to now change your trajectory or your accounts." That complete, accurate and real-time data piece is critical to the fiduciary side.

Decisions in Washington, D.C., aimed at bringing more accountability to the fiduciary role could help the industry, advisors and consumers — as long as the decisions are implemented correctly. Consumers want and need to know that they are getting the best possible advice and they can trust that their advisor has a fiduciary obligation to provide that. To have the strongest country possible, we need everyone's investments optimized and protected specifically for them, given the data about their current position, trajectory and desired destination. We need informed advisors. We are counting on them.

## Financial GPS

I see financial planning in the future being like the most advanced version of GPS you've ever experienced. It will guide you in real time with incredible insights tailored to you.

It's not like going to the dentist once every few months. Financial planning will be something that someone does on an ongoing basis. It will mimic a drive in a car when you enter directions. The phone or car determines where the driver is and even suggests destinations it thinks might be of interest based on the time of day, the driver's normal habits and other data.

My phone is constantly predicting that I am heading home, into work or to the airport based on all the information it gathers. The GPS acts like a humble, unobtrusive servant, suggesting, but always making sure the consumer is in full control. The consumer has no need to even answer the suggestions if he or she doesn't want to. The consumer starts driving and the GPS constantly updates with new relevant info on potential destinations, nearby places of interest, traffic patterns and the like. Maybe it is a joy ride. But if the consumer needs to get somewhere specifically, he or she can choose a suggested destination or tell the digital guide where the consumer wants to go and the device will find the most optimal route with alternatives ready if needed. Taking traffic patterns and the newest construction into account, the consumer is guided to exactly where he or she wants to go. Now cars are even starting to do the driving for the consumer. The result is constant guidance based on myriad data streams and data points, with the consumer controlling the desired outcome the entire time. If a consumer changes his or her mind mid-trip, no problem. The GPS reroutes instantly. If the consumer wants to make a few stops along the way, no problem. The GPS routes the person from place to place, providing updates the entire time on how these stops are changing and how long it will be until you reach each destination. Now take that entire process and apply it to the financial world and you will see the change that is rapidly occurring in the financial industry and where it is heading. That is the future of financial guidance, services and advice.

Imagine an advisor saying, "You have the right asset allocation, but yesterday when you bought a lot of company x's stock our system noticed that one of the mutual funds you have invested heavily in already owns a lot of company x's stock. This is fine in isolation, but combined with your individual purchase, it puts your concentration in that one company a little too high for your desired risk. Here are the three most comparable companies to which you could shift that investment. Would you like to have us make that change for you?" or "We're currently seven years into an upswing, and so the likelihood of a decline is great given historical trends analyzed over the last 30 years. There's expected financial traffic for two or three years of downturn. You might need to shift your portfolio in one of the suggested paths below. Just click on one and the advisor will make the adjustment for you and reroute." Every day this financial plan GPS looks at the market, pulls all sorts of information, and gives real-time advice on risk, spending and if you're on or off track.

I can say, "I want to go to this location as my first stop, that location as my second stop and this as my third stop." I can say, "I want to send my kids to college, I want to pay off my house, I want to retire and then I want to buy a lake house." I can map out that whole route to my destination. This software will, every second of every day, analyze one of the most critical things in my life - my finances - telling me whether I'm on track or not on track, provide the relevant detailed information, and most importantly, provide options in an optimized prioritized list. If done in the right interface, users will log in again and again.

## Protecting one of the great innovations

Modern society has mostly forgotten what the world was like prior to the invention of currency. Currency is one of the greatest innovations of all time. It is a foundation, fabric or operating system upon which endless innovation and efficiency has grown. Almost all current innovation would not have been possible without currency. Currency is listed as a top 10 innovation of all time on many lists. When listing innovations that changed the course of human history, history.com lists currency third. Mankind could only drive basic innovation without getting past the impossibly indiscrete and limited barter system. Once currency took hold, innovation rapidly accelerated.

Currency gave us an ability to exchange highly discrete value in an untimed manner. Before its invention, if you had a cow and I had a chicken, I might say, "I'll trade you a chicken for a cow." But you'd have to kill your cow and give me part of it to make it a fair exchange. It was very difficult to do distinct trades. They had to be timed to when both sides wanted to trade or they had to have highly localized trust that the person in their small village was good for it and would honor the debt. This precluded most large scale and distant trade, which precluded highly specialized occupations, which precluded increased skill through specialization, which has driven the modern age of innovation. Well beyond the farmer and the iron worker, today's innovation needs highly specialized database engineers, designers, mobile engineers, etc. Currency and the systems that manage currency either enable that innovation to occur rapidly or can essentially bring all innovation to a crashing halt when the financial system slows or seemingly collapses due to mismanagement.

This industry protects and guides one of the greatest innovations of all time. It provides an innovation that all other innovations in turn count on being stable, efficient and optimized. We all really need to think about that.

Financial advisors, banks, credit unions and all the related software providers are who our society counts on to protect and to guide one of our world's core innovations. No building could be built, no plane could be flown, no computer could be assembled, no cancer could be cured if we didn't have the highly efficient systems managing currency. Guiding the proper leveraging of that asset, the proper leveraging of that innovation, is a privilege.

Once invented, a fabric's or operating system's value goes so far beyond itself. It's analogous to the internet with its protocols. The internet clearly is also a fabric. The data packets flying across the internet may seem like just unimportant ones and zeros, but they can end up meaning something powerful — a phone call, a web page or a critical piece of cancer research. Those ones and zeroes mean little unless you realize what information is riding on top of them, which makes them mean everything.

Finances and currency as well seem to mean nothing by themselves. They are simply a bunch of numbers on balance sheets and transaction tables. However, they provide a fabric that every single asset, investment and transaction in the entire world rides on top of. When people in the financial services industry feel and understand that truth, they realize they're guarding one of the greatest innovations of all time. It is what we, mankind, built and build all of our innovation on. We have a moral imperative to take that responsibility seriously.

This industry should be made up of people who are deeply concerned about how they are impacting mankind. If not, they're not the right fit for such an important industry.

We can continue to shape this industry into what the world needs. We can leverage real-time data and the newest technology to help turn every person into an informed investor with clear meaningful goals. We can make our middle class strong, informed and resilient. We can play our key role in protecting one of the world's greatest foundational innovations, so that the entirety of mankind can continually benefit from the innovation they stack on top of it.

## Mark S. Casady
**Chairman and Chief Executive Officer**

**LPL Financial**

Fourteen

# Understanding Money Relationships

### About the Author
Mark S. Casady leads LPL Financial as chairman and CEO. He has over 30 years in the financial services industry and brings significant leadership experience to LPL. Prior to joining LPL, Mark held senior level positions at Deutsche Asset Management, Americas - formerly Scudder Investments, Concord Financial Group and Northern Trust.

### About the Company
Formed in 1989, LPL Financial is a wholly owned subsidiary of LPL Financial Holdings Inc. (NADAQ: LPLA). As a leader in the retail financial advice market, LPL provides proprietary technology, comprehensive clearing and compliance services, practice management programs and training, and independent research to independent financial advisors, banks and credit unions. LPL also supports financial advisors licensed and affiliated with insurance companies with customized clearing, advisory platforms, and technology solutions.

—––w––—

## The role of common sense

Whenever someone poses the question, "What is good advice?" I respond first by pointing out that it is based on common sense. While there are undoubtedly skills and knowledge that are important to investors achieving good outcomes, at the most fundamental level, good financial advice is rooted in ideas that are not that far from the common sense our parents taught us. Asset allocation aside, when you think about how you spend money or how you make financial decisions, more often than not, the best advice is really fairly basic and filled with common sense.

Of course, the next question is usually "Well, if it's so basic, why do people need advice at all?" In the answer lies the true skill of any good financial advisor: good financial advice reflects a careful assessment of the client's behaviors and his or her relationship with money. It helps us reduce the noise from other impulses or emotions that may affect our thinking and get to the core of our thoughts and actions around money.

Most of us have known someone in our lives who just spends and spends and doesn't think through the need to save money for an unexpected event or for retirement. These folks tend to live in a world where they spend every penny. It doesn't matter if they make $50,000, $500,000 or $5 million a year, they will spend it all. To work with that behavior a good financial advisor, with the intent to provide good financial advice, will focus on understanding the amount and rate of money coming in and going out as the first step to helping shape decisions involving both sides of that equation.

But more than that, in my experience, the best advisors come to thoroughly understand a person's relationship with money. An advisor may learn that the client's relationship with money is a result of how he or she grew up. Regardless of the reason, good advice stems from understanding the root cause of that behavior.

Let me underscore that seeing the root of the behavior and how it manifests itself in daily life is not enough. An advisor telling a client, "I recommend that you reduce your spending," or "You ought to be saving more," is not going to be terribly effective.

The advisor needs to help the client understand the importance of the recommendation through an exploration. The advisor may say, "Let's understand why you're spending and what you're spending it on. Why do you feel the need to go on that type of vacation or buy a new car every three years? Why do you feel the need to change houses even though your family hasn't expanded?" This series of "whys" serve to spark self-reflection and cause the client to think whether a particular expense is prudent or not. Whether it's a car, a kitchen, or a cabin in the mountains, those spending activities are all behaviors. The advisor will need to get to the root cause.

Those "whys" prompt a frank conversation over what has happened and is happening in the dynamic of the client's finances. Time after time, the light bulb figuratively clicks on in the mind of the client. The client realizes his or her "why," and whatever the reason, and it's all OK. We are who we are for a set of reasons. Financial advisors are not about creating guilt; they aim to create awareness and understanding.

In an absolute manner, spending without control can last just so long. Knowing that, an advisor has a real obligation — if only as one human being speaking with another — to get the client to think about consequences and some alternatives.

The opposite of the spendthrift presents a different set of challenges with which to contend. Consider clients who grew up in difficult circumstances, and, as a result, don't spend any money, living in a style well below their means. These types of clients may not be availing themselves of opportunities to get into better financial shape or to create a better outcome for their families.

For example, let's imagine a client that has the opportunity and means to move to a better school district. Education is important to the family but because the client worries about money and never having enough, he or she does not move. This is more than just a lifestyle choice. It's about a life, that of the child. Moving is a kind of investment in the future of the child. And, in my opinion, a good education tends to yield a good return on investment.

I offered two examples on both ends of the spending spectrum. When I share those behaviors with advisors I often hear about a different type of spectrum. In this case, the choice is either keep every dollar clients make or they give it all away. Advisors who see clients in one camp or the other, but almost never both, often insist the most important question to ask a prospect or an existing client is, "When you pass on, do you want to give money to your children or perhaps a charitable organization?" No doubt, this question would also help reveal attitudes and beliefs about money that may be lingering beneath the surface and yet having a real effect on a client's spending or investing behavior.

For example, an advisor has a client who is involved in charitable activities and is predisposed to giving a lot of money to worthwhile causes. You might expect the advisor to work with the client to determine the right amount to give away, or even how the gifts should be structured. But consider how much more valuable it is when the advisor helps the client think about where the money goes — to a charity, family members or to others who may be in need.

The point is that there is not one standard way to talk with a client. Each client is unique. Each conversation is distinct to a client's specific situation. Of course, there are some routine questions, but they are the elements of an initial discovery that evolves into a deeper dive toward determining the root cause underlying people's decisions.

Notice that I've yet to cite a single financial modeling theory. Without knowing what's at the root of the client's beliefs and behavior all of that has no purpose or, for that matter, value.

## The role of trust

No two client situations are the same and neither are any two advisors. Just like every client is different, so are the people who give advice. They may have attended the same school, completed the same training programs and worked for the same firm, but they are still going to be different in the way they approach their practice and their clients.

That difference manifests itself in how an advisor asks the questions needed to get to the core beliefs and behaviors of clients. It starts with building a relationship on trust.

But before advisors can establish trust with a client, they must first understand their own behaviors and beliefs. Said another way, you have to know yourself before you can really know other people. Is the advisor affable, warm and open or more of a technocrat, like a medical doctor? Perhaps he or she is not warm and fuzzy, but is clearly an expert. Other advisors may connect more through what I call the lifestyle approach. This is where the advisor establishes relationships through common ground. It could be something as simple as golf. The advisor plays golf and everyone he or she advises also plays golf, which becomes the common ground that fosters a strong connection.

Of course, the advisor-client relationship is not about golf, being best friends or the financial services equivalent of someone in a starched white lab coat. Whether the relationship is built on a shared interest, camaraderie or respect for expertise, the aim is to develop a relationship built and based on trust. There are as many ways of doing that as there are types of people and interests and ideas.

Once the advisor has a true understanding of himself or herself, the advisor can determine the best way to go about forging the connection necessary to be able to ask those meaningful questions that get to the root of a client's financial behaviors and views toward money.

## The role of outsourcing worry

I think a few anecdotes that frame how all this plays out in an advisor-client relationship will help connect the dots and make clear how these principles can be applied.

The first story involves an advisor I know who was having lunch with a client who had been retired for a few years. Once the food arrived at the table, the client smiled at the advisor and said, "I've outsourced my worry to you."

The client, a former senior level executive who cared deeply about his work, acknowledged that it may not have been necessary to worry about his retirement as much as he did, but he was intense about success and making it all work. Like he did during his career, he wanted to make sure things went well. When they didn't, it worried him, causing a few sleepless nights.

As soon as he retired, he realized what his advisor was allowing him to do. He said, "I can just outsource my worry to you, go on vacation and enjoy my retirement."

The now-retired, hard-driving executive was actually someone who had over-saved. His advisor recommended that he have more fun, explaining, "You have the means to do it, you're going to be able to accomplish all of your goals in terms of having enough capital through your life with a high degree of certainty, and you're going to have plenty of ability to give away to your grandkids. On top of that, you have access to savings, and you ought to enjoy it. You ought to go on vacation. You ought to have fun."

That advice made a tremendous difference in the quality of that person's life in retirement. And it was the trust the advisor had built with his client, and the knowledge the advisor had of what motivated the client, that made the advice credible and actionable enough for the client to feel his worries were well managed and could be let go.

## The role of human concern

As I've described, any good advisor must come to understand his or her clients. The advisor must devise a holistic financial plan, implement it and check in with clients on how they're doing. But even with technology that lets us probe, analyze, plan, measure and communicate with clients anytime from anywhere, there's much to be said about doing so face-to-face.

Here is another tale. An advisor's client moved to Florida. The advisor went to visit, in large part because the client told him he had some money to invest. This gentleman had been in retirement for about six months, so the advisor was also checking in on how that was going.

The advisor told me, "I went to spend a day with him, but, as things turned out, I needed to stay over and work with him a little longer." When he told me this, I asked, "Was it a wealth issue? Did the financial plan require a rework?" He responded, "No. It wasn't any of that. We covered the financial matter in about 15 minutes. I spent most of the first day and almost half of the second counseling my client and his wife about how to get along in retirement."

The client had been the administrator of a large hospital, where he enjoyed a great deal of authority and led with a very direct style. After retiring, unfortunately, he had moved his work demeanor to his home. He was in a beautiful home in south Florida, treating his spouse more like an employee than she wanted to be.

The client had been in a highly structured life for a long time. Now that structure was gone and he needed some counseling about how to make retirement work. The advisor helped the couple understand this was a classic development that could be addressed by getting involved in something like a sport or community activity.

That example reflects the dimensions of an advisor-client relationship that is built on trust. Whether listening as a financial services professional or a concerned person, in either case, it is effective, because it leads to understanding what's going on with an individual client and family, en route to being of greater counsel regarding his financial assets.

## The role of human connection

Technology advancements are helping firms make light of work that had been drudgery and tedious; it lets them drill deeper into data to draw richer conclusions, provide substantive advice in an automated manner and prepare a complete financial plan. While personal preference and convenience are certainly factors, the primary appeal here is cost. I like to say technology has driven the cost of basic financial understanding way down.

However, I cannot overemphasize the need for advisors to develop and nurture connections, human connections, with their clients to make the advice relevant to their experience, and as a result, make it actionable. While the cost of understanding may be dropping with technology advancements, the price of advice and counsel by a living, breathing advisor is in my view, priceless.

The good news is that with technology taking over the hard labor, so to speak, of financial planning and asset allocation, advisors have more time for their clients — more time to talk about what's important to their clients and how they're going to achieve their goals. It's my opinion that an individual will be happy to pay a fee for this type of advice, especially if it yields better outcomes.

## The role of technology

While it cannot replace advisors, obviously, technology plays an important role in the work of advice. There is a major shift in our industry as a result of the development of tools that enable us to see what can be done to deal with where a client is and prepare for what the future might hold. While an advisor's human characteristics are critically important, the centerpiece of the advisor's practice is how he or she takes in and analyzes data and evaluates qualitative and quantitative information.

Here is a relevant story: There's an advisor who I think does an amazing job. He walks clients through detailed intake questionnaires, asking questions ranging from where the client lives, number of children and net worth to where the assets are assigned. He also asks about the client's intent to be charitable and what types of activities are important, like hobbies and passions.

It's a very holistic view. It's not just numbers. It becomes a very personal, individual profile of the client. If the client is married, the advisor will want the spouse on hand to get the answers with his or her perspective and with a sense of the family dynamic. Along with an understanding of the client's behaviors and passions, an advisor today can use several excellent tools to complete a financial plan as detailed as this one.

When I started out, I worked at Northern Trust Bank in Chicago. I served people with a net worth of $100 million or more. Mainframe computers were used to understand asset allocation, hedging and risk because that was the only way to do that analysis. Today, I can do that same work on my smartphone. More importantly, all that was done for the seriously wealthy in the '80s can now be done for someone with $10,000 to invest.

The technology can run the data, look at what is happening to the components of the portfolio and determine the likelihood of objectives being reached, such as retiring at a certain age. It can be used to create simulations of outcomes, look at risks, and, yes, even gain insight into the financial habits of the family involved. Technology helps to run the math, which is very important. It gives a factual basis from which to discuss everything, see the findings and explore them further. With that comes real understanding.

Looking a bit further out, I see another technology that may have a positive impact on our industry by helping us to better serve clients — the "Internet of Things." Within that segment, there is a development referred to as beacon technology which is gaining traction in retailing. Essentially, as a consumer moves from home to a store and then to an aisle in the store, there is a beacon that knows where that consumer is at any given moment. As the consumer enters a store equipped with beacon technology, an offer is made that might be something that the consumer had not thought consciously about before. From a financial planning perspective, beacon technology might serve as a way to alter a client's behavior in the moment, and actually help him or her to manage their budget in a smarter way.

## The role of efficiency

Technology has not only been a tool for financial advisors and their clients for learning, planning, executing and monitoring. It has also had a transformative effect on the industry as a whole. Consider the discussion today around active and passive investment management. Related to that is much of what has been discussed around machine learning and algorithmic trading, all important to market efficiency and to garner returns. There are entire firms doing that and then selling the derived product through an advisor. On its own, that's all good.

But imagine with much more computing power and much more data to analyze, we'll have active management that's more efficient without the human behavioral bias. It's very easy to imagine the money management world being quite different in a decade's time with many more data scientists than MBAs and Chartered Financial Analysts (CFA®s).

## The role of data

Another emerging trend that has enormous potential is analyzing data associated with an advisor's practice. We are just starting to do this at LPL.

Essentially, we look at the data that shows what an advisor holds in accounts for clients A, B, and C, and then look at similar practices — same size, geography, type of wealth, zip codes, etc. Maybe they're 80 percent advisory and 20 percent brokerage. Whatever it may be, it can serve as a set of points of comparison to other practices.

This is not about finding a product to push — quite to the contrary — it is about helping the advisor effectively serve clients and grow the practice. This process offers suggestions on how to more effectively talk to clients about insurance or more portfolio diversification. We can see that because we've analyzed the data of similar practices. We might suggest the advisor attend an online training class, or we might provide a report that lets them pinpoint areas they might want to think about to improve their relationships with clients or how to solve problems in a different way. It can also empower the advisor to enhance and expand his or her skills in evaluating client behaviors. In my view, this kind of analysis and best practices counsel can quickly become an industry standard.

Through this, I see technology as a way to strengthen the human qualities of advisors, not diminish, worsen, or eliminate them. We are seeing the introduction of artificial intelligence (AI), technology that controls an assortment of functions and offers information based on oral requests. That technology is about assessing behavior and then predicting what the given human being will want or need, based largely on past evidence — a form of predictive analytics. This technology is powerful, and will get more so and, certainly, more affordable quickly.

As I've suggested all along, good financial advice, and the quality financial plan that is developed as a result, comes from thoroughly understanding the financial behaviors of the client and encouraging common sense to prevail. If AI tools can aid that effort, I urge advisors to embrace them and use them. When they do, advisors will only increase, not diminish, the trust in the advisor-client relationship. And what could be more human than that?

**Caroline Dabu**
Vice President and Head, Enterprise Wealth Planning

BMO Financial Group

Fifteen

# Coaching for the Financial Marathon

### About the Author

Caroline Dabu, Head of BMO Financial Group's Wealth Planning Group, has more than 20 years of experience in the investment industry. She leads a team of professionals across Canada and the U.S. who provide wealth planning solutions and services. As a regular spokesperson in the media, Caroline focuses on financial and retirement consumer trends and behavior.

### About the Company

Established in 1817, BMO Financial Group is a diversified financial services provider based in North America providing a broad range of retail banking, wealth management and investment banking products and services. BMO conducts business through three operating groups: Personal and Commercial Banking, Wealth Management and BMO Capital Markets.

—◊—

### Financial planning is a marathon not a sprint

Training for a marathon can be a very rewarding experience. It can also be very frustrating. Declaring that you're going to run one is the easy part. Sticking and committing to the training is more challenging. You quickly learn that everyday life can get in the way of your goal and the unexpected — injury, sickness, bad weather and challenging conditions — can derail you on race day. You'll encounter many setbacks and you may have to reset your goals. Having a good plan can get you to race day healthy, injury free and in the best shape of your life. A bad plan can leave you disappointed, injured and demotivated to try anything like that again.

Developing, managing and following through on a financial plan bears many similarities to running a marathon. I've trained for and run eight marathons over the years and I've learned many lessons that can be applied to financial planning.

It's important to set a goal, plan a strategy, create a plan and prepare for the unexpected. First and foremost is getting to the plan. I've found that for the most part, people don't inherently love to plan, especially when it comes to health, fitness or finance. How many times have we heard: "I'm too young for a plan, I know what I'm doing, I don't need a plan, or my situation isn't complex enough to warrant a plan."

Financial planning requires discipline, focus and the ability to recalibrate when things go wrong. The role of a financial advisor and planner is much like a running coach. It requires the ability to listen, establish a plan and develop strategies to be successful. Like a coach, a financial advisor and planner works alongside the client providing solutions as well as support and encouragement. And like the best coaches, the best financial advisors and planners keep discipline and focus on the plan even when the going gets tough.

## Identifying and setting aspirational but realistic goals

When a client comes in with a problem or specific need, it is human nature to provide a solution as quickly as possible. But good financial advice starts with a conversation that seeks to understand and uncover the goals of the client.

While some clients can clearly articulate their goals and specific needs, others benefit from the comprehensive approach that is the hallmark of good financial planning. A planner should understand what keeps their clients up at night, their hopes and dreams for their family and the next generation, as well as the risks that may compromise their lifestyle. It's with this 360-degree view that the plan can actually start.

After identifying goals, assessing a person's ability to get there is what determines the kind of plan that will be most successful. In the case of building the right marathon training plan, a client's goal may be to run faster, but does he or she have the ability and determination to invest in the training needed as well as the recovery and nutrition required? An overly aggressive plan can lead to burnout and injury while an overly conservative plan can lead to disappointment and may not maximize a person's potential. The right balance is critical!

A coach needs to understand a runner's starting point, current fitness level, racing history and performance, health and any injuries. It's also important to understand the tools, resources and support for that runner during training. A coach also needs to understand factors that could derail the plan. With an understanding of current ability and future potential, the coach develops a plan that is both aspirational and achievable. A runner may have the desire for a personal best (PB) but if he or she can only put in three days of training per week, a PB may not be in the cards. Understanding a person's ability to stick to the plan through thick and thin will help determine the plan's success. Similarly, if a financial plan requires a 20 percent reduction in spending, a planner has to be confident in the client's ability to make this significant behavioral change or the plan is bound to fail.

Good coaches recognize the broad set of factors that help or hurt a runner. They know that each plan needs to be customized for the individual in order to be successful.

## Financial planning that brings everything together

Good financial planning takes into consideration all aspects of a client's life, how they intersect, and the financial impacts of each. A financial plan is a comprehensive roadmap of the strategies and actions that will help achieve a client's life goals.

But there are a number of key questions clients need to ask themselves before embarking on their roadmaps. Can I commit to this? What support do I need to reach my milestones? Do I need additional resources from my advisor or elsewhere? Do I truly understand what I need to do to make the plan successful?

It's been said that financial planners are pessimistic by nature. By the same token, the best marathoners think about the worst that can happen and prepare for it. Planners have a responsibility to ensure clients have a financial plan that protects them even in the worst scenarios. Not doing so can create hardships for family members, compromise lifestyles or compromise the security of future generations.

It's a planner's responsibility to raise the tough questions and issues that may be difficult so that the plan can truly be all encompassing.

## Establishing milestones to encourage discipline, focus and ongoing motivation

As a running coach, you can put together a marathon training program for your client. At the end of the day, though, you're not the one running the race.

One of the biggest mistakes we see with financial planning is that a plan is "completed" and then filed away. A financial plan is a living document that should guide day-to-day financial decisions and long-term decisions. In short, it should be revisited regularly. It also requires engagement from a client, especially when the success of a financial plan means sticking to a specific budget or savings plan. Like a coach, advisors need to give feedback, check-in and provide encouragement along the way. And when they can, help clients make the behavioral changes they'll need to be successful. Setting smaller goals along the way often makes the aspirational goals less daunting and more achievable.

Think about running a marathon. Running 26.2 miles is daunting! By focusing on your end goal, you run the risk of being overwhelmed and intimidated. But, by setting milestones along the way, building up your endurance and your pace, putting in some practice races and setting smaller goals, you'll stay focused, energized and motivated.

The importance of setting milestones along the way is even more important when it comes to financial planning. If retirement is 30 years away, making changes to daily spending and giving up a purchase isn't all that motivating. But if your client's goal is to save $5,000 annually, it's more achievable and more real. Seeing the correlation between smaller goals and longer-term goals is a powerful motivator. There's quantifiable evidence that those with a comprehensive plan do better and are more confident. A study by the Financial Planning Standards Council of Canada showed that 81 percent of those with comprehensive financial plans feel on track with their financial affairs versus 44 percent of those who do not have plans. Further, according to the study, 62 percent of those with plans report they have improved ability to save versus 40 percent with no planning.[1]

## Recalibrating when things don't go according to plan

As Robert Burns once said, "The best laid plans of mice and men often go awry." You can establish the most comprehensive plan for your client and anticipate many hiccups, and yet derailments beyond anyone's control can happen, such as an unexpected health event, sudden job loss or market volatility. Hopefully these events don't derail your client's long-term goals. But when they happen, it's important to recalibrate.

---

1 Financial Planning Standards Council of Canada, Value of Planning, 2014

Coming back from a running injury may mean adjusting one's goal or putting off a race goal. Who hasn't experienced some setback that requires re-examining the plan? In some cases, good advice may be not going through with a race. Marathoners push themselves and coaches sometimes need to remind runners to pull back or they risk long-term injury.

When a financial plan is derailed, taking stock of the situation relative to the goal is critical. But it's often the hard trade-offs and decisions that a client may need support with in order to make the needed adjustments — lengthening the time horizon of certain goals or in some cases replacing them with new goals or making hard trade-offs in the short term.

## "A goal without a plan is just a wish" — Antoine de Saint-Exupéry

What I've learned over the years of running marathons is that following a plan works. When I look back at my best times, those races were precipitated by ambitious but achievable and detailed training programs, programs that pushed me but also kept me injury free. I trained in every weather condition to be ready for whatever could come up on race day.

Good financial plans require the right type of roadmap aligned to the client's goals and aspirations and it forms the basis of a strong partnership between advisor and client. But it must be regularly reviewed and adjusted as needed. It needs to include milestones and goals to keep engagement high. All too often financial plans set a long-term goal that seems too far off in the distant future to motivate any real focus, action or behavior change in the short term.

Our challenge as financial planners is to help clients manage all the complex financial pieces, and simplify where we can. And like the running coach, we need to provide guidance and support to clients and call out potential obstacles while identifying risks and developing strategies that increase the potential of a client achieving their goals and reaching their personal bests, regardless of whatever life may throw their way.

**Marco De Freitas**
Managing Director, Head of Retail Products and Strategy

**Lule Demmissie**
Managing Director, Investment Products and Guidance

**TD Ameritrade**

Sixteen

# Driving Engagement with Choice and Voice

## About the Authors

Marco De Freitas is responsible for managed products, mutual funds, ETFs, fixed income, retirement, cash management, margin, annuities and workplace solutions in his role as Head of Retail Products and Strategy. He also leads the Strategy and Analytics team for TD Ameritrade's Retail Business serving individual investors. Marco has over 23 years of experience in financial services.

Lule Demmissie is responsible for product development and management of investment products and retirement. She has extensive expertise in investment management, modern portfolio theory, financial planning issues and general retirement matters. Her prior experience spans analytical, financial consulting and program/product development through Morgan Stanley, Merrill Lynch and JP Morgan.

## About the Company

TD Ameritrade has been providing investing and trading services for individual investors, and custodian services for independent registered investment advisors since 1975. The Company, headquartered in Omaha, Nebraska, leverages technology to make investing easier and more efficient.

～〜Ⅲ〜～

## Success in planning is often incremental

Lofty financial goals are a nice-to-have, but in order to create a truly effective financial plan — one that endures the test of time — we need to climb down from the loft and make planning "real" for investors. Gone are the days of cookie-cutter strategies and passive planning. Financial planning today must be personalized and delivered in bite-size increments that are easy for investors to digest, understand and adopt. The more people fear they won't have enough to retire on, the more likely they are to feel defeated. And a defeatist state of mind can derail even the most well-intended aspirations. To overcome that mindset, investors need to feel empowered to make choices. Yet, in the traditional planning model, investors aren't often given choices. Instead, they're told, "Tighten up your belt." While this concept of "tough medicine" has its place in the planning process, it cannot come at the price of limiting an investor's sense of having both choice and a voice. It's this empowerment that ultimately drives engagement, which in turn cultivates the financial habits investors need to ultimately realize the promises of their long-term financial plans. After all, a good financial plan is one that is *used*.

Enter technology. With the rapid growth of user experience-focused financial software and powerful forecasting engines that support the planning process, the future of financial planning looks very different from its past. These capabilities have helped break down the planning process into incremental, logical milestones that can offer investors a greater sense of control — no matter how limited their choices may be. But, how do we as providers of financial services make the shift from being administrators of tough medicine to enablers of choice? The answer to that question for us is the new financial planning experience.

By taking the best planning software in the market, and coupling it with the assistance of a capable human, what was once a seemingly mundane or overwhelming process for investors is now an engaging exercise in self-discovery. The sense of involvement, understanding and personalization that this new process brings to the investor increases the likelihood of plan usage and consequently can increase the likelihood of success.

## Give clients agency

In the not too distant past, the financial planning process went something like this: financial planning providers delivered a dense "finished" document; the investor and the provider met once and reviewed the report and perhaps the recommended action steps; and after some time, the investor and the provider dusted off the plan for a review. In this process, the provider led and the investor followed. It was static and oner-ous for all involved.

Now, technology (coupled with human assistance) is opening up a new investor experience. The central premise is continuous client engagement along every step of the way. From the beginning, it is a partnership between the investor and the pro-vider. Investors are given the opportunity to "play" with their choices in a hypotheti-cal, dynamic setting. They can then develop, through visualization, an appreciation for the trade-offs associated with the choices they are considering. Rather than swallowing tough medicine, the investor is instead embarking on a process of self-discovery.

Hope is not a strategy. In this new environment, financial service providers help reduce the fear factor and support the investor along the way. The relationship between investor and provider deepens, and accountability for the plan's endurance is shared. Providers become coaches, and investors realize their own "aha" moments by tackling tough questions.

How does my spouse see investing? How do we reconcile our views? Can I stomach delaying my Social Security payout? How do we ensure that we don't abandon our plan at the first major challenge, like a tough market environment? Should we consider major life changes down the line, like moving to another state or country? Can we really afford to retire, or do we need to supplement our income in retirement through work? Will our health allow us to work in retirement?

A meaningful dialogue between investor and provider is essential to help quickly turn these "aha" moments into actionable plans.

## Imagine more engagement and simplicity

An engaging planning experience is no longer one big linear event. Rather, it should and can be a palatable, creative process, shaped by the role of the financial provider as coach and the intuitive, interactive digital experience that powers each stage of the journey.

It should be something an investor can log into on his or her own, or share with a spouse or domestic partner at the dinner table. It should enable and encourage an investor to run different scenarios, adjust or improve segments of the strategy and then validate those actions with their provider. This allows the investor to co-own the process, to share in the accountability and increase his or her degree of engagement.

It's up to the provider to give support and context, which instills motivation. For example, an investor might be "playing" with his or her plan at home and have a question like, "I moved one of my goal items from a 'nice-to-have' to a 'need-to-have,' and my probability of success plummeted. I don't understand why, and I'm nervous. What else can I do to meet this goal?" For the investor, this scenario represents a tipping point, and as providers it is imperative that we remain accessible, lest the defeatist mentality take over and curtail engagement. Moments of doubt are crucial opportunities for the provider to step in and level-set — to help the investor see the pros and cons of readjustments or of sticking with the original plan.

Above all, the planning experience should be as simple as possible. Investors should feel compelled to play and engage, not to put documents in a drawer and forget about them. And, by "simple," we do not mean "dumbed down." Rather, simplicity is the more elegant packaging of complexity — so it's not overwhelming to the investor. A simple planning process can be powered by an engine that handles financial complexity, but is presented to the investor with an easy-to-navigate user experience.

## Recognize priorities and biases

A good financial plan empowers investors to dream and have a sense of choice over their destinies, but it must also provide a path for navigating the realities of a volatile and complex investing environment — not to generate fear or paralysis, but rather to encourage disciplined informed financial decisions.

By nature, we as investors lead complex lives, structured by biases that can trigger different behaviors. When the markets are correcting and headlines are predicting the worst, the desire to react, even if there is already a logical plan in place, can be overpowering. The financial planning process must account for this. The dynamic and collaborative nature of the new planning model helps humanize what has traditionally been a complex and inflexible process. It recognizes our individual tipping points and provides actionable solutions.

This is because retirement and investment returns are not really measured in dollars. They're measured in peace of mind. Investing, therefore, is not just an exercise in chasing portfolio returns. It's a means of meeting the very real, very human goals we set as individuals.

Building a good financial plan isn't about saying, "Let's build a book to give you 5 percent returns over the next 18 years." It's a conversation that gets to the heart of who we are as individuals and investors. It aims to uncover more than the clients' explicit financial goals and appetite for risk. It begs each of us to consider deeper questions about ourselves, like, "What's your desired life once your kids leave home? How do you navigate the stress on your financial future when caring for your elderly parents becomes a reality? What happens once you sell your business? What will help you sleep better at night?" These conversations map the vital intersection of investing and life — helping us attack our biases before they attack us. Planning at its best makes that navigation easier and more tangible.

A good financial planning experience should lay the groundwork for minimizing fear and addressing readiness for longer-term plans like retirement. Again, this reinforces the importance of the financial provider, or coach, in all stages of the process. A good coach can help investors navigate and track their progress, uncover the biases and behaviors that stand to get in the way and serve as that all-important lifeline in those moments when investors need him or her the most.

## Embrace the future

In the end, next-gen financial planning understands the critical role of intelligent, simple and humanized engagement models, powered by advancing technologies and supported by human coaching from a financial provider. The planning experience of the future provides a dynamic, personalized process that engages individuals in a more collaborative, human way. It encourages investors to be self-critical and develop disciplined habits that can more readily enable success. It helps investors understand that trials and tribulations are normal and a cause for course correction, not defeat.

A good financial plan is not a luxury, but a necessity. It's also one that is relevant — one that's used. As providers, we can't just say, "Do this." It must be a partnership from start to finish. There are plenty of "good" plans out there that are all but ignored. Ironically, an average plan that is used can be much better than an excellent plan that is discarded. In the end, planning is about continuous alignment between reality and one's expectations and dreams. If we can create an eye-level experience such that clients respond and refer others, as an industry we've won.

The needs of today's investors continue to evolve. We are already seeing significant shifts, with an aging population expected to live longer than ever before. Additionally, an entire generation once burned by the financial crisis now is determined to pay closer attention. At the closing bell, it's on us as a financial services industry to deliver a planning experience that meets the diverse needs of our clients.

**Dean Deutz, CFP®**
Vice President, Wealth Initiatives Senior Manager

RBC Wealth Management, U.S.

Seventeen

# Stewardship for Clients and Advisors

## About the Author

As vice president and Wealth Initiatives senior manager, Dean Deutz brings over 26 years of experience to RBC Wealth Management. Dean has led the development of RBC proprietary analysis tools and provides comprehensive wealth management advice to high net worth clients. He has previously served in senior roles at KPMG and Deloitte & Touche.

## About the Company

For more than a century, RBC Wealth Management – U.S. has provided trusted advice and wealth management solutions to individuals, families and institutions. It is a division of RBC Capital Markets, LLC and a member of the New York Stock Exchange, the Financial Industry Regulatory Authority (FINRA) and Security Investor Protection Corporation. As a global organization and a segment of Royal Bank of Canada, RBC brings diverse expertise and deep knowledge to the sophisticated financial needs of clients.

## Stewardship circles for clients and advisors

The regulatory landscape is constantly evolving to help improve investor protection and help ensure the best interests of clients are served by financial professionals.

Every new rule introduced brings change and new opportunity to do the right thing for clients. Every new rule also invites renewed interest in clarifying the meaning of good financial advice, quality financial planning and fiduciary responsibility.

RBC Wealth Management welcomes the opportunity to contribute to the conversation. We have long advocated for financial advisor rules of conduct that put the best interests of clients first. However, we also strongly believe that fiduciary rules must preserve client choice regarding the investment products they use and how they work with their financial advisors.

As professional wealth managers, we fully agree with the spirit and intent of regulatory reform: to help eliminate conflicts of interest, especially regarding advisor compensation. Yet it is our experience that it is equally in a client's best interest to have flexibility in how they invest and how they pay for professional investment services (i.e., commissions versus fees).

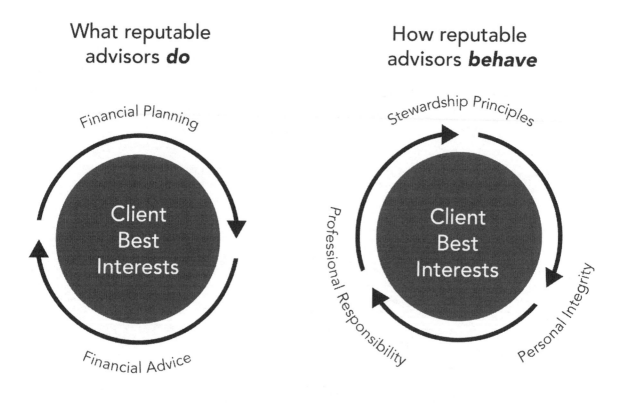

In terms of financial advice and financial planning, one may think of them as two halves of a complete circle describing what advisors do for clients. The two halves complement and complete one another. Like other dualisms (such as left and right, dark and light, positive and negative and so on) they also help define each other. Indeed, one cannot really exist without the other.

Regarding standards of advisor conduct, this is another circle describing how advisors behave with clients. This circle of conduct is made stronger when three essential advisor virtues revolve around the client in a never-ending loop: stewardship principles, professional responsibility and personal integrity.

These two circles are the framework underpinning the wealth management service model. In both cases, the best interests of the client are always at the center for reputable advisors.

With this approach in mind, let's briefly review some best practices clients should seek from any financial professional who provides financial planning and financial advice from a fiduciary perspective.

## Financial planning is the strategic half of the *Do* circle

Financial planning is client goals-based and both short term and long term in focus. A good financial plan is the result of a thorough discovery process — one that can be repeated when the client's life changes and adjusted when necessary.

It evaluates all aspects of a client's "big picture" financial life and how the various pieces fit together. It encompasses investing for retirement, college and other major expenses; protection from financial risks; managing liabilities; fulfilling charitable intentions and sharing wealth with loved ones. It maximizes tax efficiency of financial strategies implemented during the client's lifetime and at estate settlement. And overall, it establishes priorities, seeks beneficial outcomes and anticipates possible obstacles.

In this way, a financial plan serves as a kind of road map to help guide the client on his or her journey. It shows where he or she is going and why. Its purpose is to provide valuable context to help the client and advisor make well-informed decisions over time. This context provides the flexibility necessary to modify the path when unexpected life changing events — whether happy or sad — occasionally happen.

## Financial advice is the tactical half of the *Do* circle

Financial advice is needs-based and situational in focus. It helps a client answer specific questions. It helps a client solve particular problems. Or it helps a client spot potential opportunities. Good financial advice is personalized. And it always puts the client's interests first.

To continue the travel analogy, in this way, financial advice is like a GPS tracking unit. At any given moment, it helps determine which direction to go, what steps to follow and how to take them relative to the course established by the planning roadmap. Its purpose is to help achieve an intended outcome while keeping a client on track with his or her overall goals. Like any journey, there may be detours or itinerary changes along the way.

## The *Do* circle is consultation-oriented and purpose-driven

The full circle comprising financial planning and advice is both purposeful and consultative by nature. To help illustrate, one question RBC Wealth Management financial advisors often hear from clients is: "How do I set up my portfolio to provide income in retirement?"

## Planning retirement income

Here quality planning and advice come together to answer where income will come from in retirement. Does it come from a bond portfolio where interest payments may fluctuate over time? Does it come from a stock portfolio where dividend payments and stock values may fluctuate over time? Or does it come from an annuity where a fixed amount of income is paid at regular intervals? And how does income from Social Security, a pension or other sources like rental income, royalty payments or part-time employment fit in?

Usually basic needs like food, shelter, health care — the necessities — are covered by assured sources of income, like Social Security, pensions or annuities. Once the essentials are taken care of, the fun things (like vacations or how much to give to family or charity) are covered by the sources of income that may vary as interest rates, dividends or markets respond to changing economic conditions.

## Managing risk

Other questions clients ask revolve around insurance, specifically how much they should have. Again, quality financial advice relates back to being able to understand the different purposes for insurance and how it fits into the overall plan.

Is the client trying to replace income because he or she is 40 years old and wants to retire at 60 but needs to replace those 20 years of income for his or her survivors? Is it for a business purpose in which the client is trying to fund a business key person agreement? Is it for estate liquidity? Does the client have a $20 million dollar estate with a $7 million estate tax liability and illiquid assets?

Generally speaking, a client who understands why the insurance was purchased in the first place tends to believe in the purpose, commits to the plan for a longer period of time and is more likely to keep the plan in place.

But, when the client doesn't understand the purpose and receives a statement two years later, he or she is more likely to say: "Why do I have this? What was this for? Do I need to pay this premium?" That's when the financial plan tends to fall apart.

## Preserving and transferring wealth

Another question clients often ask is: "I have a large estate with an estate tax, and I want to be able to give assets to my children. How do I do that?" One thing the client needs to understand is the difference between quality gifts and quantity gifts.

A popular quantity gift is a $14,000 distribution from an investment account, to take advantage of the annual gift tax exemption. A client often does this to reduce estate tax exposure, without giving a second thought to other equally significant reasons to make the gift. The kids receive the money, but do they appreciate it? Do they know what it's for? Are there conditions or is it an unconditional gift? What's the spirit of the gift? What greater end is the client trying to accomplish with the gift? Are there values that can be taught by this gift and how is it to be shared? It is important to work through the full scenario of quantity gifts to reduce estate taxes versus quality gifts for a purpose. It can make a big difference.

## Sharing wealth with loved ones and favorite causes

Another popular question is: "Do I give to my family or others?" Quality financial advice does not just consider the "tax implications" but also the "family implications." Sometimes the difference will drive the decision. Increasingly, RBC Wealth Management financial advisors are seeing the family implications trump the tax implications because the lives of the people who receive money are affected. Suddenly it's not just about getting more — it's about how the lives of the client's loved ones are going to change.

Quality financial advice needs to include the ability to work with a client to answer these types of questions and provide long-term flexibility to change as life changes. Good financial planning provides the context that makes purpose-driven consultation possible.

## Don't underestimate the power of trade-offs

The complementary nature of good financial planning and quality advice also provides an efficient framework for evaluating trade-offs inherent in different choices.

Let's take a fairly common retirement planning scenario. Let's start with a client who is 55, with a life expectancy of 95 and $1 million in investment assets. He or she wants to save another $20,000 per year until retirement at age 66, then spend $100,000 per year and have the portfolio grow at 6 percent with inflation of 3 percent and an average tax rate of 25 percent. A financial advisor can build a base case, but what happens if the client runs out of money at age 85 in that scenario? What are the trade-offs?

There are three major categories of trade-offs.

The first category involves factors clients can control. How much did they save, how long did they work and how much are they going to spend? These are very important because clients have the ability to influence those factors and determine the numbers.

The second category involves things that are harder to control such as the investment return rate. Returns can be influenced by asset allocation. Income tax rates are similarly harder to control. If investments are not managed for tax efficiency, clients may pay a higher rate. That's a trade-off. Or, if clients do a better job of managing taxes, will the difference be enough to put them in a better situation financially? That is another trade-off.

The third category consists of things that are very hard to control, like inflation. Even though this is a factor that cannot be controlled, advisors can help clients anticipate different situations. The advisor and client can look at portfolio spending power at various rates of inflation over different time periods. This may help the advisor and client focus on what is in their power to control: how the client chooses to prepare for and respond to different inflation scenarios.

Another factor that is hard to control is a client's life expectancy. If he or she has a life expectancy of 90 years, what is more important: retiring early, spending a certain amount, maintaining a certain lifestyle or living beyond age 90 without running out of money?

Again, good financial planning and quality financial advice are a combination of the questions a client asks, the opportunities an advisor brings to the table and working through the trade-offs to deliver the solutions necessary to help the client prepare financially to enjoy the retirement he or she wants.

## Technology has made the world more interactive

In the last five years, technological advances have helped the world become more interactive. In the old days advisors would gather the information, build a net worth statement, do some cash flow modeling, create a report, put it in a binder and meet with the client. At the meeting, the client and advisor would look at the net worth statement and then the client would say, "You forgot about the $300,000 in my 401(k)." The advisor didn't really forget about it. He or she didn't know about it because the client wasn't quite ready to divulge that information.

At that point the advisor and client would look at each other and the advisor would say, "Well, let's start over again. Let's go through the plan, see what else we can find and we'll re-run it." The client would walk away, frustrated, without any answers and reluctant to schedule another meeting.

Today advisors use an interactive process and digital tools that display the client's situation on a screen. As the advisor and client review the information together, the advisor can ask questions. This allows the client to see what might have been overlooked. The advisor can add the missing data with just a few key strokes and both parties see the results of the change in real time.

With the old way, everyone left the room feeling badly. But now advisors and clients can work through the trade-offs, have the new numbers entered and see the potential outcomes right away.

This is so powerful because the client becomes more engaged. Suddenly the plan becomes his or her plan — not something presented by the advisor. When this happens, the client starts asking, "What if I did this? What if I did that?" And the advisor-client conversations become much more productive and satisfying.

It seems like most clients have somewhere between 15 and 20 "what if's." When they can share a question and see an answer right away, the client becomes more engaged in the process. Each client can see the trade-offs in such a way that helps him or her feel empowered to take the necessary steps recommended by his or her advisor.

In addition, clients are often looking for their "guard rails" to help keep them from veering off the road. This interactive discussion often helps clients build guard rails and feel more confident steering the car.

## The future of financial planning and advice

Financial planning has many opportunities to grow. The financial education of children, beginning with introducing the concept in grade school, could help individuals be better prepared for financial success as adults. There are elements of money and financial planning that should be introduced at an early age and certainly by high school. For example, there are people in college right now whose parents are paying $250,000 or more for tuition, room/board and other incidentals. That would buy a nice house in most of America. The student should understand the value of an education and the trade-offs that were made to provide that education.

The interactive component of financial planning will also continue to grow, extending the ability to be interactive and providing more ways for clients to do some things on their own. The additional information and convenience available to clients may be as compelling as the ease of receiving help when needed.

No matter how automated things become, there will still be a point where a client has to click a button to make a choice. That's where the financial advice and financial planning from professional financial advisors will be necessary. Advisors help clients understand their current situation and realize their goals. Advisors help clients understand and organize their choices and tradeoffs. And advisors uncover opportunities that help clients achieve their goals.

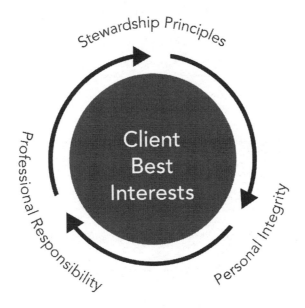

How reputable advisors *behave*

Stewardship Principles

Professional Responsibility

Client Best Interests

Personal Integrity

## Concerning the *behave* circle: What type of fiduciary are we talking about?

Many clients are not even familiar with the word "fiduciary." Of those who are acquainted with the term, many are either confused about or surprised by the inconsistencies between the U.S. Securities and Exchange Commission (SEC) rules, the Financial Industry Regulatory Authority (FINRA) rules, the U.S. Department of Labor (DOL) rules, the Certified Financial Planner Association rules — and the rules of everyone else using the term fiduciary as part of what they're doing. For the most part, regulators define fiduciary differently, yet they all define under what circumstances advisors need to act as a fiduciary and the responsibilities advisors have when they do.

The different definitions complicate matters when all a client cares about is whether or not he or she is working with someone who has his or her best interests in mind. Most clients expect advisors to uphold stewardship principles and responsibly manage the wealth clients entrust to the advisor's care. In fact, this type of stewardship may more accurately define what clients really seek.

What clients are left with instead is a regulatory puzzle. At best, it is a patchwork of complex laws difficult to understand. Is there anything the financial industry, regulators and federal legislators can do?

## Regulatory standards of care

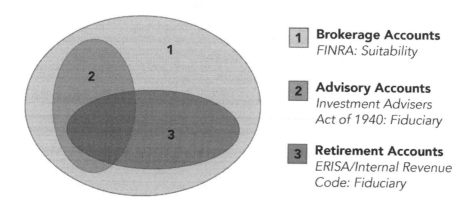

1 **Brokerage Accounts**
*FINRA: Suitability*

2 **Advisory Accounts**
*Investment Advisers Act of 1940: Fiduciary*

3 **Retirement Accounts**
*ERISA/Internal Revenue Code: Fiduciary*

When we at RBC Wealth Management hear the word fiduciary we wonder if it refers to an investment advice fiduciary under DOL rules, a fiduciary for a retirement plan, a trustee as a fiduciary for a trust, or an investment advice fiduciary under an investment advisory program at a company. Its meaning is dependent upon the context and circumstances.

Since there are many different definitions, RBC Wealth Management believes it would be helpful for clients to know which set of fiduciary requirements to apply to their advisor. The more different fiduciaries can clearly describe their fiduciary role, the easier it is for clients to determine what standard of care can be expected. For example, would the fiduciary role be clearly understood if one says, "I'm a fiduciary because I'm providing you investment advice for your retirement account?"

Yes, with a descriptor of that type, fiduciary is more clearly defined. And the purposes, roles and responsibilities are also defined. It may not resolve client confusion about the term. But at least clients will know which rule book the advisor is referring to.

Recent regulatory reform is a step in the right direction. But much work remains to be done. And until there is *one* fiduciary definition upon which *all* the legislators, regulators and financial industry organizations can agree, it is incumbent upon these parties to collaborate on unifying the standard of care which clients can expect from their advisors. Continued fragmentation of the definition and isolation among the proponents is *not* in the best interests of clients.

In the interim, regardless of what type of fiduciary a financial advisor claims to be, clients are best served by those who demonstrate stewardship, responsibility and integrity. If an advisor's behavior is consistent with these three core precepts, it does not really matter which set of rules he or she is legally obligated to follow. The outcome will be the same.

Financial advisors help clients build better futures. That's why we are in this business and excited about serving clients.

**Harold Evensky, CFP®, AIF®**
**Chairman**

**Evensky & Katz/Foldes Financial**

Eighteen

# The Human Element of Financial Planning

## About the Author

Harold Evensky, co-founder and chairman of Evensky & Katz/Foldes Financial Wealth Management, has been a leader in the financial planning and investment industry for over 30 years. He shares his extensive experience and knowledge as Professor of Practice at Texas Tech University and is an internationally recognized speaker. Harold is the author of *Hello Harold* and *Wealth Management: The Financial Advisor's Guide to Investing and Managing Client Assets*, and co-editor of *The Investment Think Tank: Theory, Strategy, and Practice for Advisers and Retirement Income Redesigned - Master Plans for Distribution*.

## About the Company

Founded in 1985, Evensky & Katz/Foldes Financial Wealth Management is a financial advisory firm based in Coral Gables, Florida that provides personalized financial and retirement planning.

—————m—————

## Unique and realistic

Good financial advice is unique to the client's needs, within a realistic framework of the real world. It takes into consideration all the realities of your client including risk tolerance, risk capacity, risk need, tax circumstances, health and, most important, goals.

Basically, good financial advice includes all of the elements necessary to assist the client in making good decisions about how to plan for the quality of the rest of his or her life, with a primary focus on the use of financial assets.

## The unawareness problem

Having described good financial advice, let's take note of all the software offered at little or no cost to help people plan for retirement. After evaluating the efficacy of the few dozen publicly available programs, my research with my associates at Texas Tech concluded that at best they're bad and, at worst, they're dangerous. They provide very misleading advice and conclusions. The problem is that the public is woefully unaware of that, and to the extent they're using this software, they probably rely on it to their detriment.

I see similar problems regarding the confusion between a broker and an advisor. Brokers call themselves advisors, even though legally they don't provide substantive advice. That can lead to a lot of bad decisions by investors, ultimately to the detriment of the quality of their financial lives. I believe that it is indeed a major problem that people can't distinguish between good and bad advice.

## Specificity and prioritization

Conceptually, good quality financial planning is very simple. It follows the classic financial planning process, which begins with the individual. What does the client want to accomplish? What are the goals? Each question needs to be answered with a great deal of specificity. Goals require both time and dollar specificity and then they need to be prioritized.

A plan that's based on, "I'd like to retire pretty soon and live well," does not provide enough information to develop a good plan. I need more information. For example: "I'd like to retire in three years, but I'll consider working for maybe another one or two, and I need X dollars annually adjusted for inflation to be able to retire and maintain my lifestyle. Also, I have an aging parent to take care of, and I need X amount annually, also adjusted for inflation and based on my parent's age and health, I estimate I'll need that for 10 years and that's a priority. So if I have to adjust some of my retirement goals, I'll do that."

All of those factors and discussions need to go into a plan, but the key is to build the plan around the unique goals of the client and the client's constraints such as health, family structure, risk tolerance, risk capacity and tax status.

Good comprehensive financial planning (as opposed to the targeted retirement planning that is the core of our practice) incorporates more than just the investment universe. For example, it also has to include risk management. While it's one of the least interesting areas to me from a planning perspective, it's the most important. If I can help someone earn an extra percent or so because of a more efficient portfolio, that's terrific.

However, if the client has a child that accidentally kills someone in an auto accident and the family does not have adequate liability insurance, it can wipe out everything. A 1 percent extra return is going to be meaningless in such a case, so comprehensive financial planning should incorporate risk management including life, health, disability and long term care. It also incorporates tax planning, cash flow management and estate planning. As for estate planning, a primary focus needs to be what I call living estate planning. While it is important to minimize estate taxes, what is far more important in the event of incapacity is how financial decisions are to be made. Who will make health care decisions? You don't want to leave those decisions up to the hospital's policy.

The responsibilities of the advisor are determined by the scope of the agreement with the client. For example, services may be limited to retirement planning and investing or may involve gathering information that includes not just financial and tax statements, but also documents for insurance and estate planning. Whatever the scope of the engagement, most important is understanding what the client wants to accomplish. What are the goals? My job is to empower clients to make good decisions, not to make those decisions for them.

The next step is to take all of that information and develop a plan, recommendations, and help educate and guide the clients on making their choices. Then, after making decisions about all those different aspects, assisting the client in implementing the plan — whether making the investments or helping to find an accountant, attorney or insurance agent — and helping the client evaluate the various solutions those professionals provide.

Then, finally, for most planning engagements, there is an ongoing relationship, because none of this is static. It's a question of constantly reviewing and, when necessary, modifying or changing all those different elements.

# Who is responsible for what?

The financial services world for the retail client is divided into two service models: The investment adviser on one side, and the broker on the other. The investment adviser is someone who provides investment advice for a fee, is subject to the 1940 Investment Advisers Act and must register as a registered investment adviser (RIA) with either the state or the U.S. Securities and Exchange Commission (SEC), depending on the assets under management. A broker is someone who holds a securities license, typically the Series 7, and is regulated by the 1934 Brokerage Act.

The confusion comes in around what's called the broker-dealer exemption in the 1940 Act. When the 1940 Act was passed, there were really very few people who were acting as advisers, providing just advice for a fee.

Brokers pretty much controlled the financial services world at the time. The broker-dealer exemption basically said that if the advice was solely incidental to the sale, then a broker would not be held to the 1940 Act; the broker-dealer could continue to operate under the rules of the 1934 Act. The fundamental difference is a broker is held to what's called a suitability standard, which is a business standard. A broker's responsibility is to the firm, not the client. Although brokers must provide advice that is suitable for a client, that doesn't necessarily mean it's in the client's best interest or the best alternative for the client. There may be all kinds of potential conflicts of interest, but there's no obligation on the part of the broker to alert the client to that.

Basically it's a caveat emptor relationship. If there's a problem, the buck stops with the client. There was a U.S. Supreme Court decision that ruled investment advisers are held to a traditional fiduciary standard. There are a variety of elements to a fiduciary relationship, but placing your client's interests first is the key consideration. The other fundamental difference between the two regulatory systems is the broker-dealer system is rules-based, whereas the investment adviser system is principles-based. Broker-dealers and the Financial Industry Regulatory Authority (FINRA) have volumes of rules that must be followed. For the investment advisers there are relatively few rules per se.

You simply must adhere to the basic principle of placing your client's interests first. Early on in the debate between these two groups, the securities industry used to argue: "We're much more heavily controlled and regulated than advisors because we've got three feet of rules and they've got two inches of rules." It made it look like the securities industry had much stronger regulation. But that's extremely misleading. The analogy I use all the time is the Ten Commandments. The Ten Commandments are principles and can be printed on a single page, but they're clearly pretty powerful principles.

Again, the difference is where the buck stops. If something is wrong in the securities world, the buck stops with the client. If something is wrong in the investment adviser world, the buck stops with the adviser.

Average investors do not understand the difference. They assume that if they're working with a broker and advisor that there is no difference, when in fact there's a huge difference.

I've been part of a group for years, The Committee for the Fiduciary Standard. We developed a fiduciary oath. Other than the title, it doesn't have the word fiduciary in it. The oath has a few "mom and pop" commitments that everyone can understand. "I will put my clients' best interests first," is really the core.

Then, "I will act with prudence that is with the skill, care and diligence of good judgment of a professional." That is a commitment to be held to a professional standard, not just a "prudent man." The oath continues with: "I will not mislead clients and I will provide conspicuous, full and clear disclosure of all important facts."

It concludes: "I will avoid conflicts of interest, fully disclose and fairly manage in my clients' favor any unavoidable conflicts."

Brokers are simply not held to these standards although that may change over time. The U.S. Department of Labor (DOL) has issued its new Fiduciary Rules that apply to IRA accounts. This new regulation will require brokers to meet minimum fiduciary standards should they provide advice for IRA account investments. A number of Congressional proposals designed to stop the DOL plan from proceeding have been introduced, substituting alternative "standards" that we do not believe make any sense, at least from an investor's perspective. We hope and believe this effort will fail.

As an example, one provision would allow clients to opt out of a fiduciary relationship as long as you tell them: "I'm not going to place your best interests first…just sign this paper and we're fine. Let's go ahead." The problem is most people sign whatever's put in front of them without any idea what it means. Real fiduciaries cannot have their responsibilities signed away.

Another provision is the ability to say: "Well, we have conflicts, but all we have to do is disclose them to you, and now we're off the hook." There's been quite a bit of research indicating disclosure is not necessarily an adequate protection. In fact, in many cases it may be counter-productive. The example that's often used is a doctor who owns a lab company. If the doctor tells you: "I'm sending you over there, but I've got an ownership interest in it. If you go there, I'm going to make some money out of it. I clearly have a conflict," as opposed to not disclosing it and sending you there anyway.

Research suggests that the patient is probably better off if not told of the conflict because if it is not disclosed there appears to be a certain moral responsibility not to gouge a patient too badly. However, if the conflict is disclosed, then it's: "Hey, look. I told you so. Now I can charge whatever I want because you know I'm doing it." That's an example of why disclosure may be counter-productive.

To the extent that an advisor cannot avoid a conflict there's a need to manage it in the interest of the client, not in the interest of the individual advisor or the firm. A classic example is bond trading. Typically bonds are not sold with a commission. They're sold with a mark-up. The way it works is the broker would call his trading desk and say: "I'm looking for a good 10-year, double A-rated municipal bond." The firm's bond trader might respond: "I've got a good one here. I can sell it to you at 102 1/2. What do you want me to mark it up?" The broker might respond, "Well, add two points onto it." He would then offer it to his client at 104 1/2. The client would only see they paid 104 1/2.

The client would have no idea what the broker was making on that or the fact that the broker made anything. I've had some very sophisticated clients come to me and say: "Oh, yeah, they charge me commissions on the stock, but I don't pay anything for the bonds." That's because most investors are completely unaware that there's a mark-up. Nevertheless, most brokers are honest, moral and competent, so the abuse of such conflicts are the exceptions. Nevertheless, under the Suitability Standard, the broker can do something that's clearly not in the best interest of their client, but would not be a conflict with the law.

Based on recent studies, brokers at major financial services firms favor a fiduciary standard. It's the institutions that are fighting the fiduciary standard and are understandably concerned about its impact.

Clearly there will be an impact on their operations and costs, but most individual brokers, the ones who are dealing with clients, are prepared to be held to all of these standards, certainly to the fairly simple principles that we put in the oath. The reason I'm so passionate about the oath is that as much as I hope that regulators and Congress will do something to change the world, I'm not optimistic that it will happen. Our best shot right now is the DOL rule.

But it's not clear how long it'll take before we see its impact, whether it will get mired in lawsuits or if a new administration may make it all disappear overnight. My personal push to retail investors is to say: "Don't count on regulators or Congress. Protect yourself. Whoever you talk to, ask them to sign this oath." Your advisor may not have a fiduciary relationship with any of their other clients, but you as a client will be in a much stronger position should a problem arise if the broker or advisor signs the oath. The ultimate protection will come from individual clients getting these types of commitments from whomever they are dealing with.

## Expect more quality

I don't think that the definition of quality financial planning is going to change. I think more quality will be offered, simply because financial planning is becoming recognized as a profession, and we are formally educating and training the next generation of financial planners.

When I started in this business, we were inventing financial planning as we went along. But today I'm talking to you from my office at a university. I just finished teaching my graduate wealth management class composed of thoughtful and dedicated master's and Ph.D. candidates. There are a growing number of people coming into the profession who are professionally qualified to offer quality advice.

The fact of the matter is the financial services world is beginning to recognize that quality planning advice is good business. It reduces a potential liability and it increases the stickiness of the relationship. Back when I was chair of the Certified Financial Planner (CFP®) Board of Governors, one of the major brokerage firms in the country would not allow their advisors to put the CFP® mark on their business card. At the time they said, "Oh, no. If you do that, it'll ratchet up our potential risk and liability."

Today, many of those same firms now encourage their brokers to earn their CFP® designation and will often pay for the training and licensing.

That, in and of itself, is a huge change. Historically, when hiring new people firms would look for someone who had a book of business or knew a lot of rich people. Today, many of the big brokerage firms are hiring students out of universities for staff planning positions at very competitive salaries. For a couple of years they do planning for the clients of the brokerage teams ultimately to move on as partners in those teams. Quality planning is now beginning to be offered much more broadly than in the past. The fact that so many major financial services firms are now beginning to use professional quality planning programs from leading software providers is an indication of the seriousness of that commitment.

## Structural change

We have been seeing and will continue to see change in the structure of the advisory world. Some have suggested all the small advisors are going to be put out of business. I think the day of the mom and pop advisor, the universe I started in, is yesterday's story. There will be small practices around, just like there are small accounting practices and small law firms and small medical groups. However, the reality from an economic standpoint is that those small operations become more for lifestyle than for economic reasons, meaning the individual advisor would probably make more money working for a bigger firm.

Furthermore, I believe that in order to deliver the quality advice that clients will come to expect and will be able to get at a reasonable cost will require scale. Just the cost of compliance and technology today, if you're doing it right, is extremely high. In addition, to be able to provide more than investment advice, firms are going to need to scale. If you're a small practice, it's very expensive to have senior people spend their time on risk management, insurance policies, estate planning, college funding calculations and similar work.

If you have a much larger practice with an accountant, an attorney, property and casualty (P&C) and health insurance people on staff to review the work of the client's professionals and to network with those professionals, you can deliver higher quality and more value at a very reasonable cost. And by adding support under your senior people, you can leverage their time and talents. Scale, I believe, is going to be extraordinarily important in the future to deliver more and comprehensive advice at pretty much the same pricing standard we use today. The reality is that what we currently do is rapidly becoming commoditized.

There are over 100 firms with over $1 billion dollars under management. Ten years ago there were probably five such firms. Along with size and scale reshaping the industry, there's a lot of discussion about changes in the compensation structure. The traditional model is assets under management (AUM).

In my view that's not a very good system. It's not very credible because it focuses on just the assets and that's not really our major value. We're not money managers.

Unfortunately I don't believe that there is a viable alternative. The alternative most commonly talked about is a retainer. Intellectually, I think that is a much more appropriate system, but it has its own challenges. First, when you use a retainer, most people are going to instantly convert that to a percent of assets anyway. Second, when the markets go up, the account grows and they add more money to it. It sounds good to say: "Well, you know you had $2 million. Now you've added another $2 million. We need to revisit the retainer."

What are you to do if the client doesn't see it that way? It's very difficult, at least in my experience, to adjust the retainer as time goes on, even if there's a significant increase in the asset base or in the responsibilities. On the other hand, experience tells me clients have no problem insisting on an adjustment if assets drop.

I do not see robo-advisors as a threat. I see it as something that we might be able to utilize for smaller clients. The problem I have with that is I often hear the argument, "Well, smaller clients, they don't need as much attention or detail."

Unfortunately, I think it's just the opposite. If I do an unbelievably bad job for my very wealthy clients, they may fire me and their grandkids may be unhappy because they inherit less, but it's not going to affect the quality of my client's life. On the other hand, someone with limited resources is the person that needs the very best planning, because very small mistakes can have a huge impact on the quality of his or her life.

A robo-advisor is attractive in making things simpler, but it worries me because it has the same issues that I see with public retirement planning software. It looks good and feels good, but in fact it's not very good. Algorithms don't think. I believe the real solution is going to be professional quality software enabling the client to do a significant amount of the work, and then a professional can step in and review that work with them. We can afford to take much smaller clients under a structure like that.

I don't see technology replacing a live planner, not just because of the personal interaction, but because of the intellectual overlay that I believe is critical for doing a good job in personal financial planning.

The human element is needed to vet the technology. It's not the technology per se that is bad; the problem is that the technology limits the quality of the input in an attempt to make it simple. Unfortunately, life's not simple. Advisors really earn their money when the market is going nuts, and it's going down a lot. Technology is not very good at holding hands or at encouraging people to hang in there. Ultimately, in the investment universe, our real value, or certainly a major part of it, is helping clients weather bad times.

Clients are prepared to pay and stay with us for decades because they're aware of that value. As we say, we can't guarantee returns, but, for the most part, our clients can sleep well in spite of what's happening in the market. They can go about enjoying their lives without worrying about what the so-called financial pundits say.

When I'm asked about those televised know-it-alls, I say, "Turn off the TV and the radio and that financial pornography and go visit your grandkids."

## Confidence and caution

People tend to make what seem like dumb decisions. We're not dumb, as research in behavioral economics has taught us, we're human. For example, we all tend to be over-confident. Many investors believe they can pick the best funds, or their managers or advisors can pick the best opportunities.

Another example is most of us are not good in what has been described as mental accounting. A client came to me in tears. A retired surgeon, he said, "I don't understand.

I made 80 percent last year and I only lost 50 percent this year. I should be 30 percent ahead, but I'm underwater." I responded with, "Well, yes, because you had a million dollars that grew to $1.8 million, and you lost 50 percent of the $1.8 million leaving you with $900,000." But that's not the way people think and it leads to the errors in their planning. If you lose 50 percent one year and make 50 percent the next year, you're not even. You're under water by 25 percent. Had a million, I lost half of it, I got a half million, now I made 50 percent, I have $750,000.

But people don't understand that kind of math when they invest in very risky investments. It takes a lot longer to catch up on a loss than one would think. There are lots of similar issues out there that we should help clients to understand to avoid those kinds of problems.

I have a friend named Nick Murry who says people confuse certainty and safety. People say: "Well, I want to be safe so I'm going to put my money in CDs or treasuries." It's certain they may have a fixed amount of dollars down the road, but as I say, it's certainly not safe because by the time you factor in taxes and inflation, they will have less real dollars and may not have the financial resources to fund their goals.

Being "conservative" doesn't necessarily mean it's safe from a financial planning standpoint. "I'm going to be conservative, let's not consider Social Security, because I don't think it's going to be around." Sounds conservative, but the fact of the matter is as a planner, if I don't factor in Social Security, I may have to tell the client, "In order to achieve your goals, instead of being 40 percent in stocks, now you're going to have to be 80 percent in stocks or, alternatively, you'll need to reduce your standard of living by 15 percent." The point is there's no such thing as just being conservative because the flip side is you need to do something to balance it that's probably not very conservative.

Again, good planning is helping to educate our clients about these conflicts. That doesn't mean coming up with a conservative solution, but coming up with a professional solution, one that is based on the best estimates, forward-looking expectations and risk tolerance.

**Chris Flint**
**President and Chief Executive Officer**

**ProEquities**

Nineteen

# Advancing Consumer Empowerment

## About the Author

Chris Flint leads ProEquities as president and CEO with the strength of over 20 years in the financial services industry. As the president of Lincoln Financial Securities and the head of Lincoln Financial Network Advisor Recruitment and Acquisition Strategies (2006-2015), Chris became known for his strategic and innovative approach to growth and his ability to develop deep relationships.

## About the Company

Serving over 1,000 financial services professionals, ProEquities is a relationship and growth-oriented broker-dealer focused on providing robust resources and support to its independent registered representatives, investment advisors, and hybrid RIAs. A leading independent broker-dealer founded in 1985 and with offices across the United States, ProEquities is a subsidiary of Protective Life Corporation.

―⟋⟋―

## Advice should mimic good planning

The financial services industry has a real opportunity to expand on what constitutes quality advice and those the advice serves. I describe this opportunity as advancing consumer empowerment through better financial literacy and improving outcomes related to the advice process. This means helping consumers become more informed and more engaged with the advice and planning process while attaining a better understanding of the solutions being presented to them. In fact, when I think about good financial advice, it embodies good financial planning and good financial planning means helping the client become more financially literate and aware in the pursuit of their investment objectives.

For example, when you consider comprehensive financial advice, it can't go unnoticed that the client may have an unforeseen financial or retirement planning need. A quality financial advisor will have a process to better understand the client. She will ask engaging questions. However, asking the "right" questions also means having the right sequence to determine whether or not there is a broader need. The financial advisor will look beyond the basic investment objectives shared by the client, by asking open-ended questions that are goals-based. This may include something as simple as educational needs or as complex as preparing for longevity needs. The client may want to fund her child's, grandchild's or even her own education, or may want to consider establishing a charitable trust that lives beyond her retirement needs. It's the financial advisor's responsibility to help lead this dialogue.

Moreover, I believe good financial advice must consider more than general investments. It must consider insurance planning, tax planning and retirement planning, as well as senior issues like long term care and basic health care needs.

I don't limit or delineate the concept of financial advice from the concept of financial planning. I think the industry has an opportunity to do a lot better at identifying where the two intersect or co-exist to create a better client experience.

Fundamentally, I think it's an obligation of all financial institutions to do a better job of providing tools, resources and training to help financial advisors improve how advice and the planning processes can integrate in a more cohesive manner. In other words, stop creating needs to fit a solution, rather, find a trusted process to meet the needs of the client.

This begins with how you pre-engage the client. That entails understanding her needs, gathering information and identifying objectives, as well as understanding what the client does or does not know about the investment and planning process. Likewise, it means the advisor needs to better understand the elements that shape the client's view of advice and financial planning.

The challenge is to routinely analyze a client's situation in a systematic way so the solutions are more consistent across the different dimensions critical to the client. Next you develop a strategy and present solutions and alternatives in a way where there's no conflict with the advice you are providing.

There is also a component centered on implementation, monitoring and reviewing the performance against changing objectives. I don't think the industry has done a very good job of this because we tend to introduce a solution that fits a short-term, immediate "need" versus engaging the client in a consistent process that evolves with the client's longer-term needs.

In order for that to happen, there needs to be a great deal of exchange, validation and re-validation between the advisor and the client when gathering information in order to properly analyze the situation and develop a solution or strategy. I think this is where there is a material breakdown in the process, which goes back to the concept of financial planning and financial advice co-existing, because they are really not two discrete functions.

The actual plan is the governing document in the financial planning process. Sound financial advice is the general objective. One of the ways to provide good financial advice to the end client is to be very systematic and one of the tools offered to our industry is the financial planning process. In order to provide good financial advice, each client deserves a good financial plan; I don't think we are doing that methodically across the industry.

## The conversation shouldn't be about returns

Individuals often talk about returns. If you look at some of the investment management companies, they cite the returns they have earned for their clients. I don't think the conversation should be about the returns. I think the client needs to separate the investment results from the relationship. It's the quality of the relationship, the plan itself, and the advice provided, that's most important.

Consumers need to focus on whether or not the advisor is a good fit. Is she listening to their needs and interpreting those needs appropriately? More importantly, a good fit includes acting in their best interest, not the best interest of the advisor or the organization the advisor works for.

# Selecting a financial planner

It took me a long time to choose my financial planner. One of my close friends is a financial planner and we have spoken a lot about the process of selecting an advisor. I think she said it best when she said most clients tell her, "I know what I want, but I don't know how to get there."

Getting there is highly personal. The process for understanding the options, the risk factors and what can and cannot be controlled all need to be undertaken in a very disciplined manner. That's why this process of the exchange of information and ideas needs to be more routine and systematic. And, this process takes time.

There is no way you can gather all the right information, ask all the right questions and completely understand the client's objectives in just one meeting. The process of analyzing the information and then understanding how various tactical actions impact the client takes time. If you need to take objective and subjective components into consideration, you're going to get different outcomes because we're human; we make mistakes. It will take time to work through these scenarios. And, if you don't have a financial planning process or mechanism in place, you're one degree removed from some of the expectations and obligations under a fiduciary standard.

When I went through my planning process, I asked the advisor about his credentials and how he is compensated. I wanted to know that if something happened to me, he would be able to work with my wife and children and they would be taken care of. The outcome of that dialogue allowed me to move forward.

I asked to see an example financial plan and we talked about his investment approach. I told him I have all my business at a certain firm; asked how he interacts with that firm; was that material for him in creating a financial plan or would the plan be compromised because my assets are at that firm. I also asked how often he checks in to make sure we're meeting the expectations of the plan, progressing toward my retirement goals and tracking the overall progress towards my objectives.

The individual I chose is very smart, but I wanted to know if he was also seeking outside perspectives. I asked, "Is there a team behind you that helps to implement some of the recommendations, such as my long term care needs, insurance and investment management, retirement goals and estate planning?" The answer to all was "yes."

I wanted to know how he selected clients and why they stay with him. I viewed it not only as me choosing him, but him selecting me. It's a two-way relationship.

# A gatekeeper and then some

As a broker-dealer, I challenge my team to be gatekeepers in terms of the types of advisors with whom we do business. I ask them if this is someone they would trust to manage their affairs or the affairs of someone important to them. We look at how they would create value for the client relationship, which could include product mix, approach and overall character. If the answer is "yes," then we would want that individual affiliated with our organization.

You need to think about the technical definition of a fiduciary, which is putting the interest of the client before one's own interest. As I look across the industry and think about comprehensive financial advice, I look at fiduciary standards and obligations back to the end client, where they have congruence and where they lack congruence. There's a great deal of ambiguity out there. A lot of the confusion is among consumers. They don't understand when someone is acting as a broker or an advisor, or understand if that someone is acting in their best interest or in the best interest of their employer.

At the end of the day, if I have to disclose that I may be compensated more for one product versus another product, or that I have a conflict when providing services to my employer versus the obligation I have to my end client, then we have a disconnect. The reason lies in the way we are presenting ourselves as an industry to the end client, "We are always going to do what's right for you," but I don't think we are doing a good job of that.

For me, the definition of acting as a fiduciary is simply acting in the best interest of the client at all times. The advisor has a code of ethics that dictates that all of her actions must live up to it. These conflicts aren't just defined in terms of the compensation structure or the costs embedded in the product. It is whether the decision I'm making for my client has been influenced by an outside force other than what can best help my client achieve the objectives identified in our initial conversations.

In our industry, if we can't stand up and say, "We don't have this conflict," then we need to fix it. That's why I keep going back to the financial planning process. If you've done a true values-based financial plan, took the time to fully understand the client's information, asked the right questions and listened, then validated the objectives before you arrived at the solution, you will have a better outcome.

## Remove embedded conflicts

A collective embrace of the role of a fiduciary will create greater transparency across the industry while also transforming the way products and solutions are developed and delivered to the end client. I think there's a great deal of momentum around that transparency, which will significantly improve the client-advisor interaction and the quality of that experience.

I don't think it's going to significantly change the solution set. I don't think it's going to change the mortality and expense (M&E) of a product or the general costs of doing business for the end client. But, I do believe there will be a much more transparent experience for the consumer because it will remove some of the conflicts that are embedded in the different compensation models and the different incentives that might be applied to selling certain types of products.

## Changes ahead

The general structure of how you get to a solution or a strategy for the client will not fundamentally change. Yes, you might call it something different. You might have varying degrees of input along each of the steps. But fundamentally, I don't think the process will change because it's a good way to interact with the end client. I think it's a good way to put a system of checks and balances in place. The financial plan becomes a better governing document around the commitment you're making to the client. Said differently, it's a roadmap for what we've interpreted, what I heard your objectives to be, how I arrived at the recommendations and how we're going to implement and monitor them.

That roadmap becomes more and more important in a post-U.S. Department of Labor (DOL) rule environment. As it relates to reasonable compensation, you're going to see technology continue to be more and more pervasive in the delivery and monitoring of the management of advice.

Forward-thinking service providers are determining how to get to a level fee structure. One of the compensation models the DOL will allow is an independently certified computer model that can support unbiased investment advice that is in accordance with the rule's structure. As such, technology becomes more and more important in a post-DOL environment, both in terms of identifying solutions, and monitoring and calibrating the solutions against the Employee Retirement Income Security Act (ERISA) of 1974 fiduciary standard.

# The financial literacy imperative

We have people today, including my children, who don't know how to balance a checkbook. "I've got money in my account … that means I've got money to spend, right?" That's how people are thinking about the basic concept of checking and banking. When you start to think about the erosion of welfare benefits and Social Security, longer life spans and having more responsibility for our own financial futures, we're not giving people the steps or the ladder to reach their objectives or even helping them to identify what those objectives might look like.

We are living longer because of technology and medical advances, which means we will live longer in retirement. What are you doing to plan for that? While the financial services industry does a good job of helping people choose a financial advisor or leverage technology to create their own financial plans, we don't do a good job helping people understand the difference between rates of return and the expense associated with the solutions that are presented to them.

People who say, "I've got money in my savings account" don't recognize that the cost of living is increasing at 1.7 percent a year and the rate of return on a checking account is ten basis points. How does that play out in a real world scenario? We need better products with better risk-adjusted returns and we need to educate individuals on exactly what that means to them.

Generally speaking, we have not done a good job of making people aware of what's important about planning for retirement and protecting themselves from some of the pitfalls around health care and long term care, and around short-term and long-term disability. We still tend to just talk about the total return of an account. We need to talk about more than that.

This is really where the fiduciary standard versus the suitability standard becomes increasingly important. We know we're dealing with investors or buyers of investment products who may be financially illiterate.

The process of gathering information and asking all the right questions needs to be much deeper because consumers "don't know what they don't know." They think they've got the right information. They think they've got the right objectives in the right order. If you ask nine out of 10 consumers or investors what they want to do, you'll hear, "I want to retire comfortably." But if you ask, "What does that mean for you? What are your objectives? What are the what-if scenarios? What if you were laid off tomorrow, what would you do? What if you had a stroke and couldn't work for the balance of your pre-retirement years?" You won't get substantive details because the typical consumer doesn't know, so the answers are easy for them to ignore.

This is where greater financial literacy and awareness becomes important. At the same time we're providing advice to consumers, we need to be educating them.

What I would like to do — especially in places like Birmingham and Philadelphia where I've lived, worked, and served in the community — is raise awareness of financial literacy in schools. Advisors and financial services companies can partner with the community to provide the educational resources to show how financial literacy can help individuals and at-risk neighborhoods better understand financial planning and investments and why it's important to be active in shaping their financial future.

Financial literacy is an issue where the financial services industry can really take a leadership role and reshape itself in the eyes of the consumer. The investing public does not have a lot trust in the financial services sector; we need ask ourselves why.

In many ways we have an obligation and responsibility to advance financial literacy for the benefit of our communities and our industry. What we do is important. We owe our clients no less.

**Deborah Fox**
Founder and Chief Executive Officer

Essential Planners, Fox College Funding and AdvisorTouch

Twenty

# Silos Prevent an Optimized Plan

## About the Author

Deborah Fox has been a practicing financial advisor for almost three decades. She developed, utilizes and teaches an innovative "integrated financial planning" process that hundreds of other advisory firms have adopted. Deborah is regularly quoted in national and industry publications and is a frequent presenter at industry conferences.

## About the Company

Essential Planners provides integrated financial planning and wealth management advice and collaborates with clients' other financial professionals. In addition to serving clients from the traditional and Baby Boomer generations, Fox's firm also serves Gen X and Millennial clients. Fox College Funding, LLC, Fox's specialty firm, provides 'late stage' college planning by helping middle- and high-income parents reduce their out-of-pocket college expenses as their children prepare to apply to college. AdvisorTouch is Fox's consulting firm for other financial advisors and their staff which helps them get systems in place to help them work more efficiently and deliver exceptional service to their clients.

—⟋⟋⟋—

## Industry evolution

I have had the pleasure of being involved in the financial advice industry in two roles. First, I have been a financial advisor for almost 30 years assisting middle-income, high-income and high net worth clients nationwide achieve their financial and life goals. In addition, for over 20 years I have personally consulted and mentored hundreds of other financial advisors to help them better serve their clients and more efficiently run their businesses. This dual perspective has provided me with insights into the many business models financial advisors have chosen and has enabled me to witness firsthand how our industry has evolved.

Over the last decade, one positive trend I've observed has been the increased number of financial advisors who provide some type of financial planning advice as part of their services. I have also noticed an increase in the number of advisors who refer to themselves as "financial planners." This is both a positive and a negative. The positive: there are now more advisors who are genuinely providing valuable financial planning services to their clients. The negative: there are also more advisors calling themselves "financial planners" whose deliverables fall short of what true financial planning services should include.

## Muddied waters

The consumer has had a difficult time differentiating between various types of advisors and what they do. Both "financial advisor" and "financial planner" are generic terms that lack specific definition in the financial services industry. As such, the lines have been blurred as to who actually delivers these services and the quality of advice. This has created confusion for both consumers and the industry, warranting a deeper look into what financial planning actually is and who is doing it.

A "financial advisor" may be an investment manager, stockbroker, insurance agent, tax professional, estate planner, wealth manager or financial planner. The advice and recommendations each delivers can vary significantly. Some sell certain types of products; some offer advice for a fee for either a single planning area or for multiple planning areas; others offer a combination of planning for a fee combined with commission they earn from product sales; while still others work entirely on a commission basis. Most commonly, financial planning is provided one way or another as an add-on to investment management services.

## The dilemma

There have never been more people who have a need for professional financial planning advice than there are today. Whether it is a recent college graduate who needs to create his or her first budget, a newly married young couple planning to buy their first home or Baby Boomers planning for a successful retirement; there is a huge market for ethical, competent financial planning advice. Consumers need the type of advice that helps them understand the various financial options available so they can be guided to make informed decisions.

Since many consumers who seek financial planning services are unable to identify true financial planners and are not sure what a real financial plan is, they are unlikely to receive the services and outcomes they desire. Research firm Cerulli Associates found in 2013 that more than 166,000 financial advisors identified themselves as having a financial planning-focused service offering. Yet Cerulli verified that only 38 percent of these self-identified financial planners actually focused their businesses on offering financial planning services!

There is plenty of in-fighting going on between the industry's professional groups about which type of advisor is best. In my opinion, it is not so much about the title advisors are using, but instead about the quality of advice their clients are receiving. Our industry needs to focus on helping each client receive the type of advice he or she is seeking from a qualified advisor with the appropriate level of expertise to deliver that advice. The advisor needs to be committed to always doing the right thing for their clients by providing as unbiased advice as possible that is in their clients' best interest. This includes being willing to turn away business if the advisor determines he or she is not the right fit for the client. Just as important, each consumer needs to find an advisor he or she feels comfortable with and can trust. Unfortunately, there are many advisors operating today who do not meet these criteria.

## Criteria for choosing a financial advisor

It is very important to know how to choose a financial advisor. Ideally, a consumer wants someone who can work alongside of him or her to co-create a financial plan. However, before searching for an advisor, a consumer must first assess his or her needs. For example, would he or she benefit most from a more holistic plan that addresses multiple planning areas or does he or she only need advice in one or two areas? Once the client answers questions such as these, he or she will be better positioned to find an advisor who can best meet his or her needs.

Many banks and insurance companies employ financial advisors who offer financial planning services. While there are certainly exceptions, the majority of them do not offer holistic financial planning for a fee. Stockbrokers from large wirehouses have also entered the financial planning arena. These institutions have traditionally been transaction-oriented to generate commissions. Advisors who offer financial planning services in this environment typically focus on using a financial plan as a door opener for selling the proprietary financial products the institution offers such as CDs, insurance, annuities, mutual funds or other investment products. However, advisors in this space who go against the firm's preferred business model have a more difficult time providing advice in the way they prefer and often take a pay cut to do so. Also, some banks and trust companies offer very high-end planning services to high-net-worth clients that do tend to be more holistic in scope but still primarily utilize the firm's proprietary products.

There are advisors affiliated with independent broker-dealer companies who are not tied to proprietary products and offer hybrid services — financial planning combined with financial product sales. Still other advisors choose to operate as a Registered Investment Advisor (RIAs) or as Investment Advisor Representatives under a fee-only model. These advisors are regulated by the state in which they do business or by the U.S. Securities and Exchange Commission (SEC), depending on the level of investment assets they manage. A growing number of Certified Public Accountants (CPAs) have also entered the financial planning space and combine their tax expertise with financial planning advice.

In addition, some advisors also offer specialized financial planning services for a particular niche. Some examples are planning for widows and widowers, executives with stock options and deferred compensation plans, specialized estate planning for high-net-worth individuals, parents with special needs children, seniors who need to optimize Social Security and Medicare, or, in my firm's case, 'late-stage' college planning for parents with college-bound high school students.

One of the hottest and most divisive discussions going on in our industry right now revolves around how advisors get compensated for their work. As I mentioned above, some advisors get paid only by commissions, others choose to only charge a fee for advice (known as "fee-only" advisors) and some get paid by a combination of commissions and fees. It is important for consumers to understand how an advisor gets paid because it can affect the type of recommendations he or she discusses.

## Best interests

There is a very important movement that has gained momentum in the financial advice industry concerning compensation. It revolves around the "fiduciary standard," the highest standard of client care under the law. Briefly stated, under the fiduciary standard advisors must place their interests after that of the client. The fiduciary standard consists of a duty of loyalty and care, meaning that advisors must act in the best interest of their clients. Fee-only advisors typically charge either hourly or flat fees for their services or a percentage of the assets they manage for their clients. This compensation method enables an advisor to be fairly compensated for his or her advice while taking their clients' best interest to heart.

Advisors who operate under a broker-dealer model are only required to fulfill a "suitability" obligation, defined as making recommendations that are suitable to their clients. Instead of having to place their interests after that of their clients, advisors bound by this standard only have to reasonably believe that any recommendations they make are suitable for clients according to their planning objectives, financial situations and unique circumstances.

Advisors under the suitability requirements, for example, would need to ensure transaction costs for their clients are not excessive, but would be able to purchase a product for a client that paid them the highest commission as long as it would be considered suitable. Under the fiduciary standard, on the other hand, advisors are strictly prohibited from purchasing an investment for their clients solely because it would pay them a higher fee or commission.

After almost six years of debate, in April of 2016 the U.S. Department of Labor (DOL) finalized legislation that created a fiduciary rule for financial advisors providing advice to clients with retirement plans such as IRAs and 401(k)s. The rule requires advisors and brokers to act in the best interests of their clients. However, there were some concessions made to the broker-dealer segment of the industry that sells financial products to earn commissions.

It will be interesting to see if broker-dealers and their affiliated brokers will be able to adapt to new regulations where their clients truly will receive advice that is in their best interest. Only time will tell if the new rule will help Americans receive better financial advice so they can accumulate more money for retirement.

## Where loyalty lies

Loyalty is a key distinction between the fiduciary standard and suitability requirements. Advisors or brokers affiliated with a broker-dealer have a duty to be loyal first to the broker-dealer. Fiduciary advisors, on the other hand, have an obligation to first be loyal to their clients.

In my opinion, advisors who operate under the fiduciary standard are better positioned to provide superior advice to their clients. Although not impossible, it would be difficult to serve as a true fiduciary to clients if advisors are set up to sell financial products for a commission under a suitability model. The potential conflict of interest created for the advisor under that model is not very reassuring to a client.

Advisors who work under a fee-only model tend to have the fewest conflicts of interest. However, to be fair, every form of compensation has some inherent conflict of interest. For example, even advisors who are fee-only and charge a percentage of assets they manage for their clients — an asset under management (AUM) fee — can have conflicts. A common AUM fee is 1 percent per year of the total value of the investments being managed. Let's say a client receives an inheritance and asks the advisor if he or she should add the money to the investment account or, instead, purchase a rental property with the funds. If the advisor recommends the rental property, he or she will not benefit from an increase in his AUM fee because the assets are not being added to the existing investment account the advisor manages. This creates a conflict. An advisor operating under the fiduciary standard needs to ensure the advisor counsels the client to choose the option that is truly in the client's best interest.

The bottom line is that consumers want to find an advisor committed to doing the right thing for them at all times. This is a matter of integrity and trust, not titles. It is important that consumers ask the right questions of any advisor being considered to make an informed decision about who would be qualified to handle his or her planning needs and also be a good fit. When choosing an advisor consumers should ask themselves: Is this person a qualified advisor to provide the type of advice I am seeking? What is this advisor's service model? Am I likely to receive unbiased advice from this advisor that will be in my best interest? Do I feel comfortable with this person? Is it someone I feel I can trust?

## A dozen questions consumers should ask and advisors should be prepared to answer:

1. Exactly what services do you offer?
2. What type of clients do you target?
3. What are your areas of expertise?
4. What are your credentials and how long have you been providing these services?
5. Do you work with clients to create a personalized financial plan?
6. For what percentage of your clients have you helped create a financial plan?
7. What areas of planning are included in the financial plans you create?
8. What is your process for working with a client when creating a financial plan?
9. How do you get paid and how much do your services cost? (Commissions, assets under management fees, retainer fees, fixed project fees, hourly fees?)
10. (If advisor earns commissions) What products do you sell that pay you commissions and what percentage of your income is earned through commissions?
11. May I see an example of the type of financial plan you create for your clients?
12. (Ask this question if everything else sounds good to you up to this point.) Can you provide at least two client references you have worked with to create their financial plan?

## What a financial plan really is

An advisor (regardless of title) who offers financial planning services should be able to expertly deliver a real financial plan. So then, what exactly is a real financial plan? I would argue the vast majority of consumers could not provide an accurate definition due to blurred lines between the various types of services advisors provide.

By my definition, a real financial plan provides holistic advice from a qualified advisor that integrates recommendations for all relevant areas of financial planning such as investment, retirement, cash flow, insurance and estate planning as well as any other specialty areas that apply such as real estate or business planning. Ideally, the advisor uses a collaborative approach to building the financial plan. This involves significant discussions between the client and the advisor about each area of the client's finances.

Throughout this process, the client would share his or her history, background, goals, hopes, dreams and concerns. The advisor would listen intently, provide financial education and share his or her recommendations. This should include multiple options for each area of planning, since there is never only one way to do something. The client would then be able to choose the options he or she feels is right. The outcome is a **co-created** financial plan that truly resonates with the client. There is a much higher likelihood that the client will be successful implementing the plan and achieve the desired results when the client and the advisor co-create a plan.

## Beyond financial calculators

Financial planning deliverables can vary significantly between advisors. On one end there are advisors who believe a financial plan is simply crunching some numbers with financial planning software. The client would typically receive a physical report that becomes the main deliverable. The report has financial projections, most often focused on the areas of investment and retirement planning. The difference here is this is not a co-created plan. This type of plan is heavily one-sided since it is created without significant discussions with the client and is mainly made up of recommendations the software has generated based on its algorithms. I call this a "pseudo plan."

A financial plan should not only be centered on algorithmic financial calculations and run-of-the-mill recommendations generated by financial planning software. A real financial plan includes deep discussions about life goals, financial priorities and expected and unexpected circumstances. It should include fully mapping out a game plan for different scenarios under various assumptions. For example, this might include the advisor and you discussing and creating a plan ahead of time for how your portfolio will be managed during a bear market cycle in the stock market when it feels really scary to stay invested. Or what if you had to provide care for an elderly parent? Or what would you do if your spouse became seriously ill or disabled? Or how will you cover the cost of college at your child's "dream" school? Or how would your financial plan change if you received a windfall from an inheritance or successful business venture?

The majority of consumers would benefit most from the creation of what I call an "integrated" financial plan, which integrates all areas of one's finances and considers the effect certain decisions made in one planning area would have on other planning areas. Integrated planning may include investment, retirement, cash flow, tax, insurance, higher education, asset protection, charitable giving and business planning. The benefit of this type of planning is that financial decisions are made from multiple perspectives. This typically leads to a more cohesive plan with superior results. For example, I describe the services of my planning firm, Essential Planners, as "We oversee all areas of our clients' finances so they work together efficiently, harmoniously and in alignment with their goals, values and passions."

## Silos prevent an optimized plan

Unfortunately, today most consumers are planning their finances in silos. Financial decisions in one area of planning are not being scrutinized to see if they would derail or have any negative effects on any other planning areas. It is very difficult to optimize your financial plan if you are planning in silos. For example, a client of mine contacted me to let me know his corporate attorney had recommended he form a new business entity to channel a portion of his income. This attorney was not aware of nor did he consider other critical information that needed to be taken into account.

I informed my client that the attorney's recommendation was likely a bad idea since he had other business entities set up with employees and a retirement plan. I believed what the attorney was proposing to my client would cause a big problem for the existing retirement plan to the point where he would be out of compliance. I suggested we confer with a few of the other professionals he works with to get their opinions. I organized a conference call with my client, his attorney, his CPA and the actuary for his retirement plan.

In less than 15 minutes of discussion, everyone agreed the new entity should not be formed. By using an integrated approach rather than planning in a silo, we averted a potential financial disaster. The collaborative, integrated planning approach ensured my client made the best overall decisions for his family and his business.

## Behavior matters

Financial modeling with the robust professional financial planning software financial advisors have access to should definitely be part of the planning process. Simple financial calculators found on the internet are not sufficient for financial planning. They do not have the ability to perform complex calculations that take into account the multiple sources of data that are needed for more sophisticated modeling.

The best financial planning software enables an advisor to model dozens of scenarios by taking into account information from almost all areas of their clients' finances. However, it is important to understand modeling various scenarios requires more than just number crunching. The numbers are only half the story.

The other half of a real financial plan includes the behavioral finance side of planning. Advisors should be utilizing their experience along with the best interactive software tools available to collaboratively explore with their clients the "what ifs" of planning. These are modeling exercises that attempt to predict ahead of time how the client will react to various scenarios, including negative results. For example, what would be the largest investment loss the client could tolerate at any given time (the client's risk tolerance)? Or how would the client be willing to adjust his or her financial plan if investment returns are lower than anticipated? Or if inflation is higher than expected? Would the client retire later? Reduce the annual amount withdrawn from the portfolio? Work longer? Move to a lower-cost area? How does the client want the estate handled when it is passed down to beneficiaries? Do they receive funds in a lump sum or only as periodic income? What happens to a plan and what should the client do if Social Security benefits are decreased in the future?

Behavioral discussions such as these are critical to have with your advisor so your money personality can be taken into account, so you can address the things that may cause you to get off track, you can fully discuss how you want your money to positively affect your children, your charitable endeavors, your lifestyle, your sense of security and, most importantly, ensure your plan is in alignment with your goals, values and passions. These types of decisions go well beyond crunching the numbers.

## A financial plan evolves

A real financial plan becomes your masterpiece, artfully co-created with your advisor. It becomes your ongoing guide to fulfill your goals and dreams. However, unlike a piece of art crafted by a master artist, your financial plan is not created just once. Financial planning is a living, fluid process that should evolve over time. Your initial plan should be created and then re-created at least once a year to keep it current as the economy changes and as you navigate through the ebb and flow of your life as your goals, priorities and perspectives change. You will want to work with an advisor who truly gets to know and understand you and who will continue to be by your side throughout the years to assist you with monitoring and updating your plan.

A financial plan should not simply be a computer-generated report created in a vacuum, of which the sole purpose is to position an advisor to sell you a product or to use as a loss leader for the opportunity to manage your investment accounts. This is a pseudo plan, not a real financial plan. Unfortunately there is still a lot of pseudo-planning going on.

A real financial plan should be the continuing documentation of a personalized planning process that not only includes relevant financial calculations, but also documents the results of significant conversations between a qualified advisor and you about your life, where you are now and where you want to be. It should also identify and take into account your beliefs and behaviors that may assist you in reaching your goals or cause you to fall short of them. Finding the right advisor with the right planning process, someone who will put your interests first, can be a powerful catalyst to help you succeed financially and get the most out of your life. The right financial advisor will likely become one of the most trusted professionals you rely on for guidance for many years to come.

**Mary Beth Franklin, CFP®**
Contributing Editor

**InvestmentNews**

Twenty-One

# The Broken Three-Legged Stool

## About the Author

As a contributing editor, Mary Beth specializes in retirement income, Social Security issues and Medicare as well as writing a regular column covering a variety of retirement-related issues. Starting out as a Congressional reporter over 30 years ago, she has written a weekly personal finance column for retirees as a syndicated columnist and has been a senior editor for Kiplinger's Personal Finance. Mary Beth is the author of *Maximizing Your Clients' Social Security Retirement Benefits*.

## About the Company

Since 1998, InvestmentNews has focused on providing news and analysis for financial advisors. From market insights and webcasts to conferences, InvestmentNews brings industry expertise to financial advisors to help them grow their businesses.

—∿—

## A holistic approach

The challenge for many financial advisors will be to expand their services beyond investment management and to take a more holistic view of financial planning that includes guidance on health care costs, housing decisions, eldercare issues and legacy planning.

At a minimum, an advisor must at least include expected expenses such as health care in a retirement plan. Otherwise, what is the value of a comprehensive plan that ignores one of the biggest expenses in a retiree's budget?

A comprehensive financial plan must also take Social Security benefits into account. Financial advisors should be familiar with appropriate claiming strategies to help their clients maximize their lifetime benefits.

While a financial advisor does not need to be an expert in every field, he or she can serve as the financial quarterback for a team of experts, helping clients to prepare for various aspects of retirement living. For advisors, linking with other professionals can create an ongoing source of referrals among their peers.

## The three-legged stool

The traditional three-legged stool of retirement income — pensions, personal savings and Social Security — is broken. Pensions are history for many Americans and personal savings are often inadequate to finance a retirement that could last 20 years or more. Social Security is a crucial piece of the retirement income puzzle as it is one of the few sources of guaranteed, cost-of-living adjusted income that lasts a lifetime, no matter how long you live.

We need a new analogy for today's retirement income plan. Rather than the old three-legged stool, a multi-layered pyramid may be a more accurate image.

At the base of that pyramid, Social Security will provide secure, dependable monthly income for most Americans, topped off by a layer of retirement savings in designated accounts such as 401(k) plans and IRAs. In addition, future retirees may find different ways to unlock the equity they have built up in their homes, whether by downsizing to a smaller house and banking some of the profits or using the proceeds from a reverse mortgage as a source of tax-free income.

Depending on their personal situations, some retirees may have access to additional layers of the retirement income pyramid such as continued employment, investments outside their retirement accounts, cash flow from rental property, an inheritance or assets from the sale of a business.

Clearly, tomorrow's retirees will face more complicated decisions about how to stitch together a retirement income plan than simply collecting a monthly pension check and Social Security benefits as previous generations did. Many of them will need the help of a professional financial advisor who can match their various sources of income with their expected costs in retirement.

# Tax diversification

Advisors are limited by the resources that their clients bring to the table. Many of those clients who have stashed the bulk of their savings in traditional retirement accounts may be in for a rude awakening. Withdrawals from traditional IRAs, 401(k)s and similar tax-deferred retirement accounts are fully taxable at ordinary income tax rates. The challenge for advisors is how to help their clients diversify the taxability of their retirement income sources to create more spendable income in retirement.

Depending on total income levels, up to 85 percent of a retiree's Social Security benefit may be taxed at ordinary income rates. At the other extreme, distributions from Roth IRAs and Roth 401(k) plans are tax-free. Distributions from health savings accounts are also tax-free if used to pay for medical expenses, which can represent a large portion of a typical retiree's budget.

Long-term capital gains are usually taxed at 15 percent or 20 percent, but clients who fall into the 10 percent or 15 percent income tax brackets — which is not unusual for some retirees — will pay nothing on their long-term gains. In 2016, a 65-year-old couple who claims a standard deduction and two personal exemptions could have up to $96,700 of income and still be in the 15 percent income tax bracket.

By having access to assets in a variety of accounts that are taxed in different ways, retirees can draw some money from each pot each year to minimize their income taxes and increase their after-tax spendable income.

# Medicare is means-tested

Income taxes are not the only concern. One of the biggest shocks to new retirees is the fact that their income level determines how much they pay for Medicare.

In 2016, most new enrollees in Medicare pay $121.80 per month for Medicare Part B premiums, which cover outpatient services and doctor visits. But if modified adjusted gross income, which includes total income reported on your federal tax return plus any tax-exempt interest, exceeds $85,000 if you are single or $170,000 if you are married, you will pay a monthly Medicare premium surcharge.

There are four premium tiers above the Medicare base amount, ranging from an additional $48.70 per month to an additional $268 per month per person. Plus, Medicare Part D, which covers prescription drug costs, is also subject to monthly surcharges known as income-related monthly adjustment amount (IRMAA).

But there are several sources of tax-free income that are not included in the Medicare IRMAA calculation: distributions from Roth IRAs or Roth 401(k) plans; distributions from health savings accounts when used to pay medical expenses; distributions or loans from cash-value life insurance; a portion of distributions of immediate annuities held in non-retirement accounts and proceeds from a reverse mortgage.

## Tax-free income

Convincing clients to convert some of their tax-deferred retirement assets to Roth IRAs could help them reduce both income taxes and Medicare premiums in the future. Roth conversions are fully taxable in the year of the conversion. One way to ease the tax burden is to convert a portion of traditional IRAs to a Roth IRA each year to take full advantage of the client's existing tax bracket without boosting income into a higher bracket.

For younger clients, urging those who have access to health savings accounts during their working years to stash money in these tax-deductible accounts will go a long way to creating an additional source of tax-free income in retirement. HSAs offer a triple tax advantage: contributions are tax deductible (except in a handful of states), assets grow tax-free and distributions are tax-free if used to pay for medical expenses. Unlike flexible spending accounts, HSAs do not have a use-it-or-lose-it feature and funds can be rolled over from year to year.

## Withdrawal order

Another challenge for financial advisors is to rethink their traditional recommendations of how clients tap their assets in retirement. Conventional wisdom dictates that retirees withdraw funds from their taxable brokerage accounts first, followed by tax-deferred retirement accounts and finally tax-exempt Roth IRAs. In the past, many advisors typically suggested that clients claim Social Security benefits as soon as possible and delay tapping their tax-deferred retirement accounts until they are required to start taking mandatory annual distributions starting at age 70½.

But this withdrawal hierarchy could unintentionally increase a client's overall tax burden.

Delaying IRA distributions until 70½ can result in large mandatory distributions, often increasing income taxes and monthly Medicare premiums. And when one spouse dies, the surviving spouse often inherits the IRA and annual distributions, significantly increasing the surviving spouse's Medicare premiums because he or she would receive the same level of annual income but be subject to a higher monthly surcharge as a single person than they were when the surviving spouse was married.

Instead, advisors may want to suggest clients begin tapping their retirement accounts before required, helping them to satisfy their income needs during the early years of retirement and enabling them to delay collecting Social Security benefits until they are worth more later. As one of the only sources of guaranteed income in retirement, holding out for a larger Social Security benefit means annual cost of living adjustments will be applied to a bigger base amount. And by having at least one spouse wait until age 70 to collect the maximum Social Security benefit, it also guarantees the largest possible survivor benefit for the remaining spouse.

## Social Security basics

Social Security benefits represent the largest single source of retirement income for most Americans. Deciding when and how to claim Social Security benefits is one of the most important financial decisions an individual or married couple will ever make. Even for the typically more affluent clients of financial advisors, an informed decision about how and when to claim Social Security benefits can mean thousands of dollars of extra income per year. For married couples, a coordinated claiming decision can boost combined lifetime Social Security benefits by $100,000 or more.

But the Social Security claiming rules are changing. In late 2015, Congress voted to eliminate two key Social Security claiming strategies for future retirees.

First, let me review some basic rules about claiming Social Security benefits. The amount of monthly benefits you receive is based on your — or your spouse's — average lifetime earnings and the age when you claim benefits. You can claim retirement or spousal benefits as early as age 62 but they will be permanently reduced compared to waiting until your full retirement age, currently 66 for anyone born from 1943 through 1954.

But if you are willing to wait longer to collect benefits, your patience will be rewarded. For every year you postpone collecting retirement benefits beyond full retirement age, you earn an extra 8 percent per year in delayed retirement credits up to age 70. That can boost your monthly payments by 32 percent more than your full retirement age amount.

Timing when and how to claim Social Security is the key to maximizing lifetime benefits. Anyone who is 66 or older by the end of April 2016 could "file and suspend" his or her benefits as a way to trigger benefits for a spouse or minor dependent child under age 18 while the benefit for the person who files and suspends continues to grow by 8 percent per year. The worker would receive nothing during the suspension but a spouse and or child can collect up to 50 percent of the worker's full retirement age amount in the interim.

This valuable file and suspend claiming strategy disappeared after April 29, 2016, as a result of the Bipartisan Budget Act of 2015. After that, a worker will still be able to suspend benefits at full retirement age, but no one will be able to collect benefits on that worker's record during the suspension.

Although the file and suspend strategy disappeared after April 29, 2016, there is another claiming strategy available to married couples and some divorced spouses for the next few years.

Under current law, anyone who is married or who is divorced after at least 10 years of marriage can file a "restricted claim for spousal benefits" when he or she turns 66. That allows a person to collect only your spousal benefits — worth half of the spouse's or ex-spouse's full retirement age benefit amount — for up to four years while one's own retirement benefit continues to grow by 8 percent per year up to age 70. At 70, you would switch to your own benefit worth 132 percent of your full retirement age amount.

But this rule, too, is changing. Anyone who was 62 or older by January 1, 2016, retains the right to claim only spousal benefits when they turn 66. They do not need to do anything before then to preserve this claiming strategy. Younger workers will never be able to choose which benefit to claim. Whenever he or she files for Social Security, the person will be paid the highest benefit to which he or she is entitled to at that age, whether based on the person's own work record or as a spouse.

Despite the recent law changes, Social Security will continue to be a keystone of retirement security. It is more important than ever for financial advisors and consumers to become knowledgeable about claiming options so they can create the best retirement income plan for their needs.

**Mark Glover**
Head of Financial Planning

HSBC Wealth Management, HSBC Holdings Plc

Twenty-Two

# Financial Planning for Universal Needs

### About the Author

Mark Glover is responsible for Financial Planning within the HSBC Wealth Management business. His 15 years of wealth management experience includes developing Barclays Wealth's international insurance activity, creating and executing international commercial strategy for UBS in London and providing planning solutions to private clients internationally with Skandia.

### About the Company

HSBC Holdings Plc, the parent company of the HSBC Group, is headquartered in London. The Group serves customers worldwide from around 6,000 offices in 71 countries and territories in Europe, Asia, North and Latin America, the Middle East and North Africa. With assets of US$2,410bn at 31 December 2015, HSBC is one of the world's largest banking and financial services organizations.

—❦—

## The uncommon common denominator

Financial advice and planning are not universally well understood. The two concepts are interpreted in many different ways in many different countries.

# Financial advice versus financial planning

Financial advice focuses on a particular investment a client might want to make to meet a particular need.

I can't offer good financial advice until I have a solid understanding of key facts about a client.

I ask my clients:

- Their age
- Relationship status
- Do they have children?

I want to understand what *they* want to get from their investments. I also establish the clients' appetite for risk. I want to know if they can bear any investment risk in return for the expected uplift from investing. This enables me to draw the clients' financial profile.

Another important part of building my foundation of knowledge is understanding the clients' level of knowledge and market experience. This varies tremendously among people and in different parts of the world. Some clients are investment savvy while others have little understanding. The advice needs to be tailored to the client.

Finally, to give good advice, I need to listen to the client to understand their investment preferences and where this particular investment fits into their overall portfolio.

There are very good instances when this narrow focus is the right thing, but I prefer a fully-rounded conversation, to understand all of the client's finance issues and their ambitions, hopes and dreams. This enables a well thought through, considered and total long-term solution to be provided to clients.

# Financial planning — thinking about universal needs

We think about how we can meet and fulfill clients' needs in a number of key areas:

**Protection:** There's always a need to protect the client and their family. How that is defined and to what extent varies. That conversation is very important. There is a lot of cultural interpretation, for example about life insurance, in different parts of the world, so you have to be careful with terminology and how you approach the subject. It's mostly inconceivable that you may have a conversation with someone who doesn't care about protecting their family.

**Education:** Planning for children's education is incredibly important. HSBC produces a report *The Value of Education* which shows that, in many countries, thinking about how children will develop and how much this will cost is incredibly high on people's list of priorities when it comes to their financial affairs.

**Retirement:** In Western countries and, increasingly, in Asian markets, we are seeing a need for retirement planning. This is growing in importance because governments can't afford to support populations that are living longer and in tough economic environments. The 2015 study by HSBC, *The Future of Retirement: a balancing act,* highlights recognizable themes: plan well and start early, think about physical health and the potential cost implications of poor health. To keep on track you may need to make necessary changes. Delivering this message as an industry is key.

**Legacy planning:** At some point, the inevitable happens to us all. Discussing what a client is able to pass on as an estate to his or her family is a challenging conversation. But it is one that has to be had — with the whole family.

Even with a deep, honest conversation of these areas we won't ever capture all our clients' hopes and dreams. Clients will always want a property or a boat or a second home to buy. It's not enough to help clients manage; we need to also help grow their wealth. For me, good financial planning is an understanding of and prioritizing those needs with our clients; learning their wants and hopes and then helping to align a client's human ambitions with the practical reality of scarce resources.

## Privileged position

I think we are in a privileged position as a trusted advisor, which HSBC is. We connect with our clients emotionally, to help them think about what's important for them and their family. There are a number of different methods to employ, but mostly they start with listening and asking thoughtful questions, then focusing on what's important for them.

I think the financial planning industry has paved the way to focusing on understanding a client's needs and then delivering them. In the past, a product would be developed, then a target market found. Today, we try to really understand what a good client outcome is.

That isn't necessarily easy. I often think about my own children. It's very easy for me to want the best for my children as it is for most parents, but how do we actually take these emotions and break them down into the hard core facts that financial people like (and need) to work with?

## The right outcome

Unless you know the destination, you'll never know where or when the journey ends. I very much see that financial planning is about clients understanding what good outcomes look like for them and then making sure we both stay on that road. Sometimes we go off the road. We hate when that happens even if we all expect it will occur. Sometimes you might need to stop. That's why it is necessary to be very clear and help clients understand what constitutes a good outcome.

## The value of going back

You need to build into the planning process the capability to keep going back, reliving the plan, keep checking that it's up to date, ensuring that the investments are on track and that you're rebalancing the portfolio to meet your client's needs. It's about making sure we can continually fine tune the plan, like you would a car, with regular service checks to maximize its performance. This approach ensures the client understands where he or she will be for the long term and not just a given point in time.

## The fiduciary obligation

The fiduciary relationship isn't something that should be entered into lightly by the advisor or the client. We need to be completely clear about what we are taking on as a business, and always be clear with clients about the terms of engagement. Taking on a fiduciary responsibility for me means having a truly long-term relationship in which I am obliged to keep effective watch over the client and their assets. That means not only monitoring the client's investment portfolio to ensure it remains on track, but understanding economic and tax changes that may impact the client's financial affairs. For example, ensuring any unused tax allowances are used in a way that's most efficient for the client.

It's not enough just to understand a change in taxation that may affect a client's affairs. We must have ongoing communication with them to explain the changes and react in an appropriate way. The client could have a new child, for example, and the plan may need updating.

In many of the markets in which we operate, the obligation is on us to ensure that our advice and plans are appropriate and feasible for our clients. If we enter lightly into an ongoing advisory relationship without proper thought, it could raise expectations on both sides, particularly the client's. Advisors must think about how they're going to deliver this service. Anything less and there is a risk that both parties will be disappointed.

In the world of more digital technology this is becoming easier, but then that pre-supposes that interacting digitally with clients includes all the necessary information, including where assets are held and how, what those assets are being used for and the client's expectations around investment growth, among other things. Even though there are some good digital solutions available, making the most appropriate use of data can be complex.

## A new remuneration model

Clients need to understand when they enter a fiduciary relationship they should expect to pay a reasonable amount for the work the advisor will be undertaking.

In some jurisdictions I am seeing a move away from advisors earning commission on selling products to charging for the services they provide. I see this in various European markets and some areas of the Americas markets. The trend in Asia is a little slower. If this model gains ground, it will require a change in advisor pricing and mindset. I believe there will be an initial fee and then an ongoing fee to ensure businesses are sustainable.

## Changes ahead

I think financial planning will change dramatically over the next five to 10 years, driven by the regulatory landscape. The pace of change will vary in different countries.

The role of the financial planner won't be to sell but to help understand the client's ambitions, hopes and dreams for his or her financial affairs.

Changing to an environment that focuses on understanding what the client wants and needs makes it incumbent on our industry to demonstrate the benefits.

While most financial planning will be online, I think there's always going to be a need for face-to-face interaction to ensure there is an emotional connection.

I like the idea of co-advising. There are a growing number of situations in which the client completes factual information online, followed by meeting with an advisor to talk through their responses. It enables the client to think a little bit more about what they've been able to do online. This is an incredibly important industry trend, but I think the real value is having a professional sit next to a client, helping them understand their results, and importantly, helping to prioritize.

No matter how automated planning may become or how broadly available advice may be online, the human element will never disappear from the advisor-client relationship.

## Scott Hanson, CFP®, CFS®, ChFC®
**Founder and Chief Executive Officer**

## Hanson McClain

Twenty-Three

# Looking at Retirement Differently

## About the Author

Scott Hanson, senior partner and founding principal of Hanson McClain Advisors and the Hanson McClain Retirement Network, is a nationally-recognized financial expert focused on providing education and independent investment advice. He is the author of *Money Matters: Essential Tips & Tools for Building Financial Peace of Mind* and the co-author of *Investment Advisor Marketing: A Pathway to Growing Your Firm and Building Your Brand.* For over 20 years, Scott has co-hosted Money Matters, a weekly radio program also available via podcast.

## About the Company

With its founding over 20 years ago, Hanson McClain committed to their mission of being a fiduciary investment advisory firm focused on the best interests of their clients and to providing education. Headquartered in California, with additional offices in Chicago, Texas and Michigan, the company also services the Hanson McClain Retirement Network made up of independent advisors focused on the telecommunications industry.

—∿∿∿—

## No time for mistakes

The other day I came across a cartoon while thumbing through a magazine. It showed an individual holding a little sign that read "A Huge Mistake" on one side and "Financial Advisor" on the other. It made me chuckle, because in my view, one of the biggest things a financial advisor can do is help people from making catastrophic mistakes with their finances.

With that in mind, getting good quality financial advice as people get older is especially important because at that stage in the client's life there's little time to make up for mistakes of just about any kind.

Good quality financial planning is not about trying to outsmart the markets or get better returns on 401(k)s. Instead, a good financial advisor should help prevent a client from making mistakes, regardless of the client's age.

Good financial advice translates into helping people make wise choices with their money and helping them to avoid mistakes — particularly costly mistakes from which they can't recover.

## There are no silly questions

There are plenty of people who call themselves financial planners and sell products and services even though they've been banned from the industry, are facing regulatory issues or are involved in lawsuits or bankruptcy.

That tells me potential clients aren't doing adequate background checks on the financial advisor before they speak with him or her. And, then when the consumer does have a meeting or phone conversation, he or she doesn't ask enough questions.

There's a financial advisor in Northern California who ran radio ads for his investment advisory services. He spoke of his uncommon approach in which an investor would be diversified in areas not tied to the financial markets, implying that this would have avoided losses during the financial crisis. Sounds great, right? Except the advisor failed to mention that he filed for personal bankruptcy in 2009 and owed the IRS more than $400,000 in back taxes.

When it comes to choosing a financial planner, there is no such thing as a silly question. Potential clients should ask questions until they are fully confident in the person and certain that their interests will be put first.

Potential clients should first determine how the advisor will be compensated. Commission? Fees? They need to figure it out.

If compensation is item #1, then item #1A is to figure out if the advisor is acting as a fiduciary. Does the advisor have a legal obligation to put the client's interests ahead of his or her own?

Next clients should determine the financial advisor's education and training. Is he or she a Certified Financial Planner (CFP®)? Does the advisor have a business degree? Is the planner truly qualified to be providing advice?

## Caveat emptor

In the financial services industry, standardized credentialing doesn't exist. There are a number of regulatory bodies. Each looks at one area, but regulators let anyone call himself or herself a financial advisor. And today, the advisor doesn't need any sort of "official approval" to be able to sell all kinds of stuff.

The consumer has an obligation to know that the financial advisor is who he or she says and is actually competent.

Working with someone who is certified as a financial planner by the Certified Financial Planner Board of Standards (CFP Board) is helpful, but often that's not enough. It's not like the Certified Public Accountant (CPA) designation, which is a true license. If someone gets a CFP® designation that means he or she is a practitioner. Stated simply, the designation means the person is supposed to abide by the CFP Board's rules, but enforcement by the Board is nothing like the enforcement of the CPA Board.

Consumers need to make sure that they conduct their own due diligence before doing business with any financial advisor.

## Designing a quality financial plan

A quality financial plan occurs when an advisor can help a client determine what he or she wants to accomplish during life, identify the resources available and then figure out how to maximize those resources.

A good financial planner looks at all those things and then says: "All right, here's what's realistic. Let's focus on accomplishing these things." If those things aren't realistic, what adjustments can the financial planner make to help the client accomplish some, if not all, of what he or she wants?

I'm not the first to make this observation: A good financial advisor is part finance and part therapist because emotions drive a lot of our financial decisions. So a good financial advisor does not just put a bunch of numbers through a program and spit out an answer to tell the client what to do. He or she creates an ongoing process that takes into account some of the emotional considerations and then helps a client make wise choices.

Financial planning comes down to dealing with individuals and making sure that they have plans they will act on. As an advisor, you need to understand their aims and abilities to execute on the plan. Remember, you are an advisor. Your clients must act, especially on the things that matter to them.

I've learned that people have certain patterns when it comes to their finances. They don't necessarily change that much. They might want to change, but they don't always do so. Sometimes, it's best to have things set up so the financial plan will work in their lives, regardless of whether they change or don't.

Do we help clients save money for the 401(k) or do we help them take the kids to Disneyland because they've been begging for two years? Those competing needs occur all of the time. Establishing a plan that balances those demands in a way that doesn't hurt a client's finances or, in this example, the family, is key for most of us.

## Planning not product

Quality, in the context of financial planning, can be defined many different ways. For a client, quality means the advisor actually puts your best interest at heart and is providing financial planning based on your needs and objectives rather than on a product the advisor wants to sell.

I started in this industry working for a life insurance company in 1990. It had a big financial planning focus but it was a life insurance company. Almost every problem was solved with life insurance. All financial planning was focused on making a life insurance sale. Whether it was for a client's retirement or the kids' education, life insurance was the answer. It really wasn't true financial planning in my mind. It was product sales.

Not everyone who worked for the insurance company was a bad financial advisor. The problem was the business structure. The main objective was to find a way to sell life insurance and financial planning was used as a tool in an attempt to illustrate the benefits.

We need to recognize that money is also a tool. Most people don't want to accumulate a chunk of money just for the sake of accumulating it. Most people accumulate money to do something with it, to achieve specific goals. They seek to use money to accomplish their goals, which could include financial independence, retirement or saving for their children's college education.

Overall, quality financial planning is helping an individual or a couple figure out what goals they want to accomplish in life and then developing strategies and tools to help them achieve those goals.

## The absence of a true standard

There are great financial advisors at some of the big brokerage firms and there are great professionals who are independent Registered Investment Advisors (RIAs). But there are also some lousy advisors at the big brokerage firms, and some lousy independents as well who act as fiduciaries, but they aren't very competent.

Further, one can come across some lousy advisors who use a fee-based compensation structure. In turn, there are some great advisors who still work for commissions at traditional brokerage firms.

One of the challenges in this industry is the absence of a true standard. If I go to a medical doctor, I can learn if the physician is board certified and I can quickly tell what his or her qualifications are. I can check with people who used the doctor before and I know that he or she is licensed to practice medicine. In very little time I can get assurance that the doctor knows what he or she is doing.

It's not so simple or clear cut with financial advisors.

## Alignment is crucial

The notion of fiduciary responsibility starts with the financial advisor being part of an organization that has its finances aligned with its core values.

If a financial advisor is in a situation that is or could be at odds with his or her core values, the finances will win. Recent business history is littered with companies that tossed out their values for pure financial gain. Remember Enron? It waived its code of ethics and succumbed to greed.

By aligning finances with values — which should include putting clients' needs first — conflicts of interest are eliminated. The individual who is a fiduciary has a legal obligation to put the clients' interest ahead of his or her own.

Most advisors who act as true fiduciaries eliminate those conflicts by recommending one financial product over another without regard to their own compensation.

For example, if a financial advisor provides fee-based asset management, he or she will get the same compensation whether the advisor is recommending a real estate investment trust, a stock, a bond or another financial instrument. The advisor won't push one thing over another because there is no incentive to do so.

This structure will help put clients' interests first. It will also help to avoid situations in which there are arrangements like soft dollars and preferential treatment that may prompt the recommendation of one product over another. Such "backroom deals" have become too commonplace in the financial services industry.

Fiduciaries do everything in their power to eliminate any of those conflicts and to make sure the finances are aligned with the values, thereby putting clients' needs and objectives ahead of their own. Then they continue to ensure that as they move forward they are doing everything in their power to make certain that finances and values are aligned.

## Changes in the air

There are a lot more financial advisors becoming pure fiduciaries. We're seeing a growth of RIAs and advisors who say they're going to act on a fee basis and not push any particular financial product. But we're also seeing some financial advisors selling a lot of non-traded real estate investment trusts (REITs). Oftentimes they do that because there's a big commission up front. We also see them selling equity-indexed annuities, another big commission product.

On one hand, there's a movement toward a fee-based fiduciary approach while on the other, people are selling products that generate large commissions that may or may not be in a client's best interest.

In light of this, the U.S. Department of Labor's (DOL) rules have expanded a fiduciary standard for all retirement plans — not just 401(k)s, but all IRAs and anything in a retirement plan. The DOL now has oversight of retirement savings after a person has left the workplace, which I find a bit ironic for a regulatory body that oversees labor.

I would love to see Congress spend some time trying to figure out how to create a system that can level the playing field and provide the same access to retirement savings, one in which we can all contribute the same amount, whether we work for a big company or a small employer.

If Congress can spend some time doing this, I think it can certainly make a step in the right direction to get people focused on retirement savings for a better future.

# Retirement is different today

I recently wrote an article about how our whole retirement savings structure is a mess. More than 55 million Americans do not have access to a company savings plan through their employers. But those who do are contributing plenty of money to a 401(k) and getting nice tax deductions. But if one doesn't have that availability, he or she is limited to things like an IRA, which is not as good as a 401(k), putting the individual at a major disadvantage.

When Social Security was put into place in the 1930s, there was much debate in Congress, but the idea gained bipartisan support. Social Security has its challenges, but it was a well thought out system. Whether you like it or not is beside the point. The fact is a lot of thought and planning went into it.

On the other hand, our 401(k) system kind of happened by accident. There wasn't any real planning. It was a bill that went through Congress, became a law and someone saw a loophole allowing for the creation of a tax-sheltered retirement plan. That's essentially how the 401(k) was created, rather than with a lot of planning and process. It just kind of happened.

I think we are in an interesting stage right now. In my opinion, retirement has been one big experiment the last 50 years. Going forward, retirement will be very different. We're living longer, healthier lives, especially during retirement. The average 65 year old today has the same health and energy as someone who was 58 four decades ago. Granted, there are things that can derail the very best of plans, but I think most people need to look at retirement differently.

The old mindset of "how can I accumulate as much money as possible so I can quit working as early as possible" doesn't apply anymore. For example: I had lunch with a friend recently. He's 63 years old. He told me about a new business he's starting. He views his retirement fund not as a stack of cash to fund his retirement, but as a disability fund to provide income in the event he becomes ill or injured. He said, "This will give me financial support should something happen and I can no longer work." But he added that he has no intention of getting to the point where he is not working at all.

I don't think many people are going to have the money to stop working at age 60 or 65, so they will just keep going without giving it a thought. The financial markets probably aren't going to produce the kind of returns in the next decade that we saw in the past few. So, people are going to have to look at retirement differently.

Retirement won't be about quitting work and never doing anything again. It will be more about getting to the point where someone is not forced to go to work every day. Once you reach that point, the idea of retirement will center on how to design a life in which a person can use his or her skills and the things he or she is passionate about and still have time to enjoy some of the things that the individual didn't have time for previously.

When someone at a later stage in life is doing things they enjoy, work can add value and meaning and then it is no longer a "four-letter word."

**Patricia Houlihan, CFP®**
President and Chief Executive Officer

Houlihan Financial Resource Group, Ltd.

Twenty-Four

# Be an Advisor, Not a Judge

## About the Author

Patricia Houlihan brings over 30 years of corporate and personal financial planning experience to her role as president and CEO of Houlihan Financial Group. For over 15 years, Patti taught investment and financial planning and co-authored the Dalton CFP® Examination Review Case Exam Book. She was the presenter of the weekly television series The Washington Forum on Financial Planning and the host of the PBS series The Financial Advisors. She has also been featured on national TV and in national and industry publications.

## About the Company

The Houlihan Financial Resource Group works with clients and their professional teams on risk and investment management, retirement, and tax and estate planning to help them meet their objectives. Based in northern Virginia, the firm was founded over 16 years ago and services clients nationwide.

—ᘓᘓ—

## See it from the client's perspective

When looking at good financial advice, I do so from the client's perspective because advice given, but not fully understood by the client, is often not enacted. An example of this is when a client goes through an elaborate estate planning process and creates a living trust but never re-titles assets in the name of the trust because he or she did not know what the requirements were to accomplish the transfer.

There is no doubt that the process proffered all sorts of good advice, but from the client's perspective, it was overwhelming. So much so that the good financial advice was never implemented. There is no question that the estate planning attorney did a great job, but the reason the advice was never taken beyond that session was because the client froze. The client did not understand the next steps and thus was unable to act.

So, for me, any related aspect of good financial advice must always be explained in a way that the client can absorb and understand from his or her point of view. If a person really understands a financial professional's advice, the client can take it and run with it. Advice that is not clear and does not result in action is not what is best for the client.

## No more thick books

Thirty years ago, creating a financial plan meant presenting a client with a heavy, thick binder that contained "The Plan." Advisors would labor to assemble these tomes and present them to clients, only to see them placed on a shelf to gather dust.

Thankfully, those days are gone, long gone. Today, advisors have a much more interactive relationship with clients. Today, clients get together with their advisors and go through all of the financial components of their life.

A quality financial plan has to begin with establishing the goals of the client and what he or she is trying to achieve. It is a plan for the client's future and it's the client's hard-earned money that is going to be invested to help provide for that future. So an advisor has to look at all the aspects of a client's life.

Everything is reviewed including investments, insurance, retirement plans, employee benefits, tax returns and estate planning documents. By reviewing all of this data, an advisor can find information the client forgot to mention. For example, many times a client will forget to mention something that the advisor can see on the client's tax return. An advisor cannot invest assets without looking at all possible elements and issues. Before a dime is assigned, an advisor must know if the client has life insurance, disability insurance, whether long term care insurance is needed or necessary and what risk the client can tolerate. I won't have a client take on more risk than he or she needs to achieve lifetime goals. For me, that's what good advice and a good plan does — helps the client work toward meeting his or her goals.

Most clients do not come in for a meeting with an advisor knowing exactly what they need or understanding what the planning process is all about. The reason is quite simple. Usually, they don't know what they need to tell the advisor. Not only do I want to know about them, but I also ask about their parents, their children and much more. Through a dialogue with the client, the advisor can bring up questions that help clients tell the advisor what he or she needs to know. Clients need to have the sense that the worst case scenario has been looked at and has been prepared for as best as it can be. I call this "looking at the parade of horribles." This awareness can be uncomfortable, but unfortunate, unexpected things can and do happen. That is why planning is so critical.

Just think about your own life and all the moving parts it has. When an advisor brings that orientation into a meeting with a client and allows him or her to share, it opens doors, sheds light and gives a broad, deep view of everything that should be taken into account.

Sometime ago I had two clients sit in my conference room; one was 88, the other was 87 years old. Both asserted they were running out of money. They were a special couple. One had had two bouts of cancer and the other had a pacemaker. I listened to the two go back and forth about who was going to die first. This couple was involved in a line of reasoning that I could not impact. They had an elder-care therapist who worked with me and our common client from our respective standpoints. Together, we helped the couple. To me that's a very special form of quality financial advice. It had little to do with financial modeling and everything to do with care, understanding and empathy.

Never overlook the fact that clients look to advisors to provide good financial advice that takes a holistic view, and is offered in a way that instills trust and creates comfort.

## There are times a plan isn't needed

Good financial advice does not always convert to a good financial plan. There are times that a client may say, "I've got $10,000 and here's my insurance. I've got it all covered. Here is my tax return. I just want to know what to do with the $10,000. What do you suggest I do? Put it in a 529 plan? If so, which one?"

This isn't about millions of dollars that need rebalancing. It's a straight-forward question that asks for a straight-forward answer. And when advisors provide it, I don't have a problem with them receiving commissions. I often told students receiving a commission does not mean you can't be a fiduciary. I don't think that's the case at all. For me, the focus isn't about the commission. Simply give the best advice; look at what is best for the client.

Let's say someone comes to an advisor and says, "I really want to pay off my mortgage. I would sleep better at night." The money would come out of the portfolio the advisor is managing, meaning the advisor's income goes down. It's the advisor who acts in the best interest of the client who knows the client's quality of life can trump the arithmetic in that scenario.

## Trust matters

I've been an advisor for 34 years. I've lost clients to death. I have sat bedside holding a client's hand while he asks everybody to leave the room and then asks me to reassure him that I will take care of things for his survivors … "just as we had planned."

When you have those kinds of relationships, you make differences in people's lives. When people trust you to that extent, there's no way you can do anything that isn't best for them. That's a fiduciary relationship.

Financial planning has always been about giving clients good advice, and, during that process, developing relationships built on trust. That's what a good advisor does. It has never been about a recommendation for the portfolio, asset allocation, stock selection or portfolio rebalancing. Clients expect you to take care of managing their portfolio. They want you there to help with their lives — not simply the portfolio. They know they have been through all of the scenarios and they know that the advisor knows the technical parts of the recommendations. Clients don't expect that they need to go and research what an advisor tells them because they trust him or her.

## Don't shoot from the hip

Clients want their advisors to be there when the phone rings. I conducted a training program titled "When the Phone Rings." It sought to help future advisors prepare for those moments when the call comes from a client who has good news or sad news, "I've lost my job." "My husband passed away." "My daughter just got engaged." "I want to buy a second home." I told every student that took this training that if he or she begins the financial planning process on a foundation of trust — when the phone rings, the class participants would be able to handle the tough issues and be able to work through them with their clients. I also told them that they should **never** shoot from the hip when giving advice. If further analysis or review is required, an advisor should inform the client that he or she will be called back with possible options upon completion of the research. This is how an advisor maintains a client's trust.

## Be a good listener

If an advisor listens to the client and responds to his or her questions, the advisor will find out more than just the answers. When an advisor is not judgmental, clients will often say things in ways they've never thought, let alone articulated. Just the other day, in my conference room, a woman said to her husband, "You've never said it like that." The husband said, "Well, I thought I had." "No, you never said it that way," replied the wife. Not influencing the conversation lets an advisor draw out information that needs to be discussed.

Every advisor must always remember that it's the client's money. And it's the client's life. Listening to what a client is saying is how an advisor develops quality advice and a quality financial plan.

## Technology helps

Technology helps to make the process easier, faster and more thorough for the advisor and client alike, whether it's research or making sure an advisor has identified investments that have performed historically to reduce the risk, enhance the return, or whatever the objective might be.

When I began in the business, I'd have to wait for hard copies of Value Line to come in each month. Now I can instantly obtain more and better information.

The technology-based services advisors provide today yield better quality, because much of the information examined is offered in real time, making that advice truly current and relevant.

You can't discuss technology today without touching on robo-advisors. For the right set of investors, I think it's a good service. I see no point in fighting technology just to fight it. Why resist new initiatives without seeing what they can do? If it can help clients, and, in the process, helps the industry, what's wrong? I look at them and see how they can work for my clients. Rather than look to see what's not good, I believe it serves us all better to seek out the positives.

Frankly, the tools we have available now are amazing.

Before becoming a financial advisor, I was a math teacher. Getting the arithmetic right has never been a problem for me. In fact, with some early software, I could tell something was wrong because I knew the math.

Sometimes the problem would be the classic garbage in, garbage out (GIGO). If the data was entered incorrectly, the output would be incorrect. Today, there are tools that prevent entry errors. There is also plenty of integration with other software so more can be done with less chance for error.

The technology is wonderful. Advisors need to be able to look at what's available and select what they are most comfortable with, as well as what allows them to provide scenarios and outcomes to clients that are possible, though not guaranteed.

I am concerned when clients go online by themselves without the help of an advisor. They plug in numbers and make assumptions, which isn't good. It gives them false comfort that it's going to be OK. Back in the '90s, when the markets were up 20 percent, it looked like the trees were going to grow to the sky. Clients started using some of the "do-it-yourself" programs and saying to me, "I don't need to save for retirement. Heck, look at how much my portfolio grew last month." I would get them to turn off the computer and talk with me, eye to eye. Very quickly I could bring them back to reality. I drew timelines and used realistic assumptions to show them and they would say, "Oh, I see now." I would say, "Let's stay on course. This is what we've committed to."

I actually have a client who's worked with me for more than 30 years. He still has the very first cash flow projection I did. Each time we meet, he brings it in. This goes to good advice. It's how we worked it through together and stayed on target. Those numbers were very close; they worked for the plan and the client. He's done everything he set out to do.

More than crunching numbers, technology helps me educate. That's most important to me; technology that helps the client understand his or her path.

The tools an advisor selects and the technology that's available today can help clients stay calm and sleep at night. I'm grateful for the tools and the technology, and I've embraced them. Actually, I've been quicker to embrace technology because I understood how it works, how it runs in the background. Clients don't want to know about that. They want to see a picture on the screen that helps them understand what the advisor is saying. That's quality.

Since 1976, when financial planning was just being born, it's been in a state of change. It is an industry that will always be evolving, especially now with everything surrounding the new U.S. Department of Labor (DOL) rules.

Technology will change us and so too will regulation. Our industry will always go through changes, but as long as an advisor stays consistent and does the right thing, is true to him or herself and clients, it will be alright.

## At the end of the day

In my more than three decades in this business, there have been two things I've said to each one of my clients and most of my colleagues.

The first is, "If it doesn't feel right, don't do it."

The second is, "If you do the right thing, you're going to be successful."

An advisor can never compromise his or her integrity. Because at the end of the day, if you don't have that, you don't have the trust of the people who are paying you to help and, therefore, have nothing.

If I were in a business where I had to do things that I didn't believe in, make recommendations that didn't feel right to me ... I couldn't do it. I'm 68 years old and I work full-time in financial services because I love what I do and the team that I work with and the clients that we serve.

Michael E. Kitces, MSFS®, MTAX, CFP®, CLU®, ChFC®, RHU, REBC®, CASL®
Director of Wealth Management, Pinnacle Advisory Group

Publisher, Nerd's Eye View

Twenty-Five

# Lemons in Financial Advice

## About the Author

Michael E. Kitces is a partner and the Director of Wealth Management for Pinnacle Advisory Group. Michael is the co-founder of XY Planning Network, New Planner Recruiting and FA Bean Counters, the former Practitioner Editor of the *Journal of Financial Planning* and publisher of the financial planning industry blog "Nerd's Eye View" at Kitces.com, dedicated to advancing knowledge in financial planning. He is a national speaker and has co-authored several books.

## About the Company

Pinnacle Advisory Group is a private wealth management firm dedicated to comprehensive financial planning and active portfolio management to help clients meet their financial goals. Founded in 1993, the firm is headquartered in Columbia, Maryland with branch offices in Miami and Naples, Florida.

—————

## Choosing an advisor ... for the wrong reasons

Anybody who wants to find a financial advisor today inevitably goes online to search and do some due diligence. But the results that come up — advisor websites — all say the same thing: "We deliver individualized, customized, personal financial advice for our clients, and have advanced credentials and years of experience."

The problem is that no consumer really knows how to evaluate and vet that information. And, ironically, the regulators don't allow any kind of testimonials, which further limits consumer information, and has curtailed the growth of any kind of "advisor review sites" where consumers might go to see how advisors have performed for other clients.

It's a real challenge. Many consumers are interested in hiring a financial advisor, but have no idea how to pick one. At best, most end up picking someone based on factors that have nothing to do with the quality of the advisor. Instead, they use factors like "is he or she a nice person" or "do they seem friendly" and "does their company appear to be well put together?" We judge by superficial things because we have no way to actually determine if the prospective advisor is competent and capable of giving good advice.

That's the first challenge for consumers: finding a financial advisor. The second is determining what even constitutes "good financial advice" to begin with.

So what is good financial advice? It has two components. The first is whether the advice is competent and accurate. Is it technically correct? Was the advisor knowledge-able enough to give a technically correct answer to: "Hey, what should I do [with this financial problem] to improve my financial situation?" The second component is whether the advice will actually be implemented, and whether the advisor can help the consumer actually do it.

What this means is that good financial advice should be judged on the outcome of whether it was implemented, not just whether it was technically correct. A good financial advisor is someone who can deliver advice in a manner so that his clients can actually do something with it. This is important because it recognizes that the quality of an advisor is determined by how effectively the advisor can actually drive changes in someone else's behavior.

## Accurate, educational, engaging

A quality financial plan will have three key elements. To begin, it will be technically accurate; whatever factors need to be analyzed will be done so effectively. If it's an investment problem, it accounts for all the relevant information. If it's a retirement projection, it accounts for the appropriate risks and trade-offs. If it's a tax question, it accurately models the tax code and how it operates.

Next, a good plan has to be educational. Most consumers are not fully educated on the dynamics of everything they need to know and what they need to do. If they knew all of that, they probably wouldn't be engaging an advisor in the first place.

The third element of a good financial plan is that it actually helps to drive a change in behavior. That means the planning process needs to include a way to meaningfully engage the client because behavior change typically requires that someone be engaged in the process in order to become part of the solution.

A classic example involves teenagers. If you want teenagers to do something, it doesn't work very well when you tell them what to do. You have to help them believe they were a part of creating the idea, and only then do they want to move forward with it because they "own" a part of it.

## Start with competence

If a client is seeking good advice, they should look for someone who is competent. Look for bona fide credentials, like the Certified Financial Planner (CFP®) certification, to affirm that the person has actually been educated in financial advice and has the relevant knowledge. After all, if the "advisor" doesn't know anything, the odds are poor that any advice will be correct, even if the person is well-intentioned.

Along with seeking technical competency, you should ideally search for someone who specializes in the problems of people like you. So, if you're looking for retirement advice, find someone who actually specializes in retirement planning and knows all the issues of retirement planning, not just a generalist that does a little bit of retirement planning on top of everything else.

Unfortunately, though, most advisors define themselves as generalists who do everything for everyone. It's a big problem, because when you're everything for everyone, you don't have any specialization at all. The fact that my doctor went to medical school and is a general practitioner does not mean he should be doing neurosurgery. The skill set of a neurosurgeon is different than that of a general practitioner. Financial advising is still very much a world where most advisors are not specialists despite the fact that most people ultimately have very specialized problems.

## Advice-centric, not product-centric

Another way to evaluate good financial planning is whether it's focused on advice about the issues that are relevant to the consumer, and not just the products that are relevant to the advisor.

When I look at financial advice today, it sadly often revolves around the financial advisor selling products to get paid. Many advisors are very in-depth on retirement planning because they manage retirement rollovers, or are in-depth on insurance because they sell insurance. On the other hand, very few do anything involving household budgeting and cash flow, even though that's crucial for consumers. If one's spending exceeds income, there's going to be a problem.

Yet most advisors don't look at these issues, because there's no financial product to sell that solves a cash flow problem. This results in most advisors being weak when it comes to counseling people about debt, whether it's credit card, student loan or even mortgage debt. Advisors need to focus on spending time talking with clients about what's relevant to them.

## The fiduciary duties of loyalty and care

While the popular view of fiduciary is that it's simply about acting in your clients' best interest, when you go to the roots of fiduciary duty, there are actually two core duties. One is the duty of loyalty. That's the focal point of fiduciary today; it's about acting in the best interest of one's clients. However, there's actually a second duty that has been under-discussed, but will become a central issue in the next couple of years. It is called the duty of care.

The duty of care essentially says you should only give advice in areas in which you have competency to give advice. If you give advice on a topic about which you don't know anything, you are breaching your fiduciary duty.

For instance, let's say I hold myself out to the public as a fiduciary with a high school diploma and a three-hour regulatory exam, and that's it. I don't have an education in finance or economics, I don't need to know anything about money or financial advice, and I don't have any training as an advisor — but I present myself to the public as a comprehensive financial planner.

That lack of training and education is insufficient to meet the duty of care and represents a looming breach of fiduciary duties. Even if I wave a magic wand and say all those people will act in the best interest of their clients, there's no way for them to act in the best interest of their clients because they wouldn't even know what's in the best interest of their clients in the first place! They've had no meaningful education to know what the right advice is.

Simply put: How can anyone give advice in the best interests of their clients if they don't have the competency to give advice to begin with?

## The DOL and a dividing line

Given these fiduciary dynamics, the U.S. Department of Labor (DOL), as it regards its Best Interest Contract (BIC) exemption rule, is weak in several key areas.

First and foremost is the issue of competency. The DOL is advancing a standard that has a duty of loyalty to act in the best interests of the client, but there is nothing requiring the advisor to actually have the competency necessary to do that!

In other words, there's a risk that the DOL has now pronounced that "all advisors now have to act in their clients' best interest" (at least with respect to retirement accounts) even if those advisors have no training about how to actually act in their clients' best interests!

As a result, fiduciary advisors may still actually fail to give good fiduciary advice, not by any failure of loyalty or desire to act in their clients' best interest, but because they have no idea what the correct advice is. This won't change as long as there is no requirement to be trained or educated to know!

The broader issue with the DOL's approach to fiduciary is the fact that it's even become necessary in the first place. If we wind the clock back to the origins of the Investment Advisers Act of 1940, at the time there was a dividing line.

On one side there were stock brokers who worked for broker-dealers and sold stocks. They got paid to broker stocks and other securities products.

On the other side there were people called investment advisers, who gave ongoing investment advice.

This dividing line worked pretty well for several decades until 1975, when fixed trading commissions were de-regulated and they were allowed to float. Competition and technology started to bring down the price of stock trading, until stockbrokers couldn't get paid well for brokering stocks anymore as the trading commissions fell.

This prompted a shift where stockbrokers became mutual fund salespeople. They sold mutual funds for 10 or 20 years through the late '80s and much of the '90s, as traditional stock broker business wound down.

Then online brokerage platforms came up and suddenly any consumer could go online and buy a mutual fund. This put pressure on mutual fund salespeople to evolve again, and they started doing portfolio management, providing value by creating asset-allocated portfolios.

The problem with this evolution is that people who started out as salespeople brokering stocks migrated to selling mutual funds and then moved on to designing portfolios. Now the job description looks remarkably similar to what investment advisors do. In the process, the stockbrokers even renamed themselves. Prior to the '80s, a stockbroker's business card said "stockbroker," but for the past 20+ years, it now reads "financial advisor" or "financial consultant." Even though, by regulation, they are salespeople for a broker-dealer, and not actually in the business of giving advice.

In other words, the problem in today's regulatory environment is that we have people who are regulated as salespeople, but put together portfolios and deliver services that are very similar to investment advisors. Which is driving the current regulatory approach, including the DOL's new fiduciary rule: If everyone is going to act like an advisor, then everyone must be accountable to a fiduciary standard as an advisor.

Yet while it's certainly appropriate that anybody who actually holds himself or herself out as an advisor should be a fiduciary, there is still a role for a product salesperson. Some consumers don't want holistic advice. They know what they want to buy. They just want to buy it from a salesperson that will explain the features and benefits and sell them the product.

It's not hard to understand this in the real world. For example, when I go into a clothing store, I don't need a comprehensive fashion consultant. Sometimes I just want someone to help me find a pair of pants in my size, make sure they fit and have that person sell them to me.

The problem we're creating with the current direction of regulation is that we're trying to properly regulate advisors, including salespeople who are posing as advisors. But we're losing the advice-versus-sales choice for consumers, as regulators would eliminate the category of salespeople altogether in the current proposals.

The better alternative is not to make all the financial services companies into fiduciaries. Allow companies to choose whether they will give advice *or* sell products (as the DOL rule ultimately did, with an exemption for order-taker salespeople who do not give advice recommendations). Then, a person who is a salesperson for a particular product or company doesn't need to be held to a fiduciary standard. But what that person needs to do is not put "financial advisor" on the business card if he or she is not a financial advisor.

What we need to do is give consumers a choice between advisors and salespeople, each of whom clearly presents themselves as such and labels themselves accordingly to the public, and then let consumers choose. That was the way the laws were originally written 75 years ago with the Investment Advisers Act of 1940. It was a good framework, and it still is – if only the U.S. Securities and Exchange Commission (SEC) had actually enforced it that way all along.

## Need to enforce

The law as written under the Investment Advisers Act states that the salespeople who work at broker-dealers need to register as investment advisers, if their advice is more than just "solely incidental" to the sale of the products and the delivery of brokerage services.

Yet while arguably many brokers at broker-dealers today have long since crossed that line, the SEC does not enforce the rule. If they did, the DOL wouldn't have needed to expand its fiduciary duty rule because those brokers providing advice (to retirement accounts) would be required to register as investment advisers and be fiduciaries under current law!

Unfortunately, because the SEC has allowed the labels to become unclear about who is a financial advisor and who is a salesperson, the public is unable to clearly identify the real financial advisors.

## Fewer lemons

The reason it's so important to separate out those providing real financial advice can be understood by the work of three economists — George Akerlof, Michael Spence and Joseph Stiglitz — who in 2001 won the Nobel Prize for their analyses of markets with asymmetric information. Their work was titled: "The Market for Lemons." It centered on low-quality damaged cars (called "lemons") and the need for lemon laws to prevent those cars from being sold.

The problem was that while car dealerships shouldn't take advantage of consumers by selling a lemon with known defects, the practice was extremely profitable. The dealer could buy them cheap and sell them for full value and the consumer wouldn't know the difference until it was too late.

Selling lemons was actually so profitable that without regulation of their sale, the low-quality car dealerships that sold lemons could become so profitable that they would out-market and outgrow the high quality car dealerships. In the end, the lowest quality providers knock out all the good ones, and the overall quality for consumers declines.

The research showed why a minimum level of regulation is so important. We have a very similar challenge today in the financial services industry. Over the course of my career, I've seen environments where some of the highest-quality, best products for consumers actually get pulled off the shelves because the lower-quality/higher-commission products sells so much more than the high-quality/low-commission products. It happens because the low-quality/high-commission products are so profitable, they can afford to pay the giant commissions that lead to those products outselling the rest … all at a greater cost to the consumer.

The positive benefit and opportunity around fiduciary rules is that many of these low-quality products will no longer be permissible. Some of them are so low in quality that it would be a breach of fiduciary duty to sell them. By eliminating some of the lowest-quality/high-commission products, there will actually be more room for the higher-quality/low-commission (or outright level fee) products to survive and thrive, with consumers benefitting.

In other words, consumers may ultimately see a significant upgrading in the quality of products available to them, by implementing a fiduciary standard for the advisors.

**Ron Kruszewski**
Chairman and Chief Executive Officer

Stifel

Twenty-Six

# The Emotional Quotient Is Critical to Investing

## About the Author

Ron Kruszewski is Chairman of the Board of Stifel. He joined the firm as Chief Executive Officer in September 1997. Ron serves on the Board of Directors of Securities Industry and Financial Markets Association (SIFMA) and was appointed by the St. Louis Federal Reserve Board of Directors to serve a one-year term on the Federal Advisory Council for 2016.

## About the Company

Stifel is a full-service wealth management and investment banking firm established in 1890 based in St. Louis, Missouri. The Company provides securities brokerage, investment banking, trading, investment advisory and related financial services through its wholly owned subsidiaries to individual investors, professional money managers, businesses and municipalities.

—m—

## Human financial advisors matter

A financial advisor must understand the individual hopes and dreams of his or her clients to formulate an investment plan to achieve those goals. This is the foundation of today's professional financial advisor, and many believe it is at risk due to the rise of "robo-advisors." I disagree. The ability to combine experience, financial acumen, empathy and a personal touch is what separates humans from machines.

## Humans versus machines

Let's give computers and intelligent software their due. As you reflect upon the advances in technology over the last decade, it is truly hard to foresee the changes which lie ahead over the next 10 years. It is simply amazing that computers cannot only win complex strategy games like Chess and Go, but also drive a car unassisted through the streets of San Francisco.

The common denominator of games like Chess and Go, aside from the fact that they are very complex, is that they are played within a defined set of rules and boundaries. Computers are very good at and will become even better at playing games with defined rules.

In financial planning on the other hand, the rules are less defined, often nebulous and different for every individual. Outcomes are uncertain. Each investor presents vastly different challenges. Financial planning is a game in which the board changes after every move.

The financial advisor's job is to help define each individual's financial board, which requires understanding the wants, needs, goals and fears of another human being. This is the core of financial planning and it requires much more than the ability to perform calculations. The key factor is imagination — the advisor's ability to come up with realistic scenarios that a client may not have thought of or doesn't want to think about.

The questions and rules will — and should — be different for each investor and may well change over time, such as: "We are no longer saving for our children's education. Now we are planning for retirement," or "We are no longer bequeathing our wealth to our children; instead, we're considering charitable endeavors."

But perhaps more important than defining the game is getting people to play in the first place. One of the most important characteristics of a financial advisor is the ability to get clients to invest at all. In the movie *War Games*, the only winning move was not to play. In investing, the only way to win is to play. Yet research shows that 69 percent of those between the ages of 18 and 29 and a third of those between the ages of 30 and 49 have not even started saving.[i] Why don't they invest? Sometimes, it is simply not a priority. Some clients are so pessimistic that they don't see the benefits of investing, while others are so optimistic that they don't see the risks of failing to. For many people, life just gets in the way. A good financial advisor helps them understand the importance of planning and investing, however difficult it may appear initially.

Finally, once the game is set and the client has a plan to achieve his or her goals, a good advisor will challenge the underlying assumptions. What happens if events outside of one's control shuffle (or even break) the game board? I am amazed by how many people don't think about insurance and estate planning, let alone the types of "what if" scenarios a person ought to account for in a financial plan. A good advisor doesn't judge or give an opinion; the advisor offers advice.

## The role of EQ

The thing that a human advisor brings to all these scenarios — the thing that a computer cannot offer — is EQ. If you want to get a job at Stifel, a decent IQ level is a prerequisite. But if you want to be a true success, you need a high Emotional Quotient (EQ), which consists of empathy, understanding and the ability to read people, as well as the ability to react to nonverbal cues or body language. A truly successful advisor needs to integrate intelligence, technology and EQ to effectively uncover a client's issues, concerns and goals.

That is why I am not as concerned about robos as some in the industry are. Robo-advisors may have a lot to offer, but they don't have EQ. They don't have empathy or understanding. They can't recognize sudden changes in a client's life, good and bad, or how the financial planning dial needs to be adjusted. This remains something that an advisor, with the assistance of technology, can do better than technology can accomplish alone.

As people interact, questions come up in a decidedly non-linear fashion, prompted by the things we learn as we get to know each other. In an advisor-client relationship, conversations about risk tolerance, family, children, goals, wishes and dreams arise naturally, not necessarily in sequence. Sometimes the client might disclose something unexpected – perhaps he or she not only wishes to retire, but to travel the world or stands to inherit a large sum from a relative.

When someone sits down at a computer to complete a questionnaire through a robo, the computer might produce useful answers, but without the interaction between the advisor and the client — the human element — the answers may not necessarily be the best for that individual, and they certainly won't be influenced by the experience a human advisor may have.

## Combining EQ and technology

The highest probability for success is to combine human insight with technology. Once you know which questions to ask, and how to weight the answers, the computers can help with the math. They help define the efficient frontier of investing. An advisor helps choose where to be on the frontier.

I've come to recognize that the best advice is provided by talented, entrepreneurial, honest people aided with the best tools, which are often based on technology. Unless computers evolve to the point where they're able to think and feel like a human and exhibit the ability to display EQ, financial planning and advising will be about people working with people and leveraging the tools available to them.

Make no mistake: there is a segment of the population who can and will plan, save and invest without the assistance of a financial advisor. New technologies will undoubtedly assist these investors. However, a significant portion of society needs advice on both the importance of saving and how to create and implement a plan. The best answer for these people is a skilled human advisor, possessing high EQ, assisted by technology as a tool.

Humans with high EQ, assisted by powerful computers – this combination makes me optimistic

---

i.  http://www.cbsnews.com/news/shocking-number-of-americans-have-no-retirement-savings/

**Jeff Magson, CRPC®**
Executive Vice President, Client Experience Officer

1st Global

Twenty-Seven

# The Science and Art of Great Financial Planning

## About the Author

In his role as Executive Vice president, Client Experience Officer, Jeff partners with more than 350 1st Global-affiliated firms across the nation to establish, expand and evolve their revenue streams within securities, insurance and advisory platforms. He draws on over 20 years of experience from various roles, including financial advisor, strategic firm development and advisor leadership roles with Ameriprise Financial and 1st Global.

## About the Company

1st Global was founded in 1992 by CPAs who believe that accounting, tax and estate planning firms are uniquely qualified to provide comprehensive wealth management services. As a research and consulting partner, 1st Global provides education, technology and support to help them build and manage their clients' wealth.

—ɯɯ—

## Good advice versus great financial planning

Good financial advice has to be a goal-driven process, and it begins with establishing objectives with clients. There is typically more than one person in each client engagement, so the process should set objectives for all involved. With more than one person involved, not everyone will be on the same page regarding goals. But there are always some commonalities, and there are definitely some differences.

Once we have a solid understanding of what's important and what clients want to avoid, we put financial advice in the context of reality. This involves a thorough discovery before any analysis can be completed — we need to fully understand all assets, liabilities, income sources, policies held to hedge risks and, of course, expenses. This part of the process also offers the skilled advisor the chance to gather emotional data. Gaining insight into how and why prior choices were made by the client can help to inform and influence how to best prepare clients to make decisions in the future.

Good advice is only meaningful if it leads to improved outcomes, so getting clients to implement your advice is imperative. A client may come to a point where he or she is faced with making a change in behavior in order to be able to implement your advice, and the client may not want to change. It's all too easy to say: "I just don't agree with the premise, so I won't act to implement the plan."

The use of modern-day financial planning software is a must. State-of-the-art modeling tools enable an advisor to analyze multi-factor risks that exist in a client's life. Ideally, clients and advisors agree upon the modeling method and are comfortable with the methodology behind the analysis prior to discussing the findings and recommendations.

Having a thorough discussion with clients about how the analysis is performed and getting them to understand what you see when you look at the complete picture helps clients buy in to your methodology, which is important and leads to better implementation.

To be good, the advice has to be comprehensive — it has to cover all the areas of financial planning. It starts with the financial position, understanding assets, liabilities, income and expenses, net worth, savings and cash reserves. Then we look at protection, or risk management. We look at the risk of loss of life prematurely as well as the risk of sickness or injury that prevents one or more of the breadwinners from being able to work. Also evaluated is the risk of any sustained health care costs, such as those incurred when a long term care stay is required. We can also look at the risks of other types of perils, such as the loss of property. If there are business owners involved, we assess the risk to the business itself. Once a client's foundation has been secured, and the risks of regressing financially are mitigated, attention can turn toward growth.

Investment planning is managing existing assets and accumulating additional assets needed for future goals. The most common goals are saving for a home or second home, college education, the purchase of a business, and, of course, retirement. All too often, this is where planning begins and ends, as it is where most of the money resides.

As clients mature in the work force, their retirement assets are often their most valuable assets and are intended to provide the freedom to live an ideal lifestyle for several decades without the need to earn income. For advice to be good, it must address at least four types of risks these assets may face in the years to come: longevity risk, market risk, inflation risk and confiscation risk.

The first major risk is longevity risk. As life expectancy continues to increase due to medical advancements and healthier lifestyles, longevity risk is the increasing chance to run out of money before one runs out of life.

There are two subcategories to that risk: entitlement risk and the risk of excessive withdrawal. Entitlement risk pertains to programs such as Social Security, Medicare and pensions. They may not deliver what was initially expected from a benefit standpoint. For example, you can compute a Social Security expectation, but to bake that in and assume that it's gospel — that it will be there for the client throughout the course of his or her life — will mean that you've just stepped into a longevity-risk trap. So, we've got to be dynamic in how we look at that component of income going forward.

The other subcategory, the risk of excess withdrawal, is, quite simply, the risk of running out of money because the client is no longer accumulating and is taking too much out of the account each year.

The next major risk is market risk. Investments are subject to market risks, including the potential loss of principal invested. That's what everybody really thinks about when they think about financial planning. This has to do with the potential to lose wealth from investments either during a downturn because of a bad decision when things are down or due to market factors beyond one's control. While that risk is always present during the accumulation phase, it could be even worse during the wealth consumption stage.

There are two types of risk that exist inside of market risk. One is asset allocation risk, which is the risk of being too conservative during the accumulation phase — not letting the money work as hard as it possibly could. It is important to remember, however, that asset allocation does not assure a profit or protect against a loss in declining markets. The other is sequence-of-returns risk. This is the risk that the stock and bond market returns will be lower than expected — or even negative — early in the distribution period. Such lower-than-expected returns can dramatically affect the amount of money you can take out of your account each year or the length of time the assets will last.

The third major risk is inflation risk. This is the impact of inflation over time on purchasing power — the ability to buy goods and services in the future due to rising costs. Associated with this is the risk of having to pay for unexpected medical expenses later in life. Sure, we're living longer, but we're living longer because medicine is enabling us to do so. We need money to pay for the treatments and drugs, and such spending can really erode savings or income.

The fourth main category of risk is confiscation risk. Much like inflation can erode wealth, confiscation risk can also erode wealth pretty quickly. For example, there's tax risk. Tax rates may change and erode wealth at too great a rate and prevent you from having adequate income in the future.

Along with the tax risk, there is relationship risk, which is about changes in relationships. A breakup with a spouse or a business partner can damage things dramatically — and more than just emotionally. Your financial situation and the way you manage your business could be impacted, as well.

Finally, good financial advice addresses estate planning. This ensures clients are doing everything they can to safeguard their estates against unnecessary financial erosion due to taxation, which is critical to keeping as much as possible of what they have accumulated. Also, making certain legal documents are in place to properly guide assets during times of transition is critically important and yet often overlooked.

The last step in the process of providing good financial advice is where science meets art. The science is the gathering of data, doing the math and running the modeling tools. The art is making sure all of the discussions that need to be held are held. The recommendations must be crafted so clients can thoroughly understand the current situation as well as the proposed solutions, and the recommendations must be discussed in a way that enables them to make decisions.

Financial planning enables you to do that. It lets you show what the situation would be relative to what the client wants. It's not enough simply to provide advice. A good advisor must enable clients to make the best possible decisions with the advice provided. Just handing over advice is inadequate.

## Great financial planning

While good advice, discussed above, is certainly an adequate deliverable for most households, a great financial planning experience — and the outcomes it can create — is another. Great financial planning involves all of the key tenants of good advice while at the same time supplementing them with a few key differentiators.

Great financial planning is provided in a tax-centric fashion by professionals, specifically Certified Public Accountants (CPAs), who are licensed and trained to also give tax advice. It is virtually impossible to make recommendations in any area of comprehensive financial planning that, if acted upon, do not have tax repercussions (good or bad) either now or later. It is critical that the purveyor of these recommendations is licensed and trained to understand and disclose these ramifications prior to making decisions.

Two advisors can give the exact same advice, one in a way that rarely gets implemented and one that goes above and beyond to get the plan put into action. The latter is the key to helping clients change behavior. Finally, there should be check-ins. Advisors should meet with clients on an ongoing basis to make sure they're doing what needs to be done, to make sure goals haven't changed and, if they have, to be able to refresh the charting. It's very rare that in a 20-year relationship between an advisor and a client the goals established on day one will be the same two decades later.

Great financial planning incorporates the key tenets of behavioral finance. Behavioral finance is a term we hear often in our business. What does "behavioral finance" even mean? It means that one is self-aware and prepared for the types of challenges that are inherent in the capital markets and in other areas of financial planning. Then, when they occur, we are in control of our emotions and are in positions to make better decisions. If we can do that, we can transfer that wisdom to our clients. It's not enough that the advisor is emotionally competent and the advice is great; the client must also be aware of these concepts in order for the advice to be great. Great financial planning is offered by a financial advisor who sees the value in making a commitment to the behavioral sciences and shares his or her insights with clients.

Finally, great financial planning is not free. I truly believe — and experience supports — that clients who are invested in the advice both emotionally and financially will value the advice significantly more than a client who isn't invested enough to pay a fee for the advice. If the advice is free, some might take it and do nothing with it, while others who invest in advice tend to invest in the outcomes they seek. Keep in mind that there are different compensation models, and in order to charge a fee for financial planning advice, an advisor will typically need to be registered through a Registered Investment Advisor (RIA).

## Fiduciary standard

Over the last couple of years, the concept of *fiduciary* has become a very hot topic. In the past, it meant doing the right thing for the client - putting his or her interests before the advisor's. It still does, but now the U.S. Department of Labor (DOL) has become the latest regulatory body to offer a new definition of fiduciary and dictate how one must act when serving clients. As a result, it's becoming more complex to serve certain segments of the investor marketplace.

If the whole concept behind fiduciary is everyone understanding exactly what he or she is doing and paying for, and what the ideal outcome should be, then we've got to be aggressive about being transparent.

Southwest Airlines has an ad campaign built around a term the airline calls "transfarency." Southwest is promoting the fact that it's very easy to know what you're getting for your ticket. The airline has become aggressive on how transparent it is. I think aggressive transparency is what our business is being forced to do.

Before clients come in or consider certain platforms or products, they need to know the real net costs and potential benefits. In the past, a financial advisor would talk about the concept, the opportunity or the problem that needed to be solved. Then the advisor would discuss the different alternatives and steer the client in a particular direction he or she thought was best. At that point, the advisor would disclose the road the client should take, the cost and the fee structure.

Everything that we think about doing now is influenced by whether this will be as transparent as it possibly could be. Beyond being in the best interest of the client, we'll look to see if there is a way to do what we're doing in a more transparent, more fee-sensitive way.

This has changed the way broker-dealers think in regard to how they serve their clients. It's going to influence product design, service models and the financial experience of firms. While the rule will likely sustain certain existing advantages to certain segments of the investing public, it will pose some challenges because it makes it difficult for all segments of the investing public to access quality financial advice. Given the demands the new rule will likely place on firms, the industry is asking how it can sustain the delivery of quality advice to all segments of consumers.

## What people want

In general, people desire joy, significance and meaning in their lives, and an advisor can partner with clients to help them achieve that. Let's recognize, however, that it takes work on the client's part, too.

Let's say you have twin brothers who want the same outcome. One has a very good relationship with a planner and a fully implemented plan that he checks regularly, making periodic tweaks. The other is simply hoping for the same outcome. You're going to see a difference in outcomes as time goes on: the brother who diligently works toward his goals by properly planning is more likely to achieve them than the brother who is taking no action.

I know a financial advisor who runs a very successful firm. One of the things he does when he meets with someone is ask, "If money were no object, what would be the one problem I could solve for you today?"

He met with a woman who was divorced and asked her that question. She shared that she was living in a house that the landlord was in the process of selling and she was terrified of becoming homeless.

She was so wrapped up in terror about not having a place to live that she couldn't concentrate on anything else.

It wasn't tax work or financial planning this particular advisor probed about; instead, he made a few calls and found a solution that helped her move on with her life.

He asked the question that most advisors never ask. He got an answer that was outside the realm of a financial advisor's regular service. Most people would have said: "Sorry, there's nothing I can do about that."

But he was able to listen and solve a problem for someone, which was far more rewarding than a $500 tax-return fee or an investment commission.

That type of commitment is something that our industry would benefit from in many ways. At the very least, it is a powerful way to cultivate a client for life.

Maybe more advisors should ask: "If money were no object, what would be the one problem you'd have me solve for you today?" You may not always be able to solve it, but sometimes you can, and that creates a dimension to your legacy that goes well beyond return on investment. It makes you a professional and a caring human being.

Frank McAleer, CIMA®
Director, Retirement Solutions

Raymond James

Twenty-Eight

# Life Advisors: Connecting a Family's Life and Financial Decisions

## About the Author

Frank McAleer brings 29 years of industry experience to his role as Director of Retirement Solutions. He leads efforts to address the evolving retirement needs of clients with effective tools, resources and education. Frank has held sales and marketing leadership positions at Janney Montgomery Scott, Merrill Lynch and Fidelity.

## About the Company

Raymond James was founded in 1962 with a revolutionary approach to serving clients that later became known as financial planning. A public company since 1983, Raymond James (NYSE:RJF) is a diversified financial services holding company with subsidiaries engaged in investment and financial planning, investment banking and asset management. As of June 30, 2016, Raymond James has approximately 6,800 financial advisors serving in excess of 2.8 million client accounts in United States, Canada and overseas. Total client assets are approximately $535 billion.

—⁓ഡ⁓—

## Life and longevity planning

To live well in retirement, individuals have to embrace change – and longevity planning. As people get older, their circumstances will continue to change, sometimes rapidly.

What doesn't change is their desire to be independent, to have social connections that enrich their lives and to participate in activities that bring them joy. Financial planning that can meaningfully address these quality of life issues can make all the difference.

Oftentimes our client does not know exactly how much he or she will have to spend in retirement or what needs, wants and wishes, also referred to as necessary and aspirational goals, the client needs to plan for. This is where the professional financial advisor is most valuable to their clients.

To manage a portfolio effectively for a specific client it really comes down to helping the client manage his or her life, which begins with asking quality of life questions. The key is to ask our clients questions and initiate discussions around those topics clients may want to avoid. Examples include the potential need for long term care or the possible need to sell a lifetime home. In fact, the 2014 Cost of Care Survey by Genworth indicated that these types of items are often not planned for because 38 percent of those surveyed did not want to admit care could be needed in the future, 28 percent did not want to talk about it and 23 percent did not know where to start. At Raymond James, the core focus within our Retirement Solutions group is to ensure that our financial advisors understand the potential solutions available to our clients for these quality of life issues and, most importantly, understand their associated financial implications.

To really engage our clients about these topics, we encourage our financial advisors to understand and be part of their clients' personal agendas. An excellent start for areas of inquiry includes questions that both affect a client's future quality of life and contain financial implications. Questions such as:

- How will you maintain your current home in the future?
- How will you ensure your ability to come and go as you please?
- Will you live in a community near family and friends?

These three questions relate to understanding both a client's concerns and desires in the future regarding housing, transportation and his or her social network.

When it comes to housing, according to a recent survey by AARP, 89 percent of people 50 years old and above want to remain in their homes indefinitely. Is that feasible in light of home maintenance needs or chronic conditions that restrict mobility? If not, what options are available? Not just the type of home or facility, but its location as well.

# Financial Implications of Caregiving

## Numbers and cost
- **10 million adults over age 50** care for aging parents
- **$325,000** in lost wages, pension and future Social Security benefits per adult caregiver

## Reasons for not planning
- 38% **did not want to admit** care was needed
- 28% **did not want to talk** about it
- 23% **did not know** where to start

*SOURCES:* Family Caregiver Alliance; U.S. Department of Health and Human Services; Genworth 2014 Cost of Care Survey

*As financial advisors, it is our responsibility to create awareness about the financial implications of caregiving and quality of life issues.*

When we discuss transportation with our clients, it's not as much about transportation per se as it is about freedom. Freedom in the sense of a client's desire or need to be self-reliant and to move about her or his world on the client's own terms.

Personally I can relate to when my mother became ill and lost her ability to drive. It was very difficult for her to call a neighbor or friend, or even me, to ask if someone could pick something up from the store or run an errand for her … it's hard for anyone to do that because it is tough to admit you are no longer self-reliant. These questions are about determining the options and costs for how to prepare for these scenarios. The most vital point to make here is one I will pose via this question: will your clients value you more because you beat a benchmark or because you helped them discover a transportation solution for them (or their parents) that enabled them to maintain their dignity and sense of freedom?

The essential reason for financial advisors to ask these questions is to help your clients manage their lives and to enable them to look their financial advisor in the eye and say, "You get me, thank you!" The decisions made around the financial implications of any of these transitional periods will have the most profound effect on your clients', and your own, financial situations in the future.

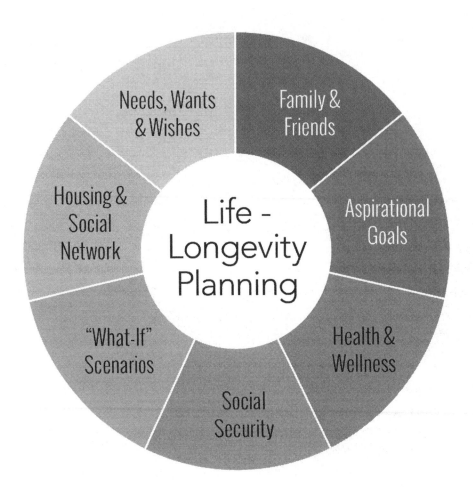

*Decisions made around the important life-longevity planning topics have a profound effect on your clients' financial future.*

The advice of a professional financial advisor is essential as this can all become very confusing quickly. According to the February 2012 Health Care Costs in Retirement Consumer Study conducted by Harris Interactive on behalf of Nationwide, 70 percent of retirees fear running out of money due to health care costs, yet 63 percent of the same population wishes they had a better understanding of Medicare! When you consider needs beyond base coverage of Medicare, it gets more complicated. Do I need extra coverage? How much will it cost? Will I need long term care? How do I protect my finances if long term care is needed for me or a loved one? When do I begin taking Social Security? What are the options?

Health care, caregiving, transportation and housing considerations all share the common denominator of money which places you, their financial advisor, at the center of choices related to these items.

Let me return to the question about one's social network. This explores the importance of a person's need for human interaction. Isolation is one of the biggest issues in aging and retirement today, especially when you lose a spouse or your children have moved away. Where will you live, what kind of community? Will it be a college community, a city or a continuing care retirement community?

A capable financial advisor will act as a guide and, in Raymond James' case, ensure that health care, caregiving, transportation and housing are discussed and planned for.

What's important is understanding why these types of questions need to be asked. The answer is: as financial advisors it is our responsibility to broach these topics with our clients due to the major financial impact any needs in these areas could cause. Clients will not ask these questions, because many times they are in denial. The answers may be something they fear and the reality is most clients don't know where to start. In thinking about these issues and the need to help your clients prepare for them, you are most likely to think about your own life and the lives of those you are responsible for. The concept that comes to mind is empathy. A good definition of empathy is not to sympathize with someone who has to walk mile upon mile in moccasins, but to understand what that experience is. As financial advisors, our lives run parallel to our clients'. Never has there been a better time to display one of the qualities our clients most desire from their advisors ... empathy.

## Matching resources

Once you have identified and prioritized your client's goals, the next step is to list their resources. This includes all of the income and assets that form the foundation of his or her financial plan. Examples include Social Security, bank accounts, CDs, investment accounts, retirement accounts and real estate. Investing has been daunting over the past several years, and this has affected our clients' decisions to stay invested in the markets. Performance and "beating a benchmark" have often been the focal points of the advisor-client relationship. Although the importance of competent and professional investment management can never be overstated, a professional advisor utilizing a robust software planning tool can help clients understand how their long-term investment strategies work to help achieve their personal goals. Our clients' goals are long term and their investment strategy must be the same. There will be "losses" in market value at times and there's real emotion wrapped up in money — security, opportunities and dreams. And, there's real value in helping our clients resist emotional reactions when personal circumstances may cloud one's judgement or when markets turn. The advisor-software combination can visually show clients how losses can occur while, most importantly, the achievement of goals remains on track.

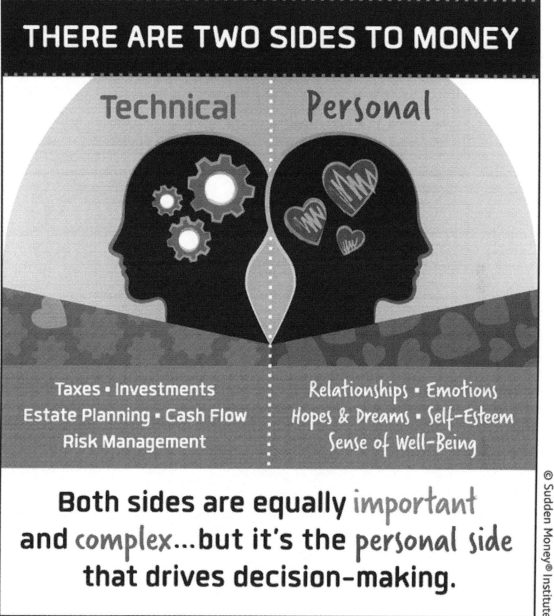

**THERE ARE TWO SIDES TO MONEY**

Technical

Personal

Taxes • Investments
Estate Planning • Cash Flow
Risk Management

Relationships • Emotions
Hopes & Dreams • Self-Esteem
Sense of Well-Being

**Both sides are equally important and complex...but it's the personal side that drives decision-making.**

© Sudden Money® Institute

*Due to concerns about security, opportunities and dreams clients have real emotion wrapped up in money which accentuates the importance of the personal side to decision making.*

## Realistic, relevant and responsive

Asking the right questions is imperative. It is the beginning of the process our financial advisors employ in order to become realistic, relevant and responsive to their clients. This process is explained below:

Realistic — Discuss with clients the realistic issues they may face and the potential financial implications, and begin to plan for them.

- As opposed to beginning a relationship discussion with financial terms, understand the important quality of life questions and how to ask them. Your client will be much more engaged in the conversation due to the personal nature of these topics. NOTE: It's not all about issues that could be perceived as negative; don't forget to also plan for fun, family and travel.
- Once the client is engaged, understand how to pivot the conversation to the financial implications and how to help your clients prepare. There are many options for each topic, all of which have different financial implications.

Relevant — Become even more relevant to your clients by understanding the various options available for quality of life solutions and the financial implications of each. Build a network of providers in your community for professionals such as geriatric care managers.

- Educate yourself and your clients about quality of life issues – housing, caregiving, health care, transportation and related categories.
- Build your centers of influence beyond accountants and attorneys. Those have been the traditional points of influence, but today this list should be extended to include, for example, certified aging-in-place specialists and long term care professionals.

Responsive — Being responsive is more than returning a call or answering an email. It's responding to the needs of the market and letting it be known in your social media postings and your website that you can help clients and potential clients manage their lives.

- Use social media and your web presence to let people know your ability to provide retirement income planning in conjunction with those quality-of-life items related to extended longevity. All age groups go online to conduct searches, whether it's to check an advisor's credentials or validate a referral provided by a friend. Making this information easily accessible on the web could make it more likely that a potential client referred to you will make contact.

- Be a source for information to your community and clients by holding meaningful, educational events. Topics that continually prove popular include Social Security, Medicare and providing care for a loved one at home, to name just a few.

With the advent of online advice, often referred to as robo-advisors, traditional money management continues to become more commoditized. It is now expected that an advisor can competently manage money. With this expectation comes continued price compression. It's the same as when you visit with your physician. You expect to have blood drawn, blood pressure taken and other vital signs read and evaluated. You expect competency in these core areas, but you also expect your physician to use that information to give you personalized advice. Similarly, it is what lies beyond the traditional core competencies of money management upon which the financial advisor of the future will be valued and rewarded.

## Interactive, collaborative plan building

The last thing an advisor should do as part of the financial planning process is print out a multi-page document and hand it to a client. Of course a client may wish to possess such a document. Even if that is the case, the document is still not essential in building a successful planning relationship.

Today, building a financial plan must be interactive and collaborative. It begins with gathering as much information from your client as possible and entering this data into your financial planning software. The next step is to meet with your client, preferably in a conference room with a big screen TV, where the plan visuals are displayed. You can then walk your client through the information provided. When verified, you can point out to your client that, based upon the information you have today, the screen displays your client's probability of success in meeting his or her retirement goals.

From there, if the client is less than satisfied with the plan outcome and/or wants to examine various scenarios, the session moves easily into creating "what if" scenarios where you can shift expense, income and investing levels. This is where financial planning becomes most interactive and collaborative and where you, as a financial advisor, create the most value. You are interacting "live" with your client and educating her or him about the different options and costs that you have uncovered. You are collaborating with your client. Because your client is now part of the process, the mystery and occasional misperception of a financial plan are greatly reduced if not eliminated. In a manner of speaking, the client is watching his or her favorite movie: "This Is Your Life," and as the plot continually changes, your client has a hand in adjusting the script. Interactive and collaborative equals buy-in and endorsement of the plan.

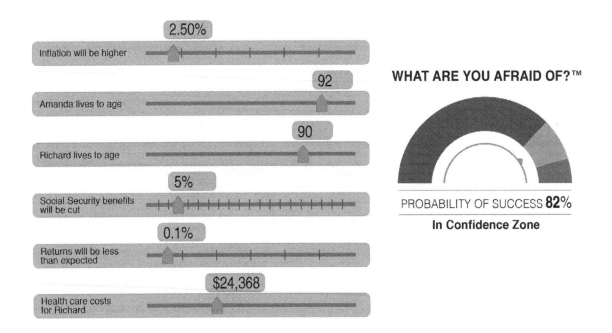

*Financial planning software enables financial advisors to work interactively and collaboratively to create "what if" scenarios for clients where you can adjust income, expense and investing levels.*

The plan, or "script," needs to be reviewed at least once a year, preferably twice, because things will change. It starts with income, assets, expenses, Social Security, Medicare and risk tolerance to determine the base level plan. Then, review a client's very personal spending and saving levels that are tied to his or her unique needs, wants and wishes. Has anything changed? It's a living, breathing process.

# DOL Fiduciary Rule

The first phase of the U.S. Department of Labor (DOL) rule related to fiduciary responsibility for retirement accounts is scheduled to go into effect on April 10, 2017 with the final phase becoming effective in January of 2018.

It seems pretty clear that one outcome of the DOL legislation around the fiduciary standard for qualified retirement accounts will be an increased focus and execution of financial planning. Is it possible to be a fiduciary and know what is in your client's best interest without totally understanding his or her life and the related financial implications? And while the rule focuses on retirement accounts, can one truly provide fiduciary advice without taking into account how any non-qualified accounts impact the full retirement picture?

Advisors will find it much easier to navigate through the requirements of the DOL rule if they are compensated. It is a certainty that after enactment of the pending DOL rules, compensation for qualified retirement accounts will need to be in the form of a flat fee, hourly rate or a fixed percentage of assets. While the rule allows for commissions to be received through the Best Interest Contract Exemption, the additional requirements that come with this exemption will likely discourage many advisors from utilizing it. What will be critical for financial advisors is to ensure we are prepared to respond to the inevitable question regarding price. Large organizations, such as Vanguard or Schwab, are utilizing their considerable marketing budgets to promote online financial advice at a cost considerably lower than human financial advice. Many clients, if left to their own devices and without understanding just what they are paying for, will leave their personal financial advisors based on price alone. Online advisors are counting on the fact that your clients believe you are charging only for investment allocation advice. If your clients believe that is all you offer, then you will find it increasingly difficult to charge a premium over the online advisors. "Robo-advisors" charge less because the service they provide is less, much less, than the value and service provided by the professional advice and planning capabilities of a professional and personal financial advisor. We embrace technology and what computers do best – to analyze data and provide insights. This frees us up to focus on what we do best – connecting with clients, their needs and their goals which leads to better advice. It will be essential in the future that our clients understand what we provide that the "robo-advisors" do not.

# Client of the future

At Raymond James, we are focused on "the client of the future," which it is important to point out has a broader meaning than the name implies. To adapt to a changing industry and meet the needs of today's clients, our advisors and the support we offer them must evolve. Financial advisors have to become life advisors, helping clients connect the dots between needs and goals, across geographies and generations. Specifically, the client of the future includes working with and for our clients and relationships of all ages in the context of the following:

- Shifting demographics
  - Longevity
  - The transfer of wealth
  - Connecting across families
- Evolving preferences
  - "Extras" are now standard
  - Robo disruption
  - Social media
- Extending our value
  - Advice, holistic and personal, beyond investing

While most of the above was discussed earlier in this chapter, a demographic aspect not yet addressed is the issue of transfer of wealth. According to a survey of 544 advisors conducted in April 2015 by InvestmentNews, 66 percent of children fire their parents' financial advisor after they inherit their parents' wealth. How do we hold onto those assets? How do we retain those relationships?

When you speak to the children, the millennials and young Gen Xers that have stayed with their parents' advisors, what you hear them say is: the advisor requested that the children be involved (which the children appreciated), and the children watched how their parents' personal advisor worked with them and helped them through the transitional, and often emotional, times of their lives. The advisor helped not only from a financial standpoint but, more importantly, with understanding and empathy.

In addition to empathy, trust and personalization of the financial plan are positive characteristics that clients seek in their advisor. Expertise in the knowledge of the quality of life issues and their financial implications continually becomes more important to clients.

The client of the future will need a competent advisor who can help clients manage their lives, their decisions regarding their future and the related financial implications.

The advisor of the future will need to be able to draw on his or her expanded local network to help clients address these issues. An absolute essential tool for the advisor of the future is having access to financial planning software that enables a continuous interactive and collaborative advisor-client relationship and having faith that the selected software provider will strive to maintain a visionary strategy and will continue to evolve the product.

## The financial advisor of the future

Our offerings to our clients must be realistic, relevant and responsive today and in the future.

Being realistic means talking about the real issues on clients' minds as they head toward retirement, while being relevant implies an understanding of the various choices available and their corresponding costs.

Being responsive is to be attuned to the marketplace, providing our clients with what they need the most — education and resources pertaining to the many different directions their personal and unique retirement path can travel.

Helping clients build the vision of their futures takes planning and preparation, but it does not have to be intimidating. A professional financial advisor working in partnership with high-quality planning software that enables an interactive and collaborative client experience is the best way to achieve this today and in the future.

**Dan McGrath**
Co-Founder

**Jester Financial Technologies**

Twenty-Nine

# The Challenge of Health Care Costs in Retirement

## About the Author

Dan McGrath is the co-founder of Jester Financial Technologies, which helps financial professionals address the costs associated with health in retirement. He has broad experience in financial services and training, is a national speaker on the impact of health care costs in retirement and is the author of *What You Don't Know About Retirement Will Hurt You!* and *Medicare: a practical guide to understanding your health coverage in retirement.*

## About the Company

Jester Financial Technologies was founded in 2013 to help financial professionals address health care costs in financial and retirement planning. Headquartered in Massachusetts, Jester's financial, health care and technology professionals provide data, education and tools.

—ɯ—

## The biggest expense and the biggest fear

I've spent several years supporting financial services firms, advisors and planners with data, education and the necessary tools to help them create better financial futures for their clients when planning for one of the biggest and most important expenses not only in retirement, but life — their health.

I learned that planning for health care costs in retirement brings angst and fear to many clients and rightfully so. Credit Suisse Euromonitor estimates that health care costs will account for 33 percent of all costs in retirement, which makes it the largest expense. The average 60-year-old couple, with each person expected to live to about 85, should expect to incur approximately $406,000 in costs just for their insurance premiums if both would like to be fully covered according to Jester Technologies' data.

This may be a somewhat larger number than some expect or anticipate and the fact that the bulk of these health care costs will be deducted directly from a client's Social Security benefit is disheartening. Published reports show that these costs will consume about 40 percent of an average person's Social Security benefits and 53 percent of married couple's benefits. Furthermore, what's alarming is that 73 percent of unmarried people rely on Social Security for 50 percent or more of their income in retirement according to Social Security Quick Facts.

Planning for health care costs has been a challenge for many advisors, but it is perhaps the most critical element of delivering a quality financial plan. If an advisor has not accounted and prepared for this cost, he or she is not giving the client the best possible financial advice nor is the advisor delivering a quality financial plan.

Studies show that less than 8 percent of Americans who are retired or thinking about retiring have taken the necessary steps to plan for the cost of health care in retirement. This is an opportunity for a financial advisor because helping a client plan for health care costs is not only very personal, but as mentioned, is usually the client's largest expense and biggest fear. If done properly, providing this service would secure a very happy client for life.

Oddly enough, health care is one of the easiest expenses to build into a plan. The advisor has all the information to figure it out. With Medicare, we have history. We know exactly how much Medicare has charged the last 48 years, at least for Medicare Part B. We also know the history of Medicare Part D since 2006 and the history of Medigap plans since 1993. In addition, Medicare tells us what the charges will be in the future. And, the federal government releases a report every August that tells us what it is going to charge for the next eight years.

The only issue one may encounter is calculating the extra surcharges that come from excessive income, but there is technology that can assist with the calculations. Granted, advisors don't know what a client is going to pay for dental, vision, and hearing which are not covered by Medicare B, but not every person is going to the dentist, podiatrist or optometrist. However, a good out-of-pocket estimate can be created based on the data that has been compiled over the last 48 years.

# Health care coverage is the only mandatory expense in retirement

Everyone must have health care coverage in retirement; it's not a matter of debate. When I mention health care coverage I am referring to the mandatory expenses everyone must pay in retirement that are associated with one's health.

These mandatory health care costs are derived from Medicare premiums and coverage including Medicare Parts A & B, which have co-pays and deductibles and excess charges. However, these costs for every state except Massachusetts can be covered through a Medigap plan policy, thus making all costs for health care in retirement just the premiums.

Please note that these health care costs are derived from Medicare, and the bulk are predicated on the amount of one's income. In other words, the more income a person has in retirement, the higher these costs can be.

The Affordable Care Act dictates that Medicare Part A is mandatory for everyone who qualifies and everyone is eligible for Medicare parts A, B and D at age 65 or older and as long as they are no longer covered by an employer's or spouse's employer's health plan. If a person is no longer covered by another plan, he or she must accept Medicare Part A. If someone is eligible and chooses not to enroll in Medicare Part A, he or she will face a series of fines that compound and grow with interest over time. To make it worse, if fines are not paid, the Treasury Department has the ability to either garnish the penalty from that person's Social Security benefit or pass the bill on to his or her children.

Once someone accepts Part A, he or she doesn't have a choice but to enroll in Parts B & D for which there is a small window. If the deadline is missed, there are late enrollment penalties which compound and are perpetual. For Part B the late enrollment penalty is 10 percent of the person's current premium for each 12-month period it is late. For Part D, the penalty is 1 percent of the current premium for each month delayed. For example, if someone chooses not to accept Medicare Part B and or D, after five years then he or she would have a 50 percent penalty on top of what the current Medicare Part B premium was for the year the person signed up. And the Medicare Part D penalty is another 60 percent on top of the current National Base Premium for Part D for that year.

Unfortunately, these two penalties stay with the person for the rest of his or her life and the person will always be charged more for health care coverage. These penalties are automatically deducted from the person's Social Security benefit, which takes funds away from the overall retirement plan. I believe that if advisors and clients are aware of the tight deadlines and penalties for not enrolling on time, these unnecessary costs and fees can be avoided, thus putting money back into the client's retirement plan.

If a person chooses not to have health care coverage, the federal government will stop sending a Social Security check. This isn't a by-product of the Affordable Care Act; the rule was created in 1993 when the federal government changed the Social Security's Program Operations Manual System (POMS) so that to collect any Social Security benefit a person must also accept Medicare when eligible. Failure to do so will lead to forfeiture of all current, future and even past Social Security benefits. This means that anyone who starts to collect Social Security at age 62 and does not accept Medicare, for whatever reason, when eligible, will have to pay back every cent of the benefits received while also forfeiting all other benefits.

## The definition of income

Financial advisors may know the basics about the mandatory nature of health care costs as part of Social Security, but in my opinion, very few are drilling down to the next level, which starts with understanding the definition of income.

Unfortunately, most of what constitutes income is what most advisors typically try to accomplish for their clients — asset accumulation strategies that are going to result in higher income, but that in the end will generate a higher mandatory cost for health care, which in turn is going to lower what a client receives from Social Security.

The definition of income is any wage plus any tax-exempt interest or everything on lines 37 and 8B of the IRS form 1040. Income also includes Social Security benefits and all capital gains, with the exception of the sale of a home, $250,000 as an individual or $500,000 as a couple and any dividend as well as interest from checking accounts, and any withdrawal from a 401(k), 403(b), a 457 or SEP IRA. It will all be counted as income.

When we look at the new definition of a fiduciary's role per the U.S. Department of Labor (DOL), it basically states the person in control of the assets of another person must place that other person's needs ahead of his or her own. For example, when a client places a dollar into his or her 401(k), the client is telling the federal government he or she would like to possibly lose a dollar in Social Security benefits. How can an advisor, in good conscious, advise a client to do that?

Fortunately, thoughtful guidance for investment strategies and products with respect to their impact on health care costs can help maximize available income. Below is a list of some of the investment vehicles that may be worth considering that are not counted as income:

- Roth accounts including a Roth IRA or 401(k)
- Reverse mortgages
- Life insurance
- A portion of non-qualified annuities
- Health savings accounts
- 401(h) plans

## The five rules of Medicare brackets and shifts

Any advisor working with a client that is just beginning retirement planning needs to say, "If you don't adhere to the guidelines, the rules and regulations, once you retire, there's nothing that can be done." The damage cannot be repaired. Even as an advisor, you can't fix it. It'll be too late. For example, the money in a traditional 401(k) can be converted later on, but the client will pay extremely high taxes, which is going to lead to a higher Medicare bracket.

Like kids said back in the day, "No backsies." Once someone loses his or her Social Security check, it's most likely gone for the rest of the person's retirement. The next step in being able to prudently plan for health care costs in retirement is to understand the five rules that may influence a change in Medicare brackets.

Medicare created five specific rules that state how someone can move or be moved from one bracket to another. Advisors need to be very aware that when a client hits a bracket; Medicare doesn't necessarily have to lower it the next year. Instead, anyone that reaches one of these brackets will receive an 11-page report from the Social Security Administration explaining the brackets and advising the client to look at their tax returns the next year, and that they may or may not lower the bracket.

An advisor and his or her client need to grasp the fact that once the damage of being in a higher bracket has been done, it may stay that way for the remainder of the client's life in retirement. Keep in mind that Medicare looks at the tax bracket, income and tax returns on an annual basis. While Medicare has dropped people's brackets, it has also left other folks in the same brackets.

The five rules of moving from one bracket to another:

- **Rule 1:** A client is retired and no longer working the same amount or decides to cut back on hours, or take a pay cut. Example: the client is 66-years old and still employed. He or she is making $125,000 a year and he or she decides to sign up for Medicare instead of opting for the employer's benefits. The client will be penalized because he or she is making too much money.

- **Rule 2:** The client gets married, a spouse dies, or they separate — the tax bracket changes. Example: the client is married; the client and the spouse make $500,000 a year. They divorce, and one now makes $300,000, while the ex-spouse makes $200,000. The client will move to a lower bracket if there is a tax status change.
- **Rule 3:** Loss of income from a rental property. Example: the client has income from a rental property that is destroyed by conditions beyond his or her control. The client may move to a lower bracket because they are no longer collecting rental income.
- **Rule 4:** The client or the client's spouse experienced a scheduled cessation, termination, or reorganization of an employer's pension plan. The client may move to a lower bracket because he or she is no longer receiving additional income through regularly scheduled benefits.
- **Rule 5:** The client or the client's spouse received a settlement from an employer or former employer because of the employer's closure, bankruptcy or reorganization. A client may move to a lower bracket because their income may decrease.

Taking into account the impact of a bracket shift is not merely something that ought to be planned for; it is a critical aspect of a quality financial plan. Here's an unfortunate example that should have been planned for. An older couple sold a piece of property, originally purchased for $10,000, for $1.6 million. With that sale, they moved to a new bracket reflective of that income level and have stayed there ever since.

## The watchful eye of the future

Looking to the future, there will be an even more watchful eye on advisors following the recent changes from the DOL to the fiduciary rule that requires an advisor to act in a client's best interest. In order to truly act in a client's best interest, an advisor must fully understand the client and develop a quality financial plan that helps achieve a retirement meeting his or her individual specifications, wants and needs. Wouldn't a big part of that be developing a retirement plan that delivers a real projection for health care costs that has been properly planned for along the way? To me, that's acting in a client's best interest.

As we move forward in this increasingly challenging post-DOL environment, advisors will eventually be asked to defend their recommendations. This is actually one area where an advisor can easily defend his or her intentions.

One potential scenario is an advisor is standing before a judge trying to explain why he or she didn't include the only mandatory expense in retirement in the financial plan they designed — a mandatory expense involving a person's greatest asset — their health. Or another scenario is an advisor sitting in front of the head of the Centers for Medicare & Medicaid Services or the Secretary of Health & Human Services, saying, "I'm sorry, it's impossible to figure out." They look at you and say, "Really? We gave you the exact numbers, and we told you what the inflation rate will be and you couldn't do it?"

Both of these scenarios can easily be avoided if you plan properly.

## Is it worth trying to beat the system?

As I mentioned, the expense is mandatory, so it's better to learn how to plan for it and just do it. Below is an example of a few folks that thought they could beat the system.

In March 2011, a judge in the U.S. District Court of Appeals of the District of Columbia dismissed a case, Hall v. Sebelius, brought by three retired federal employees. The three had reached age 65 and were receiving Social Security retirement benefits but wanted to drop their Medicare Part A coverage, which pays for care in hospitals.

Anyone who has reached age 65 and is entitled to Social Security benefits is also automatically entitled to Medicare Part A without charge. However, the three plaintiffs, one of whom was former Republican House Majority Leader Dick Armey, wanted to drop Medicare Part A coverage because they claimed it threatened their coverage under the Federal Employees Health Benefits (FEHB) program, which they said was superior.

The trio argued that the Medicare law allows them to drop out of the program without losing Social Security benefits. The judge ruled the three retirees had a legitimate point that the law does not specifically say that avoiding Medicare Part A means losing Social Security benefits. But in examining the law that Congress enacted in 1965 to create Medicare, the judge found that "requiring a mechanism for Plaintiffs and others in their situation to 'dis-enroll' would be contrary to Congressional intent, which was to provide 'mandatory' benefits under Medicare Part A for those receiving Social Security Retirement benefits."

The judge also pointed out that the plaintiffs would not gain much by renouncing their Medicare Part A coverage. Even if they were to forego and repay all Social Security benefits, under the law "their FEHB-paid benefits would be no more, and no less, than what Medicare Part A would provide."

To put it simply, the decision meant that when looking at health care costs, the average person is going to experience a 26 percent reduction in actual income received from Social Security because of his or her health care...if the person wants to be fully covered. Within 10 years, that 26 percent grows to about 40 percent and by the time someone is 85 years old, if he or she has retired at 65, 56 percent of his or her Social Security check will be eaten up by health coverage costs.

For the extremely affluent, within 12 years of retirement, not only will they never receive a Social Security check, they will actually write a check to the federal government for their health care coverage, Medicare, and then be taxed on the income never received from Social Security.

## Can't hold on to the old way of doing business

When I look at the financial services industry, instead of holding on to the old way of doing business, the industry needs to change and adapt to what is coming. The old ways are not keeping up with the regulators and all the new legislation and, in all likelihood, the industry is going to pay for that dearly.

It is my hope that if people are properly educated about health care costs and how it will impact them in retirement, and advisors truly understand all the elements related to these costs and how they affect a person's retirement income, they will automatically plan for this expense at the beginning of a client-advisor relationship. This will put the client in a better position of financial strength and may make them rethink other investment strategies and perhaps adjust how they are saving today in order to be more prepared for the future.

**Dale Niemi**
President and Chief Executive Officer

BancWest Investment Services

Thirty

# The Component Approach of Financial Planning

## About the Author

Dale Niemi leads teams that work with clients on retirement and investment needs as President and CEO of BancWest Investment Services. With over 20 years of experience, he previously served as Bank of the West Senior Vice President - Private Client Services Regional Manager and as Vice President, Regional Trust Manager at Wells Fargo Bank.

## About the Company

A subsidiary of Bank of the West, BancWest Investment Services is a broker dealer with over 400 financial professionals nationwide. Focusing on individuals, high net worth individuals and pension and profit sharing plans, the firm brings together investing and online banking. It offers a broad range of products to help clients reach their investment goals, including retirement planning, mutual funds, annuities, IRA, insurance and more.

—m—

## A real disconnect

There's a real disconnect between what financial firms and their financial advisors say about what constitutes good financial advice and what consumers see as good financial advice.

In part, this is a direct result of our industry setting the bar low insofar as what good financial advice should look like. This in turn has created much more than just a misalignment with consumers' expectations. Consumers are telling us that they're not getting sound comprehensive advice from us — but we're not listening.

## More listening needed

One of the common mistakes many financial advisors make is to do too much talking and not enough listening. They want to rush to implementing a solution instead of spending time listening to customers and hearing all of their thoughts on what goals they wish to accomplish.

Too many advisors think of financial planning as the contents of a three-inch thick binder. It contains everything the advisor thinks is needed. It's all-encompassing, very comprehensive and contains everything the consumer is thinking about.

Or does it?

Too often the advisor doesn't hear the consumer say, "You know what I really want to do is to make sure I have enough money to pay for my daughter's wedding; I really want to be able to buy that vacation home; I really want to be able to pay for my kids' education" or "I want to retire."

More often than not, clients think of needs or goals one at a time. Unfortunately, far too often advisors comingle all the components of a financial plan. Seeing all of these components together rather than separately can be overwhelming for the typical consumer.

Fundamentally, good financial advice happens when an advisor sits down with a client and listens to learn about the individual's goals and what he or she wants to accomplish. After that the advisor can develop a customized strategy to help the client achieve his or her desired goals.

## Communicate to connect

Another aspect that is often overlooked is gauging the client's confidence level of achieving these goals or, perhaps more importantly, the level of fear of not doing so. That gauge will tell an advisor where a given goal falls on the client's priority list of goals.

It is absolutely impossible to gauge a consumer's confidence level on any goal if the advisor doesn't communicate sufficiently with his or her client. Too often firms see in their customer experience surveys that clients complain: "I don't hear from my advisor often enough."

Disconnects become more so if little effort is made to create and strengthen connections. By extension, it's necessary to determine with a client the desired frequency of communication. The advisor may have created the best plan imaginable, but if the communication isn't there, then the customer doesn't know where things stand. Are the plan's goals being met? To me, good financial advice has to include communications as a key component. It should be the simplest thing we do as an industry. Yet it's the one thing that most advisors don't do well enough. Let me emphasize that good communications does not mean a phone call to offer birthday wishes or just to say "hi." Substantive, purposeful communication is what is needed.

## Everyone is in some phase of retirement

A key to quality financial planning is the advisor listening to hear the client's priorities. Once those are thoroughly understood, then the advisor can develop a plan designed to hit those objectives.

I like to remind my colleagues that everyone is in one phase of retirement or another. And, seemingly, everyone has a retirement plan of one sort or another, but there's this thing called "life" that gets in the way. It has a way of impacting the ability to hit the goals. After all, life is constantly changing. When life throws you a curve ball, what happens to your plan? Does the advisor even know that this "life event" occurred?

By the way, curve balls are not always "bad" things — they may be births, marriages or new jobs. Imagine a plan that doesn't anticipate a child going to grad school, but a four-year degree will not suffice for the desired career. That's a curve ball.

Curve balls are the realities that require quality communication, quality advice, pre-determined goals and flexibility. I like to say a quality plan has to be a dynamic, living, breathing document. It has to be able to adjust to any curve balls that life throws at you.

When an advisor sits down with someone to begin financial planning, he or she may come up with 15 goals. I ask whether the client and I should devise something that can accomplish all of those goals. As with advice, good planning calls for good listening, then pointing out priorities with a strong dose of reality. Which goals are most important? How satisfied or devastated would the client be if certain goals are not met? Those are some of the basic questions that have to be asked, answered and understood.

## The first inning

My firm launched an integrated banking and investment solution last year. Let's just call it "premier banking." It's something most institutions have. I went on a media tour to discuss this solution. A reporter asked me if we were "late to the game with premier." Many firms have had "premier" for many years — even as long as a decade. My response was, "I'm not so sure you can be late to the game when it's still in the first inning."

I hear consumers speak about how they want more advice, how they are looking for a financial institution to provide them with something they're not getting, something that's more comprehensive. Clients say they are getting things individually — one thing from financial institution A, another item from financial institution B, etc. No one's pulling it all together.

Year after year the consumer asks for something holistic and the industry doesn't deliver. If consumers continue to say they are not getting what they need from the industry, it's still the first inning.

## Transparency and the fiduciary standard

In this era of suitability we have already started to move closer to a fiduciary standard. That means we need to better understand what a fiduciary standard is because there's a lot of misunderstanding on what that really means. This will have some big implications for our industry.

I look back at 2008 and 2009, when the average consumer started to see the complexity of financial instruments and the lack of transparency. They were understandably confused.

From a fiduciary perspective, we're going to have to be much more transparent. We're going to have to make sure the average consumer can completely understand the offering, the products, the solutions, fee structures built around those and the actual benefit to them and the firm. But it won't be a simple process to deliver the true sense of a fiduciary standard.

The consumer is saying, "I need my advisor. A big part of what my advisor does is educate me, empower me, teach me, involve me." That's a different business model than what we've been operating under for many years, for many decades.

We're seeing that today. Again, customers are saying: "I want to be involved. I want to know. So you have to educate me, you have to teach me, you have to involve me before you can be my advisor."

## Don't overwhelm

Looking ahead, about five years out, I think we'll see an evolution where we'll likely get paid more on the advice that we give rather than the products we sell. The fees that we're getting today cover the advice that we provide. Yet, as an industry, it's hard to demonstrate that the fee is warranted if clients are rarely or never called. What advice are advisors giving if there isn't any dialog?

One of the changes I'm seeing is a reduction in servicing fees. That reduction is off-set by charging for advice. But that means advisors must provide that advice in substantive communications with their clients. What that advice consists of may well need to be defined. With that, we'll see good planning: financial planning, retirement planning and estate planning.

True quality financial planning is an A to Z process. Like I mentioned, a good financial plan includes retirement planning, estate planning and risk management. It's wise to break down financial planning into all these smaller increments. Instead of it being one big plan, it's a series of components.

My experience with this component approach has found that the customer adoption rate is higher when we break the financial planning down into what are essentially related, but separate conversations.

We found the uber-comprehensive plan was too overwhelming for a majority of consumers. When we broke the plan down by components, it was very well received. Our customer experience scores are a lot higher and our adoption rates are higher.

If you take the component approach, work with clients at their pace and just have a conversation, then there will not be many sales in the first few meetings. Given that, firms will have to think about compensation plans.

## Fear of the future

If a consumer knows that his or her future is secure by virtue of the financial plan, the client can now do other things. I call that "social impact." We don't have enough of that, because people aren't confident in their futures. They still have too much fear about what the future has in store for them.

If a client has a high level of confidence and a low level of fear is in place, he or she will be able to have a greater "social impact."

Clients might be able to give more to charity or set up foundations; something they aren't currently doing, because they are fearful of not having enough money for themselves, children and grandchildren. Clients can do other things when their levels of confidence are high and levels of fear are low.

**Alex Potts**
President and Chief Executive Officer

Loring Ward Financial and SA Funds - Investment Trust

Thirty-One

# Understanding the Patient

## About the Author

With over 26 years of experience, Alex Potts leads Loring Ward as president and CEO helping financial advisors deliver a positive wealth experience for their clients. Alex started SA Funds, Loring Ward Securities, and served in key leadership roles of LWI Financial, Inc. and RNP Advisory Services. He is a contributing author of *The Wealth Solution: Bringing Structure to Your Financial Life.*

## About the Company

For over 25 years, Loring Ward (LWI Financial Inc.) has been focused on empowering financial advisors with investment and advisor solutions. The firm has a large network of independent advisors in the United States and is located in California.

—⟋⟋⟋—

## Examining one's financial health

The analogy between the medical profession and the financial profession came to me when I was sitting in my ear doctor's office. As a kid, I suffered many ear infections and ultimately had to have both eardrums replaced. My doctor, renowned for his work for helping people hear better and performing surgeries ranging from cochlear implantation to reconstructing eardrums, turned out to be one of the best advisors I've ever met.

When he sat down with me, he dug deep to uncover my problem and wanted to understand the mental toll it had on me. He looked into my ears and said: "OK, yup. I see the problem. You've got an issue on your eardrum and we need to resolve that."

He then stopped, stepped back and explained to me exactly what he was going to do. He spoke plainly and in a way I could understand. He shared the potential issues and how they could be mitigated. I had no questions or concerns. I trusted his guidance. He ended by telling me, "The procedure should resolve the problem and should take about five to 10 minutes."

And it did.

In the course of the doctor's discovery I told him my other eardrum needed some attention. He looked into my ear and told me, "The eardrum looks like it's starting to fail, but you might have a year, you might have three years. If I were you, I would do nothing."

I was thinking, this guy is an ear surgeon, he makes his money doing ear surgery and he just told me not to do anything, just wait. That, to me, was an incredible experience. He clearly put my interest above his own. I think every great advisor, not just those in the financial industry, can bring an experience like that to his or her clients.

Receiving financial advice is a lot like going to the doctor. Obviously, he or she is going to ask you many questions and spend time understanding your issues and getting a broad picture of your health and life. The doctor may decide to run tests, take some blood samples and go through a series of steps to determine what ails you. Then, once your problem is diagnosed, your doctor will prescribe a treatment and ideally suggest ways you can stay healthy over the long term.

Great financial planners do almost exactly the same thing. They will work closely with clients to understand who they are, uncover their problems and learn about their goals — then they put in place the best possible long-term plan.

In most plans, the investment goals are typically solved first, since we usually rely on the growth of our portfolio to finance our goals. The advisor then focuses on planning issues such as retirement, estate planning, long term care, college education, buying a house and philanthropy. These tend to be the big issues that most clients face, the ones that tend to keep them up at night. For many of us, the biggest questions are, "How long will my money last after I stop working?" and more importantly, "Can I live the way I do now when I stop working?"

As Americans become increasingly responsible for financing their own retirement along with enjoying longer and longer lives, the decisions we make during our working years can have an enormous impact on the quality of our retirement. A great advisor can make a real difference in helping us put together retirement plans that provide the highest probabilities of achieving our goals, with suitable amounts of risk.

## Deep understanding and caring

In order for a client to get great advice, the advisor needs to deeply understand them — their needs, goals and values and any potential problems. This is why great advisors are empathetic listeners.

An empathetic listener doesn't judge and is not trying to move the conversation toward a pre-conceived end. Discussions are all about the clients and helping them understand the importance of talking about key life areas that will ultimately have financial consequences.

The need to explore the real issues that clients face is hard for some advisors. Often, they will say that they don't feel comfortable getting into emotional or psychological issues. But both are critical to understanding who clients are and what they need — and then building a great financial plan. From this discussion, the advisor ought to have a really good idea about:

- What clients need to do with their finances
- Family and dependents
- Issues that relate to work life
- What could happen if the client should suddenly pass away, suffer a serious illness or unexpectedly experience a major life event

Not only is a good plan forward-looking toward big goals such as retirement, it also helps to mitigate problems that might occur along the way, before they actually happen.

Great advisors care a lot about their clients. They're so much more than salespeople.

## It's about helping

Some of the ways advisors guide and serve their clients are just amazing, even inspiring. Some advisors help clients deal with grandkids addicted to drugs or alcohol, or children who are physically or mentally challenged, at times setting up a trust, or a foundation, to help people with kids in those situations. In other instances, advisors are making sure that elderly clients are able to access a network of care; while other advisors are providing pro bono financial advice and education to people in need. I'm reminded of what a Certified Public Accountant (CPA) once told me, "I know my client is working with a great financial advisor when I meet that financial advisor at weddings, funerals and baptisms." Trusted advisors have an immeasurable level of empathy for their clients and are integral parts of their lives.

Being a great financial advisor has always been about putting the interests of the client first no matter what. That means delivering benefits to the client and not to you, the advisor. To me, it's just common sense. For example, I've seen financial advisors help clients sell large businesses and help them convert those sales into large charitable foundations. In each instance, the advisor met the needs of the client, but didn't earn anything on the transaction.

As a client, the expectation should be that you are getting the best information and the best advice from your trusted financial advisor. That advisor should help uncover the life issues that may actually affect your financial plan.

**Knut A. Rostad**
Founder and President

Institute for the Fiduciary Standard

Thirty-Two

# It's Just Common Sense: Disinterested Advice Is the Foundation of "Good Advice"

## About the Author

Knut A. Rostad is the founder and president of the nonprofit Institute for the Fiduciary Standard. Rostad, a former compliance officer for a registered investment advisor, works with volunteer leaders and a small staff to fulfill the mission of the Institute. He's authored numerous articles, papers and comment letters on fiduciary duties, is regularly quoted in the media and is the editor of *The Man in the Arena: Vanguard Founder John C. Bogle and His Lifelong Battle to Serve Investors First*.

## About the Company

Founded in 2011, The Institute for the Fiduciary Standard is a non-profit that exists to advance fiduciary principles in investment and financial advice. The Institute conducts research, education and advocacy to benefit investors, capital markets and the economy and advocates for the instrumental role of robust fiduciary duties.

—⚍—

## What is good financial advice?

Questions of good advice and financial planning are timely. 2016 will initiate the U.S. Department of Labor (DOL) Conflict of Interest (COI) rule era, 76 years after the Investment Advisers Act of 1940, and 47 years since the "birth" of financial planning. The force behind the DOL rule reflects the "shared mission" and question that attracted the financial planning founders in 1969: Can *advice* replace *sales* as the industry's "driving force?"[i]

2016 is important to the question of "good financial advice" because regulatory, technological and market forces remind us why the foundation of good advice must be disinterested advice. In this chapter I highlight the arguments around fiduciary advice and cite the work of Rutgers Law Professor Arthur Laby that explores a basic (and over-looked) rationale for disinterested advice: common sense. Common sense informs investors' views of sales and advice, generally, and does so for "good advice" as well.

## Regulatory and market changes

The DOL COI rule resets the foundation of retirement and investment advice. For some firms, the rule will be shock therapy that requires fundamental changes; for all firms, adjustments will likely be needed. It also puts mounting pressure on the U.S. Securities & Exchange Commission (SEC) to create its own rule.

Additionally, market forces are already transforming how advice and product rec-ommendations are being delivered. New technology (including robo digital platforms), products and aroused cohorts of disgruntled investors are demanding new advice rela-tionships based on transparency, straight talk, broad planning expertise and reasonable fees. As in the TV ad for a broker-dealer firm, at the end of a father-son conversation about investing, the millennial advises his boomer father, "The world is changing."

At issue is whether these transformations rejuvenate "good advice" in securities regulation and in advisory firms. The jury is out. Much will depend on what advisors do. Will advisors speak out on and actively explain how true fiduciary advice differs so sharply from product recommendations or not?

## The current battle

The current seven-year battle between investor advocates and industry advocates is a battle over "good advice." The battle is over what most fiduciary advocates consider to be a core element of "good advice" — avoiding conflicts of interest and getting as close to "conflict-free" as humanly possible.

The two sides remain far apart. This is understandable because what separates them are not small differences or mere nuances. No, what separates them is a principle. A principle which, when fully transparent, resonates strongly. It resonates because it involves fixed notions of fair play and common sense based on everyday experiences.

The principle, as Laby points out, is that "advice" must mean the advisor is "disinterested." Fiduciary advocates espouse this principle, while industry advocates who oppose the DOL rule do not. While industry advocates claim brokerage customers' best interest are served, when their words and deeds are closely examined, it becomes apparent this claim is highly dubious. That it is highly dubious comes as no surprise, at least as long as one's primary business is distributing products and one's primary compensation is based on product recommendations.

## The "Conflicts are OK" view is prevalent in Washington

As such, key federal regulators and industry advocates implicitly argue that conflicts are OK when they explicitly espouse that product recommendations are advice and disclosure is the remedy to conflicts. I call this the "Conflicts are OK" view.

The views of the SEC, the Financial Industry Regulatory Authority (FINRA) and business lobbyists led by the Securities Industry Financial Markets Association (SIFMA) are key. Their views differ in tone but are grounded in common assumptions. The key assumption is that conflicts of interest are omnipresent and inherently part of "advice." Their presence is inevitable. As such, they are accepted as normal, and expressed as "acceptable" and "permissible." The message, now explicit, is that conflicts are permissible and need not be avoided and need not be minimized.

This "Conflicts are OK" view means the regulatory issue is no longer about avoiding conflicts — or even managing the harms of unavoidable conflicts. Instead the regulatory issue is about disclosure, sometimes with true consent but rarely with true client understanding of the nature and potential harm of the conflict (that is, anyway, according to volumes of research and experience).

**SIFMA**. The "Conflicts are OK" view is evident in the writings of SIFMA. The wide acceptance of conflicts is evident in SIFMA's July 14, 2011 comment letter to the SEC: *Proposed Framework for Rulemaking Under Section 913 (Fiduciary Duty) of the Dodd-Frank Act*. There is no mention here of why conflicts have been viewed historically as undermining objective advice, of why conflicts should be avoided if possible and why disclosures are inherently ineffective. To the contrary, there is explicit mention that proprietary products and a limited selection of product choices is not presumptively a fiduciary breach.

**SEC.** The SEC's broad acceptance of conflicts of interest is discussed in an Institute paper covering SEC recent developments; *Conflicts of Interest and the Duty of Loyalty at the Securities & Exchange Commission.* Among these developments: The March 2013 SEC Request for Information on a potential uniform rule for advisors and brokers sets out parameters which effectively encourage conflicts and narrow the reach of fiduciary duties. Furthermore, a number of recent SEC administrative decisions dealing with conflicts rest on the premise that disclosure sufficiently addresses conflicts. The question of whether the client's best interest is served is not addressed. Finally, a February 26, 2015 speech by Julie M. Riewe, Co-Chief, Asset Management Unit (AMU) SEC Division of Enforcement, provides the rationale and analysis for concluding that disclosure alone presumptively addresses conflicts.

This broad acceptance of conflicts is part of a more fundamental view, advocated by the brokerage industry, that brokers and fiduciary advisors are, for regulatory purposes, largely indistinguishable. In March 2015, SEC Chair White discussed her support for SEC rulemaking on a uniform standard. In part, she explained: *"You have to think long and hard before you regulate differently, essentially identical conduct."*[ii]

White seems to suggest that whatever differences there may be between advisors and brokers, from a regulatory view today these differences are immaterial. This would seem to mean that investment advisors, who are compensated and contractually obliged to be fiduciaries to their clients, are no different from broker-dealers, who are compensated and contractually obligated *"to distribute the very securities that they provide advice and recommendations on to investors."*[iii]

## The "Conflicts are Harmful" view is supported in law and logic and common sense — and by many investor and advisor groups

On the other side, the DOL, investor advocates, the association of state securities regulators, NASAA and advisor groups are the bulwark of the defense of fiduciary duties. These groups reject the "Conflicts are OK" premise. Instead, they advocate that conflicts of interest are inherently harmful and should be avoided. Unavoidable conflicts must be managed to minimize their harm to clients. The inherent harm that can flow from conflicts are the core rationale for the DOL COI rule, which is based on research and investor experiences. This evidence is very compelling, but it is not the only basis for concluding, "Conflicts are Harmful." Law, logic and common sense also support this conclusion.

Laby discusses the law and logic in his paper, *Selling Advice and Creating Expectations: Why brokers should be fiduciaries.*[iv] Laby starts with the Oxford English Dictionary definition of "advice" meaning "to state one's opinion as to the best course of action, to counsel, to make recommendations … (and) implicit in the "term" is that the guidance given will be the best guidance for the recipient of the advice, tantamount to a best interest standard." Laby notes, "An advisor's impartiality is implicit in the profession and the hallmark of advisor regulation."[v]

Laby notes an underlying concern of the crafters of the Advisers Act of 1940, as expressed by one participant, A. A. Berle, was "the presence of tipsters who were disguising themselves as legitimate advisors." Laby notes that "Investment counsel would advise in a client's best interest whereas other securities professionals were trying to make a sale."

Laby concludes, "When one advises another, he is purporting to provide independent, impartial information in the best interest of the recipient. This is common sense … the propensity to rely on a disinterested advisor is illustrated by a venerable common law doctrine that distinguishes between advice given by a seller and advice given by one who holds himself out as disinterested." Laby goes on to note the "rule of the disinterested advisor" dates to the 1800s and cites a case in which a court distinguished a seller of property who might be inclined towards "hyperbole" because "a reasonable buyer would understand … hyperbole (while) … the same false statement by a person purporting to be independent would result in liability."[vi]

## "This is common sense"

Laby raises a significant point that in the common discourse is rarely mentioned:[vii] That "common sense" tells us advice should be in the best interest of the recipient. Laby notes a student has a "reasonable expectation" for advice from an academic counselor to be in his or her best interest. The Oxford dictionary says common sense is "good sense and sound judgment in practical matters." Laby's point resonates — it is, "The Laby Principle." The Laby Principle should be considered broadly, as in how consumers usually apply common sense fairly well to distinguish sales and advice.

**Advice.** In practice we usually know "disinterested" advice when we see it, be it our children's pediatrician, our tax accountant or the high school college counselor. Based on our experience we reasonably believe their advice is founded on their expertise and our interests and objectives. If we were to discover our pediatrician only recommended medications from a drug company from which he received consulting fees or the counselor received payments from colleges for each enrolled student, we'd be very upset. We'd feel — at a minimum — that a trust had been violated.

**Sales.** In practice we also usually know sales when we see it; whether a real estate agent, Home Depot representative or our favorite clothier, there's no mystery. We know he or she is more interested and (perhaps) incentivized to make a sale than to carefully assess what is in our best interest. This is not to criticize; this is to say the obvious. Sales is not the same thing as advice. It's also to say most of us would probably agree that many salespeople and business owners enjoy great reputations *from* — not despite — their sales aptitude. Many consumers have great stories they tell about these people and their companies.

This is, perhaps, to also stress the obvious: It's not product recommendations and sales that are a problem; it's opacity, contradictory messages and misunderstandings over basic notions that are a problem. For 30 years many brokers have simultaneously boasted "trusted advice" while widely following broker-dealer sales rules. Have these mixed signals "short-circuited" investors? Some research suggests so. Today, it's hard for investors to know sales from advice, or much else about their own advisors. Investors can't tell the difference between an advisor and broker or fiduciary and suitability, or (if they can) they doubt it matters. They often ignore disclosures or misunderstand those they do read. Many investors don't even know what these services cost or they believe they are "free."[viii]

**Sales and BD Rules.** This reminds us of two facts. First, financial services seems associated with more than its share of inexplicable (irrational) investor behavior. Second, compared to other sales transactions, broker-dealer rules often handcuff brokers. They disallow or rebuff brokers' efforts to be transparent, clear and client-centric. How many broker-dealers allow brokers to put a fiduciary agreement in writing? Or provide clients a list of their conflicts? Or deviate from unintelligible legalese in boiler plate contracts and disclosures? Or provide complete pricing transparency?

Strict broker-dealer sales practices are common. Yet, these practices would not be tolerated in any other sales situation. Take pricing transparency. Think for a moment if your contractor refused to tell you the cost of a new home he or she just designed, or put the price in a broad range, or if the Home Depot sales representative proudly explained how he or she was paid, if you purchased the refrigerator — but refused to tell you what you would pay. You'd laugh out loud. Or walk out. Or both.

Industry advocates repeatedly remind us that *choice* is important. They have a *certain* point. Common sense is powered by logic, experiences and values. The more that questionable practices deviate from common sense and other choices are readily available, the faster these practices will be replaced.

## Common sense "good advice"

The battle to define good advice has been waged for centuries. Its course has been closely followed since the Advisers Act of 1940. 2016 is set to be a tipping point because, as the millennial tells his dad, "The world is changing." Despite industry opposition, key regulatory, technological and market forces are aligning with history and law. The DOL rule is key. A new frame for advice is fast evolving. Its core is the principle that good advice is disinterested advice and this *is* common sense — fair and reasonable and consistent with our experiences with sales and advice. This is the Laby Principle.

This is also a driving force in crafting the Institute's Best Practices for Financial Advisors. Best Practices seek to describe plainly and concretely the basis for what "good advice" requires that advisors do. The goal of the Best Practices is to contribute to the missions of industry pioneers who helped craft the Advisers Act and, then again, founded financial planning and fought for what it could become. The institute's Best Practices for Financial Advisors offers descriptions or a baseline of what good advice requires of advisors.

---

i.   On December 12, 1969, 13 men met at Chicago O'Hare Airport. "In The History of Financial Planning," Denby Brandon and Oliver Welch write, "These men came out of curiosity and a sense of shared mission: to raise the level of professionalism in retail financial services and to make "financial consulting" rather than salesmanship the driving force of their industry."

ii.  http://www.wsj.com/articles/sec-head-seeks-uniformity-in-fiduciary-duties-among-brokers-advisers-1426607955

   It should be noted that certain SEC staffers have spoken out eloquently, in their individual capacities and not on behalf of the SEC, against conflicts of interest.

   In 2012, Carlo V. di Florio, then Director, SEC Office of Compliance Inspections and Examinations, spoke bluntly about why conflicts of interest are so important to the SEC.

   http://www.sec.gov/News/Speech/Detail/Speech/1365171491600#.VRBoKI4sq6U

   "Conflicts of interest can be thought of as the viruses that threaten the organization's well-being. ... These viruses come in a vast array of constantly mutating formats, and if not eliminated or neutralized, even the simplest virus is a mortal threat to the body."

Further, of course, RIAs, are directed to "seek to" avoid conflicts in instructions on the ADV Part 2. "As a fiduciary, you also must seek to avoid conflicts of interest with your clients, and at a minimum, make full disclosure of all material conflicts of interest between you and your clients that could affect the advisory relationship."

iii. Securities attorney Michael Koffler makes this point in: "Six Degrees of Separation: Principles to Guide The Regulation of Broker-Dealers and Investment Advisers," BNA's Securities Regulation & Law Report (April 27, 2009).

iv. Selling Advice and Creating Expectations: Why Brokers Should be Fiduciaries, 87 Washington Law Review 707 (2012).

v. Ibid, 767.

vi. Ibid, 769.

vii. While I have not read all 3,000 comment letters to the DOL, the argument of "common sense" (to my knowledge) has been completely absent from the discussion over the past seven years.

viii. See the Institute paper, "Fiduciary Duties Advanced in 2015 …" at www.thefiduciaryinstitute.org

**Tricia Rothschild, CFA®**
Head of Global Advisor and Wealth Management Services

**Morningstar**

Thirty-Three

# The Freedom of a Plan

## About the Author

In her role as Head of Global Advisor and Wealth Management Solutions, Tricia provides strategic direction and oversight for software, managed portfolios, data and research solutions globally across online brokerage, broker-dealer, RIA and hybrid advisor channels. With over 20 years of experience, she brings deep experience in investment research, product development, sales and marketing.

## About the Company

Morningstar is a provider of independent investment research in North America, Europe, Australia and Asia. It serves individual investors, financial advisors, asset managers and retirement plan providers and sponsors. Headquartered in Chicago, Morningstar has offices in more than 27 countries.

—⁓𝍦⁓—

## My love/hate relationship with financial plans

I have to admit it — I don't like planning. And I don't simply mean financial planning. I'm really just not a planner in general. In a small internal meeting a few months ago, our CEO commented that I was the most organized person in the room. The president of our firm, whose desk is next to mine and who sees me in action every day, actually laughed out loud at that notion. And it's true … if I'm being honest, I believe that planning can be hard, boring and offers no immediate gratification. I like the spontaneity that comes with *not* planning. Some of the best outcomes in my life — and my work — have unfolded without a plan. In my mind, too much planning stomps the spark out of an opportunity that might lead to an adventure or an amazing outcome that you otherwise just couldn't have imagined.

Even though I'm not a planning poster child, I am ambitious — and I care deeply about meeting my goals. And therein lies the paradox. I want to feel confident enough in my future that I can take risks from time to time. I do recognize complexity when I see it, and I understand my limits. I know that I don't want to spend my limited free time thinking about how to minimize taxes. I also know that my Chartered Financial Analyst (CFA®) coursework didn't begin to cover the impact and financial tradeoffs related to caring for my elderly mom, managing college costs for my three children, evaluating the potential sale of my husband's business or accounting for our future health care costs.

Yes, it's clear to me that financial planning ranks right up there with access to quality medical care in terms of what I — and others — need in order to live life to its fullest. So why is it so hard for me to prioritize it? Why has it been so hard for our *industry* to prioritize it? Do we even have a shared definition of what we're talking about when we use the phrase "financial planning?"

## Can we call it something different?

First of all, I think we have the language all wrong. A plan sounds like something that nags at me; it implies something that is either really tedious or that I'm not likely to complete. At the very least, I am likely to fall short of the ideal plan, "…the best-laid plans of mice and men, often go awry…" as Robert Burns' poem says. It's kind of depressing. A "plan" doesn't draw me in; it doesn't inspire me. I would love to see a re-labeling of financial planning — maybe "financial roadmapping" or "financial journeying," or even something more staid like "wealth development." Something with a bit of optimism, a sense of ongoing change and possibility and an expectation of fulfillment.

## Inverting the value stack

Second, we in the industry really need to embrace the new "value stack" of financial services. By this I mean that what we focused on yesterday is not what we should focus on in the future. We have failed as an industry to cohesively articulate the tremendous value delivered to an investor through a comprehensive financial plan. By and large, we've done a fine job of establishing liquid markets that enable a wide range of folks of varying income levels to participate democratically. But a large portion of the profits that we've made in our industry has been based on the investment piece of the puzzle — not the planning piece of the puzzle. There is something about trading and transactions and short-term, benchmark-driven scorecards that is inherently more alluring, less "messy" and actually easier to manage than the intimate and idiosyncratic business of a client's personal situation. The best advisors in the industry know this. Even though they perhaps haven't explicitly charged for it, they work nobly to deliver the behavioral coaching and "financial concierge" services that a commitment to financial planning requires.

But this value hasn't been widely articulated. Rather, investment "products" are where the value stack has historically been weighted. I remember when I was a young mutual-fund analyst in the mid-1990s, and I heard someone in the industry refer to a mutual fund as a "product." The term was appalling to me and my Morningstar colleagues. A mutual fund is not a tube of toothpaste! But, little by little, I started to understand how and why fund manufacturers needed to create products that would sell, that would be differentiated from the competition and that would attract customers … and it started to seem that maybe the toothpaste analogy was not too far off the mark.

And, investing in a vacuum — without an actual client portfolio — is clearly easier to measure and easier to compensate for. It's easier to sell the tube of toothpaste than it is to coach and manage a patient toward a life of good dental hygiene! Yet, thankfully, the value stack is inverting, such that the perceived value of investment selection and "investing in a vacuum" is beginning to wane and the perceived value of financial planning is on the rise — and this I would argue, is well-deserved.

## Re-tooling for the future

It is going to be extremely hard for many of the largest firms in our industry to adapt to this reality. I applaud all of the firms that are trying to reorient their businesses to continue to serve investors in a more holistic way. But I think we need to be honest about the re-tooling that is required in order for us to fulfill the potential opportunity in front of us.

This re-tooling will require at least three things. First, we need to be clear on the skills required. The skills that brought success to many people when "investment products" were at the core of the value stack are not going provide success in the future. The broker of yesterday does not necessarily have the skills or the interest in delivering high-quality financial planning services. It's impressive that one of the country's largest wirehouses hired a psychologist to sit with each branch of advisors to discuss how the advisors could add value through behavioral coaching, and how they could shift the conversation from the investments themselves to the emotions (including fear, ambivalence and anxiety) that investing might provoke. It's great to see automated-advice firms attract people who would never pick "investor" out of a list of words that they use to describe themselves. The simple and visually appealing websites that these innovative firms are designing make the investing process relevant for thousands of "non-investors." But there is much work to be done to equip the majority of advisors with the tools and support they need to have these essential conversations — particularly across generations and genders — and not just with the archaic "head of household."

Second, we need to restructure the industry's standard fee and service model so that it is more tailored to the client's need. For people who have a straightforward situation and modest means, 100 basis points per year in fees is probably too high. For people with complex situations and considerable means, 100 basis points may be too little. And for people whose situations are in flux — meaning they had been in the "simple bucket" but are moving toward the complex end of the spectrum or vice versa — the successful advisory firm will find a way to meet these folks where they're at and offer a service model to accommodate them. I'm encouraged by the conversations that I've had over the past year with thoughtful independent Registered Investment Advisors (RIAs) who are revisiting the spectrum of services they provide. Many of the more progressive, larger firms are also clearly focused on segmenting their client bases in a way that is more logical … albeit potentially risky to some of the established fee structures. We can move beyond the one-size-fits-all model of financial advice that we've accepted for so many years and actually begin to provide the right service, at the right price, to the right family members, at the right time. What a concept.

Third, we can use data to our advantage. It is both cool and scary to be able to collate and analyze so much data — cohort studies and predictive analytics will undoubtedly help us influence behavior for the better. This is true for many industries, not just ours. But, due to the privacy and security of financial information — unlike, say, movie preferences or travel recommendations — we need to be very clear on who owns the client's data, who owns the advisor's data and what rights are associated with these various data sets. Using the client's data to best meet his or her needs is the fundamental challenge — and promise — of the future of financial planning.

One way to accomplish this is through the creation of personalized, goal-based performance reporting. I can't wait for the day when the closing level of the Dow or the S&P (Standard & Poor's) is not reported nightly on radio broadcasts. Instead, I'll be personally and automatically alerted that my total wealth barometer is still in equilibrium. (Inevitably, the next alert I receive will tell me that my son is waiting for his allowance to be automatically deposited into his account ... but that's OK! Progress works both ways.)

## What is a quality financial plan?

So this brings me back to the underlying question of what constitutes a good financial plan. Let me sum it up. A quality financial plan is:

1) Energizing and engaging, not pejorative or painful.
2) As important as high-quality medical care ... and worthy of the same level of care and thoroughness. It's not a "loss leader" on the way to selling something else.
3) Delivered by people with skills that are likely to be quite different from those previously fostered and rewarded by our industry's traditional emphasis on "investment product" sales.
4) Paid for via a modular "fee for service" pricing model rather than the historic "one-size-fits-all" pricing model.
5) Backed by solid data that is not generic and readily commoditized, as has traditionally been the norm. Rather, the data is gathered from all of the relevant sources in the investor's life, is thoughtfully analyzed in a way that is uniquely relevant to each client and yields insight and influences behavior.

If we can do all of these things — and work together within our industry to bring this kind of positive change to the people who trust us to collaborate with them along their financial journeys — even I might be inclined to say: "Planning? Can't live without it!"

**Steve Sanduski, MBA, CFP®**
Founder

**Belay Advisor**

Thirty-Four

# Automate the Money and Focus on Transforming Lives

## About the Author

As founder and president of Belay Advisor, Steve Sanduski focuses on financial advisor coaching, business consulting and professional speaking. With more than 20 years of experience growing companies, Steve is an active blogger, podcaster, a New York Times Bestselling author, and the co-author of *Tested in the Trenches: A 9-Step Plan for Success as a New-Era Advisor* and *Avalanche: The 9 Principles for Uncovering True Wealth.*

## About the Company

Belay Advisor focuses on personalized coaching for financial advisors, strategy, technology, media and growth consulting and keynote and panel speaking. The company leverages its founder's extensive experience along with a nationwide team of experts to deliver solutions.

—ⱮⱮ—

## Good financial advice is personalized, objective and easy to understand

Good financial advice is completely personalized for each client. In order to do that, you must ask a lot of questions to learn the hopes, dreams, fears, obstacles and goals of the client. And the questioning goes way beyond money.

Advice must be objective, and therefore must present both sides of the coin. With every recommendation, there will be potential benefits and, in many cases, downsides. But good financial advice wouldn't be good without the presentation of both the upside and the downside.

It's easy for financial professionals to get caught up in jargon and insider language. Good financial advice is presented in language the client can understand. Only through a conversation with a client will you truly be able to determine if he or she clearly understands the ramifications of your advice.

Effective advice has to be based on solid research and sound principles, not hunches and rumors. It's important to take into consideration the behavioral aspects of that advice. For example, you might offer the best advice you can give, but for some reason, the client doesn't want to follow it. Maybe he or she thinks it's too complicated or there's too much risk. If you believe this is the best advice, but the client won't follow through with it, then it means nothing. Advice is only good when it is acted on.

## Quality through collaboration

In the days before the Internet, financial planning was mostly top-down. I'm the advisor, I'm the expert. I've got access to information that you, the client, don't. Back in the '80s, for example, if you wanted to get a stock quote you had to call your broker.

Today, all of the information that once was available only to financial professionals is now widely available on the Internet. Now because there's so much more information out there that consumers have access to, financial planning has become a collaborative process.

The financial advisor and the client identify where he or she is today and where they want to be in the future — together. Then they collaborate on the plan's creation and implementation and make any necessary adjustments to get to the desired outcome in the smoothest way possible.

Quality financial planning must also be comprehensive. It considers more than the financial aspects of a person's situation. It ought to lean toward what I call life planning. It's hard to do quality financial planning without recognizing the impact the financial plan will have on the client's life. What will he or she do with that money and how will it enable the client to live a fully realized life. It's about optimizing life outcomes, not just financial outcomes. It's about helping clients understand the trade-offs in life and making smart decisions that will generate the most happiness and well-being.

## Built-in flexibility

Planning done well means developing a financial plan that is flexible. Things happen in life, so a quality plan must have built-in flexibility. I should add that planning is never a one and done type of thing. Planning is an ongoing process and the plan should change as needed to accommodate any changes that might take place in the client's life.

## Better technology makes for better advice

I've been in this business more than 20 years. But just in the past few years, the pace of change in the technology area, as it relates to helping financial advisors do a better job with their clients, has accelerated to a near-blinding speed.

We have things like 24/7 access to client portals. We have account aggregation that enables a client and the financial advisor to see all of the client's accounts at one time, updated in real time. An advisor and a client can easily get a 360-degree view of the accounts and better information, so an advisor can deliver better advice.

Big data is another recent technology development. The trick when dealing with lots and lots of information is to be able to make sense of it. The aggregation of large amounts of information enables advisors to discover some of the nuanced information about their clients which they can then use to offer better, timelier and more personalized advice.

## Human insight

While computers are great at following commands and sifting through data, the financial advisor adds value by interpreting what the data actually means and how it applies to the client. Yes, technology automates some of the more mundane aspects of running a financial planning office. As a result of that, advisors are able to spend more time on the higher level advice that can only be delivered by humans.

Let's always remember that clients are not data. Data and the technology behind producing it should be used to enhance the client experience and deepen the client relationship. Accurate data can be used as facts. But facts don't move people. Add your insight and imbue the facts with emotion; that's when you can move people to take action.

# A renaissance in financial planning augmented by technology

As the millennial generation becomes a bigger part of the financial industry, it will be important to harness technology to make changes, particularly as to how people deliver financial advice and financial planning.

It can be a simple thing like using video over the internet to discuss the plan. The client doesn't need to come to a conference room anymore for a meeting or a discussion.

Technology already is and will continue to have a significant impact on people's ability to access advice. Take robo-advisors (online computer-driven investment management platforms), for example, they have driven down the price of basic investment management to near zero.

One of the benefits of robos is that they are dramatically expanding the range of people who can get access to professional advice.

A lot of young people I know in their 20s are using robo-advisors to fund accounts with a few thousand dollars and they're getting their first taste of financial advice and investment management. To me, that is huge. In my opinion, the earlier people can start investing, the better off they're going to be over the course of their lifetime.

Since these robo-advisors are driving down the price of basic investment management, it will force financial advisors to dramatically enhance the quality of advice and planning they deliver so they can maintain their profit margins. A successful advisor who delivers tremendous value to their clients is good for all parties.

Some firms are implementing technology that enables financial advisors to onboard clients more effectively. Making that process more efficient leaves more time for the financial advisor to have conversations with clients, to better understand their needs and therefore deliver better advice.

How you go about delivering value well beyond basic investment management is the key question you have to answer in order to thrive in the future. I believe the definition of financial advice will expand and evolve over time and, at the high end, will center around enhancing people's lives.

You will have to consciously choose a business model in order to survive in the next 10 years. Do you want to use technology to limit your client interaction and work with thousands of clients for a low fee and deliver automated, call-center type advice that is powered by artificial intelligence? Do you want to use technology to work with a small number of clients, be their human-to-human financial and life coach and deliver personalized guidance that they will pay a premium for? Technology is creating numerous possibilities for you to deliver your services. Advisors who continue with the status quo will quickly find themselves ill-equipped in a world that has passed them by. Computers will not put you out of business; they will massively change the way you do business.

Ultimately, all signs point toward a renaissance in financial planning. Financial planning will morph from focusing on money and products to focusing on a broad palette of life- and lifestyle-enhancing issues. It will shift from focusing on the destination (retirement), to the experience of living a full life in the here and now. It will go from trying to "beat the market" to "how can I transform my clients' lives?" And of course, the training to become a financial advisor will have to dramatically change, too.

## Accept and expect only the best advice

This should be really simple. An advisor should do what is best for the client using the advisor's knowledge, skills and ability. Think of a doctor. You don't go to a doctor and ask: "Are you giving me the best diagnosis and the best prescription you can based on your knowledge, skills and abilities, or, are you just giving me something that you think is suitable, may not be the best but it won't kill me?" Of course not. You expect the best the doctor has to offer as the default, period, end of story.

So then why should we expect financial advisors to act any differently? All financial professionals who offer advice and counsel to clients should, as the unbreakable default position, offer their clients their best diagnoses, their best prescriptions and their best behavioral guidance that they believe is in their clients' best interest and is the most likely course of action to get the clients to where they want to go in the smoothest way possible.

Financial advice should be more than just "suitable," but even that's not good enough.

An advisor could give his or her best counsel. But if it's bad advice because the advisor has little training or experience, the client suffers.

Rather than just having a long list of rules and regulations determined by regulators, (yes, we need some), we should dramatically raise the standards to become a financial advisor. The requirements to become a financial advisor today are ridiculously low. Pass a few tests, fill out some paperwork, and bam, you're a financial advisor. Again, using doctors as an example, they have to go to school for many years and engage in extensive on-the-job training. Accountants have rigorous training requirements, too. By raising the standards to become a financial advisor, we'll weed out those who are in it to make a fast buck, attract those who are serious about their work and dramatically elevate the profession in the eyes of the public.

We need to have the core regulatory structures in place. We need compensation models that support correct behavior as opposed to models that might encourage people to focus on how much money they can make. Ultimately, the better job you can do for your client, the more business you'll have and money you'll earn.

As time goes on and technology continues to advance, putting more information and tools into the hands of clients, financial advisors are going to need to focus on doing what is absolutely best for the client. The reason is clear: The client is getting smarter and has the information to call out the advisor if he or she is not acting in the client's best interest.

## Can quality advice be standardized?

No, you cannot standardize quality financial planning advice. People are like snowflakes; each one is unique. Advice needs to be personalized based on the specific needs of the individual client. It needs to be delivered or offered by an advisor who meets a minimum level of competency (determining that level of competency is for another book).

I am making a distinction here between investment advice and financial planning advice. Investment advice can and has been turned into a relatively automated service through so-called robo-advisors. Once we understand a client's objectives and ability to absorb risk, we have the data to develop, monitor and adjust portfolios in an automated way to reasonably meet what the client is seeking.

Financial planning advice is a different story.

You can't automate emotions, and much of financial planning is about uncovering the deep-seated desires of the client and collaborating with him or her through the stages of life. You can't automate "holding the client's hand" during turbulent times in the market and discuss how changes in portfolio values may or may not affect the client's ability to retire with dignity. You can't automate the seamless coordination of a client's tax, estate, insurance, philanthropic, investment and retirement planning goals.

Here's my simple definition of quality advice: guidance and counsel delivered by a rigorously trained financial professional that is personalized to and in the best interests of the client.

## The future for advice is bright, but...

As life continues to become more complicated and full of choices, the need for financial and life advice will continue to grow. Knowledgeable, well-trained and empathetic financial professionals will be in demand for the foreseeable future. What will change is the variety of options people have to receive advice. There may be so many choices that it becomes overwhelming for the typical investor.

Through the growing use of technology and the evolving business models of traditional financial advisors and major firms like Vanguard, which offers a technology-based investing platform with remote access to a human advisor all for a traditionally very low fee, investors now have a multitude of ways to receive advice.

Financial advisors have to make sure that we evolve in a way that is empowering and uplifting for our clients. We have to walk a mile in our clients' shoes and understand exactly what they need so we can deliver advice that fits them perfectly. We have to stop bickering about the difference between what's "suitable" for the client and "what's in the client's best interest."

Frankly, everything we do should be in the client's best interest and then we should build businesses around that. If we do that, our industry and our clients will thrive.

**Richard Scarpelli, CPA, MST, MBA, ChFC®**
Executive Director, Head of Financial Planning

UBS Financial Services, Inc.

Thirty-Five

# The Objectivity of Empathy

## About the Author

Richard Scarpelli, Head of Financial Planning at UBS Financial Services, Inc., draws on over two decades of experience working with high net worth and ultra-high net worth individuals. Richard began his career at Chase Manhattan Bank and subsequently worked at Arthur Andersen in the Private Client Services division before joining UBS. Richard is a CPA, ChFC® and has an MBA and MST from Fordham University.

---

*The views expressed herein are those of the author in his personal capacity and may not necessarily reflect the views of UBS Financial Services Inc.*

—ⱳ—

## The Process

Financial planning is more than just recommendations on various investments like stocks and bonds. It's about comprehensive financial advice that goes far beyond basic investments. Many people, including many in the financial services industry, use the term "financial planning," but the definition varies depending on whom you speak to and most use the term loosely. To most, financial planning probably means a basic retirement projection with a simple asset allocation. But financial planning goes much further.

Comprehensive financial planning involves assessing, at a very minimum, the following items:

- Client goals and objectives
- Asset allocation
- Insurance (long term care, life, disability, auto, homeowners, excess liability, etc.)
- Education planning
- Estate and gift tax planning
- Charitable planning
- Employer benefit planning
- Income tax strategies
- Advanced wealth transfer planning
- Retirement projections
- Social Security planning
- Medical and health care planning
- Concentrated equity position planning

The above list is a great foundation for financial planners. These are areas that financial planners should explore with their clients but the list is not all-inclusive. Some clients' financial situations will be more complex, resulting in a more comprehensive list of items to examine.

Before we get into the most important parts of good, high-quality planning, it is important to understand the advisor/client experience that is necessary to get the desired and optimal results. Financial planning is an ongoing process and it is very important to use an organized approach to be successful. A financial advisor should work closely with the client to properly go through the following steps:

- **Discovery and understanding:** The most critical of all steps. This is where I feel many advisors fall short. It is important to take the time to ask questions that will enable you to get a true sense of the client's goals and to collect the data needed to run a quantitative analysis. Get to know each client well, not just on a superficial level but at a very personal level where you can gain a better understanding on what actually makes clients "tick." Some thought provoking questions include:

- o Describe the one thing in your life (other than family) about which you are most passionate?
  - o What financial wisdom would you share with your children or grandchildren?
  - o What is your greatest achievement and why?

- **Analyze:** Assess the client's current financial position. First, put together a balance sheet, which will be the basis for many of the projections and advice. Run a projected cash flow analysis based on the full life expectancy of the client (and spouse, if there is one) and for unforeseen circumstances, such as the passing of a spouse or a long-term illness. Don't forget about conducting an estate analysis. How large will the client's estate be, what are the estate tax implications, what do the current documents say? Sit down with the client and discuss the analysis based on the client's current situation. Does it match the client's current goals and objectives?

- **Develop and propose a plan:** After reviewing the client's current financial position, strategize and tactically develop a detailed financial plan, including alternatives for his or her specific goals. Analyze those alternatives to ensure they quantitatively make sense, and don't forget the qualitative side. If the financial plan doesn't align with the client's goals, then it's not the right plan for that client. Reconsider the previous steps. Did you thoroughly examine the client's financial position and financial goals? Did you develop the plan with those in mind? If not, then the resulting plan will be flawed. Time and time again I have seen clients who have already done significant planning, but the plan they put in place does not meet their particular goals. One client distinctly stands out. The client wanted 90 percent of his net worth to go to charity and thought this was in the original estate plan that the estate planning attorney had implemented. But the reality was nothing was going to charity, nothing at all. So we had to make some pretty big adjustments.

- **Propose:** After conducting a quality analysis it is time to propose a financial plan that the client agrees with and desires to take the next step — putting the plan to work. In order to help facilitate this there are a number of different items planners can prepare for clients. These include: checklists, action plans, executive summaries or timelines. These items can be very valuable and help guide planners and clients down a path towards achieving a successful end result.

- **Ongoing review:** Review plans with clients on a regular basis. The review does not have to happen all at once. A quarterly approach may work better for some clients. For example, in the first quarter you can review the overall investment strategy; during the second quarter you can talk about budgeting, college planning and insurance planning; for the third quarter you can shift to estate and gift planning and in the fourth quarter you can discuss year-end planning, including charitable and income tax planning. This is just one example. You should customize the review process for each client's specific situation. Of course, if any major events change in a client's life, then those should be addressed promptly.

## See the client, be the client

An objective advisor needs a great deal of empathy where you almost have to "be the client." Become the client, focus on his/her interests, needs and goals and make decisions and recommendations from that perspective — as if you were that client — putting his/her interest first.

The human element of the advisor-client relationship is extremely important. By taking the aforementioned approach of being empathetic, open and objective, an advisor will satisfy clients and be successful over time.

## Start digging and don't stop

As I mentioned, financial planning is an ongoing, dynamic process — an in-depth discovery that continues as personal or financial situations and goals change over time. Advisors should look to develop a good, strong working relationship with their clients over a period of time. It shouldn't be one meeting and done. Financial planners who take a "one and done" approach may find their clients seeking out others who understand the need for an ongoing, evolving, dynamic relationship.

When preparing a comprehensive financial plan designed to uncover and address a client's full financial picture and plans for the future, a good financial planner will conduct an in-depth discovery exercise. This discovery exercise goes far beyond simply filling out a questionnaire and jotting down a client's goals. Anyone can do that.

Let's say a client has a goal to travel in retirement. A good advisor will dig deeper to discover as much as possible by asking questions like: "Where do you want to go? What do you like about that location? How do you want to travel — rent an RV and tour the country or explore Europe and Asia traveling first class all the way? How much do you think you're going to spend?"

Many don't ask: "Travel with whom?" There is a big difference between traveling with your wife or traveling with your wife and four children and potentially grandchildren. The point is that there are a number of thoughtful questions that can be asked that should flow like a great conversation which leads to appropriate advice on how to achieve goals. Comprehensive financial planning is about getting to the core of a client's goals and grasping what motivates clients, all while learning what the individual client wants to accomplish.

It is hard to get to know someone well enough to be able to dispense good advice. It doesn't happen in an hour or two. It takes time and patience as the client's situation is always changing.

## Don't expect all the answers right away

It's not unusual to have three or four meetings with a client before he or she is comfortable divulging personal information around sensitive topics like the current state of his or her marriage or personal feelings towards the children.

Many clients are extremely private about their medical or health conditions, but this information can significantly impact a plan and the advice you provide. In one instance, I developed a plan for a client, and he never told me he had a terminal illness. Six months later he shared the news just as I was presenting the final recommended plan!

As a financial planner, the more information you have, the better your recommendations and advice will be. After the discovery and information gathering process, it is much easier to perform analytics to make sure the financial plan makes sense. Until now, I have not mentioned software, calculators or tools because the human element of a planner working together with a client will always be a top factor in the quality of the financial plan. Without a quality planner, it can be difficult to get a quality plan. High quality advisors should be comfortable with the quality and comprehensiveness of the tool they use. Knowing the client first and then conducting the analytics puts advisors in a solid position to assess quantitatively and qualitatively the economics behind certain strategies.

## Going flat fee

Proper planning takes time, a lot of hard work and intellectual capital which in turn provide the client with tremendous value. Some advisors provide planning as an incidental service and don't charge at all for the service, others charge a separate flat fee, and some incorporate the costs into other fee arrangements, such as an asset management fee, but don't really break it out for the client.

The future of the industry, specifically financial planning, should be explored. The process and the service will continue to incorporate technology advances into the client experience and it appears inevitable that how financial planners are paid for advice is going to change.

I see a trend toward a separate flat fee for financial planning. It's in its infancy right now, but I see it coming up more often with clients and advisors. To be clear, I'm not talking about a wrap fee where you have a basis point calculation on a certain amount of assets under management (AUM). I'm talking about a pure flat fee of $5,000, $10,000, $20,000 for planning and planning related services. The value of financial planning services are becoming more apparent and important to clients around the globe, so it makes sense to them that they would pay a separate fee for that service.

In most professions, the fee structure is transparent. For example, attorneys charge by the hour, it's very straightforward and it's a number that doesn't necessarily fluctuate year to year. Going forward, I wouldn't be surprised to see more of this type of fee for planning services. It might not be by the hour, but I expect to see more flat fee arrangements.

## Technology and experience

The proper application of technology will enhance financial planning. It will reduce time-consuming tasks advisors have historically done manually that sometimes yield errors and don't add any value to the client like gathering account values from paper statements or going through credit card statements to gather expense information. Technology is improving every day where auto downloads of this type of data directly into planning software is possible.

There are also many firms providing clients with direct access to technology-based financial planning tools and possibly leaving the human advisor out of the mix. In simplest form some of these technology-based tools are provided by "Robo Advisors" where clients fill out a questionnaire, provide their current asset allocation and then click a button to get the proposed allocation with specific product recommendations that can be implemented with another click of the button. No advisor needed. This may be acceptable to some clients, but the process is missing what I believe is a critical component of developing a quality comprehensive plan — a knowledgeable and experienced financial advisor.

I expect that we will continue to see technology improvements, particularly with software that enhances the client experience. But for comprehensive planning, that type of technology ought to be used in conjunction with advisors to enable them to develop more in-depth, robust plans for their clients. Working closely with the client, and asking those meaningful questions to gain a deep understanding of the client's wants and needs, the advisor can determine the right elements for a customized plan.

Discovering and building trust between a client and an advisor will remain a human-to-human experience. Software engineers will try to replace that human element, but I don't believe they will be successful in the long run. It seems that even the most likely individuals, millennials, would rely more and more on non-human technology driven advice, but that may not necessarily be the case. The UBS Investor Watch, 1Q 2014 survey found: "While most millennials do not have a professional financial advisor, that does not mean they are self-directed, in fact, only 9 percent made their last key financial decision without consulting someone. More than any other generation, they look to their spouse, parents, and friends for financial advice, and then make a decision based on this input from multiple sources. While some do research online, they are actually no more likely than other generations to use online sources for key financial advice."

## It's hard to define it

Whether you are a client or an advisor, a large firm or a small firm, I think everyone struggles with the definition of quality financial planning and what constitutes a good quality plan. There isn't one consistent standard definition. The focus of many definitions is usually on the "plan" — the actual document that contains the analysis, assumptions and planning recommendations – and the "planning" is often overlooked. There is a difference. One is the actual document and the other is the action of taking a client through the process and generating solutions. Technology can often help with the plan but an advisor is critical for the planning. Having a highly trained and technically competent advisor can be key to getting a high quality plan and planning experience.

**Chris Scott-Hansen**
Head of Retirement

**Rose Palazzo**
Head of Financial Planning

**Morgan Stanley**

Thirty-Six

# A Purposeful Plan

## About the Authors

Chris Scott-Hansen is a managing director of Morgan Stanley Wealth Management in Investment Products & Services based in New York City. As Head of Retirement, this includes financial planning, insurance, annuities, trust services and the overall individual retirement account business of the firm. Chris spent 18 years with Morgan Stanley in the advisory and asset management space.

Rose Palazzo, Executive Director and Head of Financial Planning for Morgan Stanley Wealth Management, is responsible for managing the development and support of Morgan Stanley's financial planning offering. Rose has over 16 years of experience industry experience in financial planning and retirement income planning.

## About the Company

Founded in 1935 in New York City, Morgan Stanley operates in 43 countries and specializes in providing personalized boutique-like attention and service through the creativity of top financial professionals and global resources. The firm focuses on individuals, companies, institutions, and government agencies providing a wide range of investment banking, securities, wealth management and investment management services.

—◎—

## It starts with the client

Good financial advice begins through the discovery process — an ongoing collaboration between financial advisor and client. A good financial plan at its core is centered around the client's specific goals and investment objectives as identified through this iterative collaboration. The financial plan is the core of the relationship between the client and the financial advisor. It should play an integral part of every conversation.

Once a financial plan is formulated, a financial advisor can propose solutions which put the financial plan into motion and help the client on the path to achieving their goals. Sometimes the solutions may be product-oriented, in other cases advice-oriented, but good financial advice should always be aligned with the client's financial objectives. Everything that a financial advisor does needs to tie back to, and be consistent with, achieving the client's specific goals and needs as outlined in the financial plan.

Any time there is a course correction or deviation, the financial plan needs to be reviewed and perhaps amended to reflect new situations and assess the impact of those decisions on the client's overall financial wellbeing. Financial advisors can no longer afford to simply be brokers — the service model has evolved and their practices are evolving to reflect the transition of advice delivery from sporadic, point-in-time conversations to a continuous, ever-evolving dialogue around the client and their needs.

## Start by doing inventory

There are numerous ways to create a foundation for a good financial plan. We often begin by taking a financial inventory — a thorough assessment of the client's assets, liabilities, expenses, risks, loans, or other items that can impact the asset base. This inventory then is tied to actual portfolio implementation and ongoing management of the financial plan and the investment profile of the client. Planning that is not tied to implementation or ongoing monitoring can be helpful, but it may not lead to desired outcomes for the client.

## Sometimes it's too much

A financial plan should leave room for development and improvement over time. The initial conversation does not need to map every detail or model every scenario. Those that try to bake everything into the initial financial plan often run the risk of intimidating or pushing away the client because planning irrefutably brings to light uncomfortable conversations — conversations around death, wealth transfer, financial priorities, and moral understandings. These conversations, which are very important, can be off-putting and intrusive to clients if not based on a solid relationship and understanding with the financial advisor. Discovery informs the financial plan so it needs to be ongoing.

In many respects, financial planning can be likened to building a house. If you set a solid foundation on good ground, you can always expand to meet your evolving needs. Building too much before you are sure what your needs will be may lead to trouble down the line. In the same way, we are never going to have a perfect financial plan at the very outset that will account for all of life's possibilities. It would be foolish to try to and impossible to do. We have not seen a software package or a solution out there that does that.

What is important from the outset, however, is that the assumptions and projections which are factored into the initial financial plan be communicated to the client in a clear fashion. The factors should be realistic and the client should understand the implications of changes.

The effort the financial advisor puts in pays off when the client can express how he or she feels about potential loss, risk, or the priority of certain goals over others. All these components married with proper advice and counsel help to yield a holistic financial plan. Advice without a financial plan or standalone investment recommendations will only take an advisory relationship so far — the deficiencies will be felt over time and the client's assets may be deflected to those that can provide a balanced approach to investment advice which incorporates planning, solution advice, and implementation.

## Don't overlook emotions

One of the most valuable aspects of creating and implementing a financial plan is that it can mitigate the impact of irrational, emotion-driven actions on financial decisions. Make no mistake, money is very emotional. Goals are emotional. Life plans are emotional. Families are emotional. A smart financial advisor knows that one of his biggest hurdles is defusing these very emotions — fear when the markets are volatile, selflessness when it relates to wealth transfer, uncertainty of what the future holds, etc. Once these emotions take a grip of the conversation, it can be difficult to steer the client back. A financial plan helps chart the course. Potentially detrimental deviations from a set financial plan can easily be identified and addressed in a timely manner before they lead the client towards undesired consequences.

## Manage expectations

In many cases, an effective way to prevent negative emotions from taking over is to manage expectations through financial planning. If clients fully and completely understand their financial plans, financial advisors can keep things calm and emotions will stay in check.

A way to frame a purposeful financial plan is to explore with the client possible events. For example, what would happen if there was an unexpected death of a spouse? Obviously, we cannot predict the future, but we can try to put clients in the best situation possible by identifying and exploring as many "what ifs" as we can over time.

## Clients want people, not robots

The financial industry is constantly evolving and is one of the areas most impacted by disruptive technologies. As a result of these innovations, a dichotomy has arisen between those who feel that financial planning can be fully automated and those who purport that true financial planning can only be executed by an experienced financial professional.

We believe that neither extreme will win out in the end — the human financial advisor, empowered by sophisticated planning software, will be the ultimate victor. While there is room for standardization in planning and solution delivery through technology, the human financial advisor will not be displaced. Every client is different, their needs are different, and the approach a financial advisor should take to manage that client is different. A computer algorithm will never be able to fully account for the very human nature of financial advice delivery. The human financial advisor is capable of factoring in human emotion, human behavior and relationships. No computer to this point can empathize in the same way, nor can a computer take on discretion over financial decisions.

## Adapt to regulatory change

The industry should consolidate for its own good. There are too many firms that don't have scale, process, capabilities, infrastructure, or consistency to act in a way which responsibly supports clients in this new environment.

It is our view that larger firms have the means to quickly react to regulatory change by building out capabilities to better serve clients — many will and others have already. Smaller firms may have a harder time demonstrating to regulators that they have a process, consistency, controls and capabilities to best serve their clients. This may lead smaller firms to consider new partnerships with their larger counterparts who are well-positioned to continue to act in a world undergoing regulatory standardization.

Firms should look within themselves and ask if they are truly well-positioned to serve clients or do they need to enact change, whether subtle or radical, to better serve the client.

## The problem with standards

While regulatory standards are especially important, one of the biggest challenges we face as an industry is technological innovation outpacing the speed to implementing regulation. By the time a rule or standard is passed, interpreted and enacted, it may already be outdated. Smart, purposeful change that makes us all better is the change we should seek. Regulations should be flexible enough to accommodate the pace of innovation. We, as service providers, need to be engines of change — we cannot allow the industry to become stale and encumbered by outdated standards. Questioning the status quo is the only way we will improve. Not rethinking our approaches leaves us and our clients exposed to risk. Change needs to be encouraged even in the face of the challenges it may present.

**Joseph Sicchitano, CFP®**
Senior Vice President, Head of Wealth Planning & Advice Delivery

**Lauren Oyster, CFP®**
Senior Vice President, Wealth Planning Manager

**SunTrust Bank**

Thirty-Seven

# Moving Clients from "Could" to "Should"

## About the Authors

Joseph Sicchitano is a senior vice president, leading Wealth Planning and Advice Delivery at SunTrust. With over 23 years of experience in financial services, he led Practice Management & Consultative Sales at TIAA-CREF and Financial Planning at AXA Equitable. He began his career as a financial planner at IDS/American Express Financial Advisors.

Lauren Oyster brings over ten years of financial planning experience to her role as Senior Vice President, Wealth Planning Manager at SunTrust Bank. Starting her career with Smith Barney, she has been in roles of increasing responsibility through SunTrust Bank.

## About the Company

SunTrust Bank provides a full suite of financial services and products to meet the needs of consumer, business, corporate and institutional clients. Operating primarily in Florida, Georgia, Maryland, North Carolina, South Carolina, Tennessee, Virginia and the District of Columbia, the Bank focuses on helping clients and communities achieve financial confidence.

—————

## What is good advice?

Author Anais Nin said: "The purpose of planning is to bring the future into the present so you can act on it today." Those words serve as a perfect explanation of what a financial advisor should strive for whether framing a plan or offering advice.

Good financial advice is something a client can understand, follow and implement, and also allows for measurable advancement toward the achievement of their goals. If it doesn't do that, it's not good advice. It must also be specific, not nebulous like: "You should save more money." Of course the client should save more money, but the more important questions are how much and how should it be allocated? If a financial advisor can't answer those questions, he or she is not providing good advice.

Further, good advice is only good if it is taken. And if you want it to be taken, you have to make it easy to do. The minute a client gets frustrated he or she will stop.

Clients will realize they have received good advice if the advisor has listened, collaborated and engaged them during each conversation, and made the advice very personal and specific to their situation.

## The purpose of planning

Financial planning is a "process" through which a plan or deliverable is developed.

When thinking about financial planning, it's important to start with the assumption that financial advice is "the plan" or "deliverable" that helps a client achieve his or her goals and is really the application of wisdom. It is very specific and action-and-recipe oriented. It is the pursuit of a goal that's personal to the individual receiving or executing the advice.

By contrast, financial planning is the process of gathering the necessary personal information and applying knowledge and expertise to the unique story of your client in order to make an appropriate recommendation to your client.

This combination leads to a thorough analysis of the established plan.

## The process

When you Google "financial planning" the search produces 208 million options. But if you type in "financial planning and retirement," the number of options drops from 208 million to 35.1 million.

Many clients today are all too aware of how many options are available, but it is the job of the advisor to help clients ferret through those options and determine which are best for their unique situations.

So what's the process? How do you help clients cut through the noise of 208 million options and focus on the two or three that are best and most appropriate? It's the marriage of two things. The first is being a really good advisor — a source of wisdom, whose expertise can help to reduce the number of choices to something more manageable.

The second is marrying it to the personal context of the client — the client's unique story. How did the client get to where he or she is? What is the client trying to accomplish and what are his or her priorities? What resources does the client have available? All these unique personal elements are going to naturally shrink the universe of options.

After an advisor has determined the best option, clients often wonder how they can trust that it is in fact the best option for them and their unique situation. It goes back to the quality financial planning process mentioned earlier.

Clients cannot reach their goals with knowledge and advice alone. It's through the planning process, and the application of wisdom and advice from an advisor that enables clients to make progress toward reaching their goals. Winnowing those options down to the two or three that a client should do and then moving a client from "could" to "should" — now that is the result of great advice.

## What's a priority?

The key to being able to identify the best option is to have a clear understanding of the client's priorities. Make no mistake — the way each client looks at retirement, education or any goal may be different.

A client may say, "Given the choice between my child graduating college with debt or me handling it, I would rather deal with the debt." Or a client might say, "Being able to retire on time is a top goal." While another might say, "I will delay my retirement in order to allow my child to graduate college with no debt."

The clients are talking about the same goal, but may want to get there in different ways. It's not enough to just say, "My goal is retirement planning or my goal is education planning." You have to understand the order of their priorities.

Every goal usually has personal opinions, history and experiences. One client may prioritize education over another because of family history. Maybe the client is the first person in the family to go to college; it's important to know that.

With a few exceptions, all goals typically extend over a long period of time, which means to stay on track to meet those goals clients have to stay committed to the course of action. That's why it is so important in the early part of the planning process for both the advisor and client to understand the client's motivations, objectives and priorities.

In the end, it is the client's emotional connection to their goals and priorities that become the fuel needed to see the plan through to its conclusion.

## Financial planning is not just math

If financial planning was just math, we could hand everybody a calculator, give them the formula and they would hit their goals. But it's not that simple.

Of course, there are lots of calculations. How much the client needs to save, how to save and how to allocate those savings. But advisors need to act as counselors or coaches in addition to being financial experts. Without doing this, advisors often lead clients down the wrong path.

A well-thought-out financial plan considers all the client's resources. It takes into consideration the client's current situation like how much he or she is saving; what capacity the client has to save; and, how much money he or she is spending now.

Another important factor of good advice and planning is collaboration. If the client is involved in how the plan is developed, he or she is more likely to trust that the calculations are correct, and accurately reflect his or her needs.

For example, if you go to a doctor and the first thing he or she does is put your X-ray on a light box and says, "You see this shadow over here? That means this, that's your concern. See this line here? This is a real problem and we have to fix it."

As the patient, you're nodding away, thinking, "Yeah, yeah, that looks really serious." The doctor says, "Well, because of this I recommend this course of action and I really think we should start treatment today." You say, "I agree that is a serious problem and it should be taken care of right away, but there's one problem. The name on the X-ray is not mine."

Collaboration between the client and advisor allows both parties to see the problems, recommended solutions and how they are connected to the client's personal goals that were defined at the beginning of the process. This kind of transparency is not only vital, but has become increasingly expected.

Many times we see an advisor go through an elaborate process, but because he or she hasn't done a good job collaborating and involving the client throughout the entire process, the advisor gets to the end and realizes that the wrong goal has been solved or something has been seriously misinterpreted.

## What could happen?

Not executing a plan consistently over time and making mistakes when life throws a curve ball are the most common reasons clients do not achieve their goals.

Even though the objectives of the plan are defined and are the focus of the process, a good advisor goes beyond that. A good advisor stress tests the plan and does some contingency planning by asking, "Okay, what could possibly happen that could derail the plan?"

When there's an emergency in life, clients become emotionally charged and surrounded with the gravity of a difficult situation. They are more likely to act irrationally and are not going to be at their best for decision making. That is why there is a real need to anticipate what could go wrong and to form contingencies based on those situations when stress levels are low.

A good financial plan will look at multiple scenarios and make assumptions about what could go wrong like if a client dies early, is injured, falls ill or if the markets take a sudden tumble. If any of these were to happen, we need to know our options and what we would do.

If you can anticipate what could go wrong and determine the course of action in advance, when that situation does occur you can say, "We already planned for it." And at that moment, you can calmly execute that contingency plan and react intentionally in the context of the goals the client wishes to achieve.

## The importance of being flexible and dynamic

Let's look at the doctor example again. Practicing good medicine is not just treating one issue, but trying to treat the underlying cause of the illness, which is often uncovered in regular check-ups. It's also about staying ahead of the issues before they become acute or untreatable.

A good financial plan will shift and change over time. Therefore, the last aspect of a good plan is the ability for it to be dynamic. A good plan allows for check-ins that are purposeful, deliberate, disciplined and scheduled. These check-ins help to determine if a client is on track to achieve his or her goals and if not, the plan must be dynamic enough to allow for changes to the original calculations.

An advisor needs to follow-up with a client and collaboratively check the status of the plan and its progress. They need to diagnose if the budgeting plan or commitments are being met and that the client is being held accountable for decisions made during the planning process sessions.

Remember, being a coach sometimes means taking a client to task for his or her own good. It's equally important that the advisor guides the client in addition to holding him or her accountable by saying, "Yes, this is your goal. You said this is how much you were going to spend. Right now you're overspending." Simply put, it is critical for an advisor-client relationship to make sure that the client never runs out of money for the things that are important to him or her.

Consider pharmacists. They not only understand the potential side effects of a certain drug, but they also understand how different prescriptions interact with each other. Some drugs, if combined with certain others, could kill you. A good advisor has a similar awareness. If my spouse and I are doing a really good job accumulating money for retirement, with every dollar we accumulate, that's one less dollar that's available for me to pay for life insurance should one of us die unexpectedly. Our success in accumulating money for retirement planning contributes to the success in insulating us from an unexpected death. In contrast, there's an impact for every dollar I don't save for retirement.

Similarly, for every dollar that I accumulate for retirement, I'm continually building my estate. If I do a good job of that, while I may not have a life insurance need, I may be creating an estate planning need. I have survivorship issues with how my heirs will inherit this money. The way my wife will inherit this money is very different from the way my children will inherit it.

Good financial planning extrapolates the client's actions into other areas of the plan and understands the impact and implications of those decisions while keeping the client's goals front and center.

## The fiduciary standard — piece by piece

Fiduciary means that you're acting in the best interest of the client. As a standard, it's also the way you treat all your clients, every time. It's defined that way by the Certified Financial Planner Board of Standards (CFP Board), and now by the U.S. Department of Labor (DOL).

Best interest is defined within the context of the client's interest and only happens if you understand the client fully and completely, and do the things that we have discussed.

Let's take the fiduciary standard piece by piece.

The first piece of acting in the client's best interest is to understand the full context of the client's situation. This means the advisor thoroughly understands what the client wants to accomplish and why, then weighs that against other priorities and fully understands the resources that are available to achieve that goal.

The second piece is the math, the calculations of how clients will achieve their goals. The numbers need to be correct and based on sound data and assumptions.

The third piece of best interest is the connectivity of decision making. Understanding the implications of executing any advice against all other areas in a financial plan. For example, a decision executed by a financial advisor in one area of the financial plan may be in the best interest of that goal, but may not be in the best interest of the long-term goals when measured against the impact it has on the full financial plan.

The fourth piece implies that advisors have a standard of care that requires them to anticipate other issues or scenarios that could impact a client's goals. For example, the same decision can have different implications for different clients, like owning a rental house or if a client is a business owner and has additional risk because of how their business operates. What does that do to their liability? If you want to say that you're acting in the best interest of the client, a good financial plan requires you to anticipate these types of situations. Again, this is the implication that we're not doing this exercise simply to provide information.

The standard of care extends into making sure the actions of the plan are taken, well executed and continue to be appropriate over time. A fiduciary puts the client in the position of being able to take action and the client is able to do this because they know the process to get there was in their best interest, because it was collaborative and transparent.

## Access to Information

One last thought. The balance of power in the financial services industry is shifting at a rapid rate. There have been lots of articles and books recently like "Age of the Customer" and "To Sell Is Human," that explore how the balance of power has shifted.

It used to be *caveat emptor*, buyer beware, because the information was always in the hands of the experts, but that is no longer the trend.

Think about the old days of buying a car. When a consumer went to a dealership, the keeper of the information was the salesman. But now, with the ubiquitous availability of car data, the consumer walks onto the lot well informed, if not better informed than the salesman. The availability of information has absolutely changed the buying experience and it's the same in financial planning.

The average consumer walking around with his or her iPhone today has access to lots of information, far more than what they could get, with considerably more effort, five or 10 years ago. Access to all this information means clients expect a lot more from a service standpoint and advisors need to find a way to differentiate themselves.

A well-informed client who is holding the knowledge of what's important to him or her and what they are trying to accomplish has the advantage over an advisor. The advisor has to understand what the client is trying to accomplish just to level the playing field and catch up to the present.

An advisor must demonstrate that he or she understands the client and demonstrate that he or she has incorporated the client's unique situation into the math of the financial plan. An advisor must also be able to connect the dots as to why his or her recommendation is going to take the client closer to his or her goals and they must be specific enough for the client to execute the plan with a well-actioned recipe to achieve those goals. If an advisor is unable to do these things, the client is going to go elsewhere.

And, with the new ruling from the DOL, the advisor of the future has to understand that if he or she doesn't act as a fiduciary, the likelihood of a prospect becoming a client will be greatly diminished.

———❦———

**Don Trone, GFS®**
Co-Founder and Chief Executive Officer

3ethos

Thirty-Eight

# Standards: A Sword and a Shield

## About the Author

Don Trone, GFS® is one of the industry's foremost leaders of the fiduciary movement. Besides being the co-founder and CEO of 3ethos, he is the former Director of the Institute for Leadership at the U.S. Coast Guard Academy, founder and former President of the Foundation for Fiduciary Services, and principal founder and former CEO of fi360.

## About the Company

3ethos inspires and engages leaders who have legal, financial, professional or moral liabilities for their decision-making processes. The company develops standards, training programs and assessment instruments to help professionals understand the interrelationships between leadership, stewardship and governance.

—∽∿∿∽—

## Giving rise to a fiduciary standard

In the U.S. there are more than 8 million men and women with the legal responsibility to manage someone else's money. They are investment fiduciaries who manage more than 80 percent of our nation's liquid investable wealth. They serve as trustees, financial advisors, financial planners, portfolio managers and investment committee members of pension plans, foundations, endowments, personal trusts and money management organizations. But as critical as their function is to the fiscal health of this country, little has been done to educate and train these 8 million men and women on what it means to serve as a fiduciary.

If an investor asks a financial planner, advisor or broker whether this is the time to buy Facebook or Google – and that is the sum total of the relationship — that would not give rise to a fiduciary standard.

If a client or couple sat down with a financial planner and asked, "We have young children and would like to start saving for college. What's the best way to begin saving for their education?" If that was the extent of the relationship, it would not call for a fiduciary standard.

The term "fiduciary" comes into play in conjunction with comprehensive financial planning and investment advice, which includes discussions to fully understand a client's goals, objectives, assets and time horizons. Such planning and advice is continuous and not something offered in a single meeting or discussion. The planner or advisor needs to follow-up with the client to see how he or she is progressing toward goals and whether investments need to be readjusted.

The law is fairly clear that when somebody has a legal responsibility for the management of someone else's assets, he or she is held to a fiduciary standard of care. That standard is defined in terms of a procedurally prudent process. By law, if you are a fiduciary, you have to show the details of your decision-making process. That's what it means to be procedurally prudent. But the lack of an industry standard or the details of an industry fiduciary standard of care caught my attention 30 years ago and are what got me involved with the fiduciary movement.

Whether we are talking about a standard of care for financial advice, financial planning or a fiduciary responsibility — the challenges are the same. Regulators don't understand the industry they're charged with overseeing. Many "advocates" for industry standards are motivated more by ego and greed than by the best interests of the public. Additionally, the sales culture in the financial services industry is resistant to any initiative to define higher, professional standards of care.

## From the Coast Guard to Wall Street, with checklists

As a graduate of the United States Coast Guard Academy, I have a propensity to be concerned about the welfare of others. That's just part of the Coast Guard ethos. We serve so that others can live or, in the case of this discussion, we serve so that others can be financially more secure. I was a helicopter pilot in the Coast Guard. It placed me in an operational environment with a need for comprehensive checklists, particularly when dealing with emergency procedures.

When I came to Wall Street from the Coast Guard and began working with investment fiduciaries, I was startled to discover that the men and women who have this legal responsibility didn't have checklists and there was no defined standard of care. That's been my focus — finding the details of that checklist.

When we talk about standards, particularly fiduciary standards, the 8 million people I mentioned have a direct impact on the quality of our society. The same can be true for investment management and financial planning.

If I addressed an audience of financial advisors or planners and asked who thought he or she was doing a great job of managing their client's assets and financial plans, the vast majority would immediately raise their hands. But, if I let that question hang, you'll start to see the advisors in the audience begin to slowly lower their hands when they begin to realize that in order to answer that question effectively, they need to compare it to some sort of standard.

When they think about it for a second, their hands begin to waver and you will see the expressions on their faces change as they start thinking — compared to what? What's the benchmark? What do I measure my services against?

There are a lot of people, associations and organizations opposed to standards. People don't want to be marked or evaluated against a standard. But what our industry must understand is that standards are both a sword and a shield.

If you're not doing your job, a standard is a sword used against you. But if you are doing your job, the standard can be a shield. You can have a disgruntled client tell you that you mismanaged his or her assets or financial plan. If there's no defined standard, it's very difficult to defend yourself against such claims. On the other hand, if you have a defined standard you are hopefully able to reason with the client or his attorney that you have followed the generally recognized best practices in the industry.

## Three disciplines, five steps

In a fiduciary engagement, the process is the same whether we're talking about developing a comprehensive financial plan or an investment strategy. I would describe it as a five-step process which drills down to three disciplines: financial planning, investment management and fiduciary responsibility. All three of those disciplines share the same five-step process.

The first step is to analyze the needs of the client and determine who the key decision-makers are in the client relationship.

The second step is to gather the input that will be used to develop the client's strategy, whether that's a financial planning strategy or investment strategy. That input goes by the acronym "RATE."

The R stands for the sources and levels of the client's risks. What kind of risks is the client facing — are they investment risks, financial planning risks and the risks of the fiduciary in managing someone else's money? What are the risks?

The A represents the assets. What assets do we have at our disposal? The assets could be liquid assets, cash, stocks or securities. They could be intangibles. The assets could be goodwill, the brand or intellectual property of a company. The assets could be advisors who are available to the client. A knowledgeable client is an asset.

T is the time horizon associated with the client's goals. What are the client's goals? How much time do we have to achieve those goals?

E is the expected outcomes or short-term objectives that have to be accomplished in order to reach the client's long-term goals or objectives. For example, if a long-term goal and objective is retirement, what rate of return do we have to earn on their assets today to build a retirement account up to the necessary level for the client to reach those goals?

Once we have those inputs, the third step is to develop a strategy. What strategy has the greatest probability of achieving or covering a client's risks, assets, time horizon and expected outcomes? After the client has agreed and understands the strategy, we develop the plan into a written statement, or in the case of financial planning, it's the financial plan. In the case of investment management and a fiduciary standard, it's the investment policy statement.

After we have a financial plan or an investment policy statement, the fourth step is implementation. We start by identifying the key decision makers that need to be brought on board to implement the strategy or to implement the financial plan.

We need to reassure the client there's a clearly defined due diligence process in the selection of those key individuals. In the case of financial planning, it might be the same process as identifying the appropriate insurance carriers. If it's investment management, it may be the due diligence process to select the investment options. If it's a tax strategy, it is the due diligence process to select the appropriate accountants. With estate planning, it is the due diligence process to select the proper attorney. As it relates to implementation of an estate plan, it is establishing a budget to get the work done. By budget I mean identifying the expenses we are willing to assume to properly implement the plan.

The budget covers the necessary tools and technology. What kind of budget do we need to have in place to properly execute this strategy? In the case of investment management or investment decisions, this is also where we have the conversation about active versus passive investment strategies, conversations about using mutual funds or collective trusts versus separate account managers. Then there's the need for a conversation about a custodian. Do we want to use a broker-dealer or a separate trust agreement at a bank?

The fifth step is monitoring. We should periodically evaluate the performance to see how well the client is progressing against his goals and objectives. Here we get back to fees and expenses. Has the client been fully informed of every party that has been compensated from his account? Can we demonstrate that the compensation is fair and reasonable for the level of services being provided? We also want to step back and periodically monitor for potential conflicts of interest. Whether we're talking about investment management, financial planning or a fiduciary standard, it's the same.

## It's not a job — it's a profession

Much has changed in the 30 years since I made the transition from military pilot to investment consultant. There are more products, more investment strategies, more technology to support the financial planning and investment decision-making process and, of course, more rules and regulations. However, what has not changed are the training and licensing requirements for brokers, financial planners and investment advisors.

In most states, barbers and beauticians still undergo more training and testing. That prompts me to ask: "What will it take to make the financial services industry a profession?" To examine this question we need to define a standard of excellence for investment advice, financial planning and fiduciary services.

I should note that it's not the job of regulators to define a professional standard of care. Their job is to define the *minimum* requirements that must be met for one to conduct business. Unfortunately, regulators tend to devise complex rules and regulations that make it harder for honest investment advisors and financial planners to properly service their clients and easier for dishonest advisors and planners to hide behind the complexity of the rules. The public should never make the mistake of thinking there is a correlation between a robust regulatory environment and trust, integrity and prudent decision-making.

## Compassion and discipline to protect

People have a disdain for the subject of fiduciary. As a result, we weave the concepts of leadership and stewardship into most of today's writings about fiduciary.

We define leadership as the ability to inspire and the capacity to serve others. Stewardship is a passion and discipline to protect the long-term interests of others. Here it's important to note the distinction between stewardship and fiduciary. As the fiduciary I have a legal responsibility to manage the best interests of the client. With stewardship I have a passion and discipline to protect the long-term interests of the client, which evokes a higher standard of care.

In effect, fiduciary is a floor; the minimum legal standard of care that has to be met. In contrast, leadership and stewardship defines the ceiling. Leadership and stewardship is what defines a professional standard of care. There's a lot of attention being placed on fiduciary. The public needs to understand that fiduciary is merely a minimum standard that a broker, advisor or financial planner has to meet in order to conduct business. It's the minimum. Leadership and stewardship are the hallmark of a professional standard. That's what the public should be seeking.

## The 10 attributes of a trusted professional

Survey after survey has revealed that the vast majority of investors do not know the differences between various industry standards, particularly the variances between a fiduciary and suitability standard; nor do they care about their ignorance in this regard. What they care about is whether they can trust a financial advisor or financial planner. So important is trust, it has become the new currency of Wall Street. With that in mind, here are what I believe to be the 10 attributes of a trusted professional.

1) **Aligned:** The professional must demonstrate alignment — a consistency and continuum between his or her character, competence and courage; that he or she is passionate and disciplined about protecting the long-term interests of others.
2) **Attentive:** The professional must be an active listener and be observant; someone who can promote inclusiveness and gather information about a particular situation and use it to engage others and to foster shared reflections.
3) **Agile:** The professional must accept vulnerability and recognize that he or she doesn't have to win every argument to be in control; someone who is able to absorb more risk and be more resilient.

4) **Adaptive:** The professional must have the capacity to evolve and be able to pivot as new ideas and challenges are presented.

5) **Accepting:** The professional must be able to breakdown stereotypes, be inclusive of others and be more transparent about his or her feelings. The professional must be able to accept uncertainty with fortitude and calm.

6) **Articulate:** The professional must be genuine in both written and spoken word and be able to adapt and customize his or her communications to the audience, and be someone who can be inclusive of contentious points, yet also be affable and capable of demonstrating a sense of humor.

7) **Ardent:** The professional must be able to keep a sense of perspective in the face of adversity and to be able to see optimistic outcomes despite known risks.

8) **Action-oriented:** The professional might be the smartest person in the room, but doesn't have to prove it. He or she will have a sense of vision and feel confident to move forward when others want to gather more facts.

9) **Accountable:** The professional will be able to generate a greater return on investment (ROI) because he or she is able to do more with less and will collaborate with team members who have diverse talents and ideas. The professional will focus on issues that can be controlled and won't get hung up on missed opportunities.

10) **Authentic:** Perhaps the most important of the 10 attributes – the professional must be connected with a sense of purpose, be passionate about his or her life's work and have a well-defined process for managing key decisions.

Taken together these 10 attributes stand as a gold standard for financial planning or fiduciary best practices. They allow us to define higher, professional standards of care, not merely to articulate a baseline. They give clients a way to hold financial advisors, financial planners and investment fiduciaries accountable — as leaders who can demonstrate the capacity to be the point of inspiration for moral, ethical and prudent decision-making.

## Training the wrong way

Having spelled out the characteristics of leaders of planning and fiduciary practices, it strikes me that we've been training financial planners, advisors and brokers the wrong way. We've been teaching them all the complexities of the law and estate planning, insurance planning and investment management and all the legal liabilities. In turn, they share all of this information with their clients thinking that if they show how much they know, the clients will trust them more. In my view, this has the opposite effect and is one of the reasons why the vast majority of financial plans are never executed. It is also the main reason why the vast majority of investment strategies are abandoned at the first sight of market volatility.

## People skills are needed

Planning and investment management have become modular by bringing together the best pieces to build a more cost-effective and stronger financial or investment plan and is a trend that will obviously continue. While a robo-fiduciary or a robo-advisor may accelerate that process, the human element will not — cannot — be fully removed from our industry.

The evolutionary change we're seeing in medicine today, where technology enhances the impact of people, will be readily evident in our industry as well.

Let me provide some context by relating a tale involving a friend of mine. She was diagnosed with cancer two years ago. She has undergone major surgery and dramatic treatment. Throughout her procedures, her medical team of five doctors exhibited outstanding leadership. They showed all the qualities that I spoke about, especially the ability to inspire and the capacity to engage.

The medical world has realized that proper patient care is not quick nor does it simply involve inconsequential contact with the patient. It's about real human interaction and coming across as a person that can be trusted, that is passionate, and who obviously loves the people for whom they are caring. Love is a key word of leadership and stewardship. You'll find that the most successful financial planners and investment advisors love their cause. It's a genuine, heartfelt love.

In turn, the clients will feel that love while they are working with their advisor or planner. In the coming years, the industry is going to have to learn that lesson. I have been fighting the Certified Financial Planner Board of Standards (CFP Board) on this for six years now. The CFP Board made a determination that leadership and stewardship have absolutely no ties to financial planning whatsoever. From a theoretical practice management construct, I'd agree. But in terms of affecting a thorough financial planning process that applies a fiduciary standard, one that yields benefits that will be good for clients and makes them feel good in the process, I couldn't disagree more. This has been, is and will be a people business.

**Marcia S. Wagner, Esq.**
Founder and President

The Wagner Law Group

Thirty-Nine

# Moving Toward a Fiduciary Standard

## About the Author

Marcia S. Wagner specializes in ERISA, employee benefits and executive compensation. A *summa cum laude* graduate of Cornell University and a graduate of Harvard Law School, she has practiced law in this field for three decades. Ms. Wagner is recognized as an expert in a variety of employee benefits issues and executive compensation matters. She is a prolific author and is widely quoted in business publications and on television.

## About the Company

The Wagner Law Group was established in 1996 in order to provide premier ERISA, employee benefits and executive compensation advice. Representing a wide range of domestic and international clients, from financial advisors to publicly-traded corporations and tax-exempt institutions, the firm has offices in Boston, California, St. Louis and Florida.

—m—

## The evolution of fiduciary standards

This chapter examines existing rules relating to fiduciary duties under ERISA and the securities laws, including finalization of the expanded definition of a fiduciary and the scope of fiduciary duties under these laws. It then proceeds to consider how the conception of fiduciary duty is evolving outside the law and what may be needed to satisfy this alternative view of exemplary fiduciary conduct.

## ERISA fiduciary duties

Statutory Definition of Fiduciary. The Employee Retirement Income Security Act (ERISA) identifies when a fiduciary relationship arises and establishes the scope of fiduciary duties owed to retirement plan investors by a plan service provider. Aside from fiduciaries specifically named in the plan document, ERISA provides for three classes of fiduciaries:

- Persons who manage plan assets;[1]
- Persons with discretionary authority or responsibility for a plan's administration;[2] and
- Persons, commonly known as investment advice fiduciaries, who provide investment advice with respect to the moneys or other property of a plan for a direct or indirect fee or other compensation.[3]

Plan sponsors and financial advisors should be aware that these functional definitions, which focus on a person's authority and/or activity, can override the terms of an agreement for plan-related services by redefining the relationship between the parties and revising their respective duties.

Fiduciary Duties under ERISA. Reflecting the principles of the common law of trusts, ERISA also sets forth four standards of conduct that those who have fiduciary status must obey:

---

1   ERISA §3(21)(A)(i) provides that a person is a fiduciary with respect to a plan to the extent "he exercises any discretionary authority or discretionary control respecting management of such plan or exercises any authority or control respecting management or disposition of its assets."

2   ERISA §3(21)(A)(iii) provides that a person is a fiduciary with respect to a plan to the extent "he has any discretionary authority or discretionary responsibility in the administration of such plan."

3   ERISA §3(21)(A)(ii) provides that a person is a fiduciary with respect to a plan to the extent "he renders investment advice for a fee or other compensation, direct or indirect, with respect to any moneys or other property of such plan, or has any authority or responsibility to do so."

- Loyalty to the plan and its participants;
- Prudence, particularly in dealing with plan assets[4];
- Diversification of plan investments so as to minimize the risk of loss;
- The duty to follow the terms of the plan to the extent that they comply with ERISA.[5]

Failure to adhere to these standards can result in legal liability for plan losses. With increasing frequency, these standards are being enforced by private class action lawsuits.

## ERISA standards do not guarantee good advice

The overarching duties of an ERISA fiduciary are loyalty and prudence. The first requires a fiduciary advisor to be guided by the needs of the retirement plan client even if they conflict with the financial interests of the advisor. The second duty, prudence, is usually viewed as a procedural requirement so that it is held to be satisfied if an advisor engages in a process of thoroughly investigating a proposed investment, evaluating whether it meets the particular needs of the retirement client and documenting the rationale for either approving or rejecting the investment. The loyalty standard is intended to prevent the corruption of this process which, if followed, will result in a decision that ties in to the design of the particular retirement plan. However, neither of these standards guarantee good advice or take the long-term planning interests of plan participants into account. For example, they do not ask an advisor to step back and recommend whether participants or the plan sponsor would be better served by a defined benefit pension plan with lifetime payouts, a 401(k) plan with individual accounts or a compromise between these approaches, such as a cash balance plan.

---

4  ERISA §404(a)(1)(B) requires a fiduciary to discharge his or her duties "with the care, skill, prudence and diligence under the circumstances then prevailing that a prudent man acting in a like capacity and familiar with such matters would use in the conduct of an enterprise of a like character and with like aims." This standard of prudence is sometimes referred to as the "prudent expert" standard.
5  ERISA §404(a)(1).

# Expansion of ERISA fiduciary definition and related duties

As noted above, fiduciary status can be imposed on a person that renders investment advice with respect to plan assets for a fee or other compensation.[6] For this purpose, fiduciary status may be based on the person's conduct rather than his title or formal designation and without regard to whether the person acknowledges, accepts or is aware of such status. In order to determine when fiduciary status attaches without consent, the U.S. Department of Labor (DOL) has issued regulations specifying the criteria to be applied in deciding whether or not advisory services are fiduciary in nature.

Old Five-Factor Test. Longstanding DOL regulations set forth a five-factor test to determine whether an advisor was acting in a fiduciary capacity. This test looks to whether the advisor for a direct or indirect fee or other compensation (i) renders advice as to the value of securities or other property, or makes recommendations as to the advisability of investing in, purchasing or selling securities or property (ii) on a regular basis, (iii) pursuant to a mutual agreement, arrangement or understanding, with the plan or a plan fiduciary that (iv) the advice will serve as a primary basis for investment decisions with respect to plan assets, and (v) the advice will be individualized based on the particular needs of the plan. For purposes of the last factor, the particularized needs of the plan include such matters as investment policies or strategy, overall portfolio composition and the diversification of investments. However, advice of a more general nature, such as which asset classes are consistent with long-term investing, would not necessarily be considered particularized advice.

Over time, this definition came to be seen as outdated and no longer protective of the interests of retirement plan investors. One example of the regulation's perceived deficiency was that an advisor could take the position that advice was not provided on a *regular basis*, giving the advisor a way to escape any fiduciary responsibilities under ERISA for a one-time recommendation even if it was understood that the advice was of major importance to the recipient. Similarly, the advisor could argue that there was no mutual understanding that the advisor's recommendations would serve as a *primary basis* for the plan's investment decisions. The DOL has responded to such criticism by

---

6  ERISA §3(21)(A)(ii). The statute indicates that it does not matter whether the fee is received directly or indirectly. The receipt by a broker of a commission may be sufficient for this purpose, even though no payment has been specifically allocated to the provision of investment advice. Indirect forms of compensation, such as soft-dollar arrangements and revenue sharing under which an advisor receives something of value from an investment provider, are likely to be taken into account for purposes of determining whether an advisor has received a fee for purposes of determining fiduciary status.

seeking a considerable expansion of the definition so that it includes a much broader group of advisors.

New Fiduciary Advice Definition. The revised definition of investment advice, which will become effective in phases from June 7, 2016 to January 1, 2018, will include recommendations or advice relating to certain specified matters. As under the old rule, the subject matter of fiduciary investment advice would include recommendations relating to securities or other property, but this has been expanded to cover recommendations to take a rollover, as well as investment recommendations for rollover assets. Fiduciary advice can also consist of recommendations for hiring investment managers.

To be taken into account as fiduciary advice, these recommendations need to be made pursuant to an understanding between the advisor and the retirement plan client, but it would no longer be required that this understanding be mutual. Gone also is the requirement that the advice be a primary basis for the plan's decision, and all that is needed is that the advice factored into the decision. Moreover, if the advisor makes covered recommendations (such as investment or investment management recommendations), the advisor will automatically be deemed a fiduciary if it represents or acknowledges that it is serving as a fiduciary with respect to the advice that is being provided to the plan or IRA client. The representation or acknowledgment does not need to be in writing and could be verbal.

Exemptions. The broadening of the definition of fiduciary investment advice is so far encompassing that the DOL has found it necessary to issue a series of exceptions from the definition. These exceptions, along with the expansion of prohibited transaction exemptions, are intended to facilitate the continued delivery of investment advice under traditional business models, since it was feared that the restrictions on potentially conflicted advice and the forms of compensation received for such advice would make many advisors unwilling to continue offering this kind of service. One of these relief mechanisms, the Best Interest Class Exemption (referred to as the "BIC" Exemption) is designed to enable the new regulation's expanded class of fiduciary advisors to earn variable compensation, such as commissions and 12-1 fees, with respect to services rendered to plan and IRA clients. Retirement clients covered by the BIC Exemption include plan participants and IRA owners, as well as certain sponsors of plans with less than $50 million in assets.

Best Interests Requirement. The central requirement of the BIC Exemption is a written agreement between the fiduciary advisor and the retirement client that must contain certain mandatory provisions and warranties. This agreement must acknowledge that the advisor is a fiduciary for purposes of ERISA or the Code, as applicable, with respect to the advice to be provided under the agreement. It must also incorporate what is called the "impartial conduct standard," meaning that the advice will be in accordance with the "best interest of the retirement investor."

Even when an exception from the requirement to enter such a written contract is available, fiduciary advisors seeking to qualify under the BIC Exemption must acknowledge that they are subject to this impartial conduct standard. This new fiduciary standard is a refinement of ERISA's "prudent man standard of care" and requires an advisor to provide investment advice that reflects "the care, skill, prudence and diligence under the circumstances then prevailing that a prudent person acting in a like capacity and familiar with such matters would use in the conduct of an enterprise of like character and with like aims *based on the investment objectives, risk tolerance, financial circumstances, and needs of the Retirement Investor, without regard to the financial or other interests of the Adviser... ."*[7] (Italics added.)

To qualify for the BIC Exemption, the agreement between advisor and retirement plan client must also provide that the advisor will only earn reasonable compensation, and that no misleading statements will be made. Further, it must include various warranties from the advisor, such as the advisor's promise that it will comply with all federal and state laws, that the advisor's firm has adopted compliance policies reasonably designed to mitigate conflicts of interest, and that any incentives encouraging the advisor to make recommendations inconsistent with the "best interest" fiduciary standard have been eliminated. Finally, the agreement must not limit the advisor's liability for contract violations.

Additional conditions to qualify for the BIC Exemption include comprehensive disclosures to the client[8] and provision of a range of investments broad enough to enable

---

7  Best Interest Contract Exemption, §II(c)(1).

8  The disclosures must identify the advisor's conflicts of interest, which would presumably include the fact that the advisor can influence its own variable compensation. There must also be disclosure of the client's right to obtain complete fee information from the advisor. The advisor must indicate whether the advisor offers proprietary products or receives third party compensation such as revenue sharing. It must also include the address of the advisor's webpage disclosing all relevant compensation.

In addition to including disclosures in the written contract, the advisor must also provide certain transaction disclosures. An upfront disclosure that includes a chart displaying the cost of making the recommended investment for 1-, 5- and 10-year periods must be made. Annual disclosures of all investment and fee activity during the relevant period must also be provided to the retirement client. The advisor must also maintain a webpage with disclosures of compensation from all investments held by the client during the preceding 365-day period.

the advisor to make recommendations with respect to all of the asset classes that are reasonably necessary to serve the best interests of the client.[9]

Potential for Biased Advice. From a big picture perspective, the DOL is seeking to impose a "best interest" fiduciary standard on all types of advisors to plan sponsors, participants and IRA owners. Rather than devising a detailed "rules-based" exemption, the BIC Exemption follows a "principles-based" approach that is similar to the existing legal framework for regulating investment advisors, requiring heavy disclosures and the adoption of compliance policies. Under this standard, advisors will be expected to act prudently based on their plan client's objectives, risk tolerance and financial circumstances without regard to advisors' own financial interests. It is interesting to note, however, that the new fiduciary rule embodied by the BIC Exemption does not outlaw conflicts of interests; it merely extracts a promise that procedures will be implemented to mitigate them so that, in theory, they will not influence fiduciary advice and decision-making.

For advisors, such as brokers, who rely on product sales and commissions, there will always be an unconscious psychological bias that favors plan acquisition of insurance, annuities and other commission-laden products. Conversely, even where these products meet the needs of a plan, they may be rejected by advisors with a fee-only business model, because they are viewed as tainted by conflicts of interest. Neither of these predilections is a good basis for the delivery of prudent advice, but they are permitted under the DOL's new regulatory regime.

## Halting steps toward a uniform fiduciary standard

The 2008 Dodd-Frank financial reform law authorized the U.S. Securities and Exchange Commission to promulgate a uniform fiduciary standard for retail investment advice, and shortly before the DOL issued its revised fiduciary proposal, the chairwoman of the SEC publicly remarked that the Commission should implement a uniform fiduciary duty for broker/dealers and investment advisors where the standard is to act in the "best interest"

---

9  An advisor is permitted to offer a more limited range of investments if certain conditions are met. The firm must make a written finding that limitations on the range of investments offered do not interfere with the "best interest" fiduciary standard for providing advice. And written notice must be provided in advance to the retirement client describing the range limitations.

The advisor must also notify the retirement client if the advisor does not recommend a sufficiently broad range of investments to meet the client's needs. The DOL contemplates that an advisor may have range limitations because the firm in certain circumstances may limit its investment offering to proprietary products or investments for which the firm receives third party payments or revenue sharing.

of investors, presumably including retirement plan investors. Until such a rule, which has yet to be proposed, takes effect, investment advisors will offer advice under a best interest standard while broker/dealers will continue to adhere to a suitability rule under which recommendations must meet the client's financial situation and risk tolerance but commission-based compensation, along with its attendant conflicts of interest, is allowed.

If, as seems likely, the best interests standard is applied to broker/dealers when a uniform standard is adopted, it will not necessarily mean that brokers will be prohibited from receiving commissions and other compensation that varies depending on the product purchased with plan assets. The DOL BIC Exemption represents one way in which old compensation models could conceivably be retained. Thus, conflicts of interest might continue to be tolerated if accompanied by heavy disclosures and a contractual commitment to be guided by the client's best interests. There will be a strong incentive to adopt this approach, because fee-based advisory services may not be economically feasible for smaller accounts. Traditionally, these accounts rely more heavily on advice from brokers who can be compensated by commissions, but brokers might choose to restrict their services if this source of compensation were no longer available.

Fee-based service models are arguably geared to larger and more complex accounts and forcing smaller accounts to seek advice from advisors using this model may not result in economically efficient advice or even the best advice for these clients. On the other hand, many think that compensating advisors based on the sale of a product is an outdated concept that allows investors, large or small, to be abused. The SEC will face significant challenges in developing a uniform fiduciary standard that protects investors and still encourages good advice.

The SEC will also need to find a way to harmonize its standard with the DOL's new fiduciary rule, which as noted above, extends the ERISA standard to IRAs. If the agencies cannot reach a compromise, a broker with a client who has a brokerage account and an IRA will operate under two different standards when communicating about the different accounts, a situation which the client is almost sure to find confusing. Such a compartmentalized approach would likely result in planning and advice inadequate to meet a client's needs, because of the failure to consider all of the circumstances relevant to the client.

## Fiduciary stewardship beyond regulatory parameters

Government regulation of fiduciary relationships represents a minimum standard of conduct. From a practical perspective, these efforts aim to ensure that the amount of an advisor's compensation is no more than reasonable and that the circumstances in which compensation can vary depending on the investment product being recommended are restricted. In other words, government regulation, by its nature, is limited to preventing advisors from taking advantage of their clients and does not necessarily encourage advice that best fits the needs of plans or plan participants. Moreover, regulators are even less interested in trying to deliver assistance with respect to the long-range planning many retirement investors seek.

Fortunately, another set of expectations with respect to fiduciary services has developed on a track parallel with government regulatory efforts. In contrast to regulatory prohibitions, this alternative view emphasizes the positive benefits that can be derived from fiduciary guidance that focuses on a multitude of factors, lifetime events and needs. Planning that focusses on the investment of plan assets is only one component of the advice rendered by this new breed of fiduciary who might be described as a steward.

Financial planning by such a steward will entail predicting future asset values, cash flows and withdrawal capabilities based on all relevant factors that can be known about the client. The factors to be taken into account will include, but not be limited to, the client's life goals, wealth transfer objectives and anticipated expense levels. A quality financial plan will ensure that this person has enough money to take care of him or her in their retirement years, and good advice will mean recommending the actions that must be taken to smoothly transition from one financial phase to another.

Individual Clients. When dealing with individual clients, such as an IRA owner, this holistic approach to lifetime planning goes beyond mere asset allocation and how much of a client's assets should be placed in stocks, bonds, cash or real estate. It seeks to learn the client's personal as well as financial goals and makes a point of addressing them in the context of life events, such as marriage, divorce, the cost of educating children, as well as retirement. It builds a complete picture of the client's net worth based on a thorough analysis of bank accounts, business assets, personal property, qualified and nonqualified retirement accounts, IRAs, Social Security, annuities, investments, health insurance, life insurance, residential property and other real estate, as well as the client's liabilities. Only from this information can the advisor prepare an accurate retirement income projection, without which a truly reliable life plan cannot be developed. Having evaluated this knowledge, the advisor can then create a cash flow statement that includes the client's fixed and discretionary expenses over time. This will enable the advisor to set forth the client's options with respect to pre- and post-retirement expenditures, as well as estate planning possibilities.

Plan Clients. The evolving fiduciary standard requires a similar comprehensive approach when dealing with retirement plan clients. As with individual plan participants, plan level advice must go beyond the investment allocation of plan assets. This is not to say that investment issues can be de-emphasized. Most plans today are participant-directed individual account plans, such as 401(k) plans, and an advisor has the responsibility to ensure that such plans offer a broad range of investments covering all asset classes reasonably necessary to serve the plan's best interests. In this regard, an advisor should assist the plan sponsor in preparing an investment policy statement (IPS), which is a written document that provides the plan's investment fiduciaries with guidelines for investment management decisions.

An advisor should discuss the importance of the IPS with the plan's sponsor and, if the plan already has an IPS, determine if it needs to be modified to meet the plan's current investment needs and objectives. For example, shifting plan demographics may call for adjustment of the risk and return profile of the plan's investments. An alert advisor should identify whether this is needed and, if so, propose a change to the sponsor.

A further evolution of this concept is to include guidelines in the IPS (or in a separate fee policy statement) for reviewing the fees and expenses charged by the plan's investment funds. A separate fee policy statement may be advisable as a guide to determine reasonable compensation that may be paid to plan service providers. It is also a common best practice for plan fiduciaries to meet at reasonable intervals in order to conduct reviews of plan investments and service providers in accordance with the performance and fee standards set forth in the investment and fee policy statements. Advisors should facilitate and be prepared to provide technical assistance in these reviews.

Plan Design Issues. As noted, the scope of the fiduciary steward's holistic recommendations goes beyond investment matters. A proper matter for such an advisor's attention is whether all of a plan sponsor's benefit arrangements, welfare and retirement, and in the case of retirement plans, tax-qualified and nonqualified, taken on a stand-alone basis and in the aggregate, meet the current needs of the sponsor and plan participants. In short, a fiduciary advisor should ask whether these plans fit together.

Advisors taking a broad view of their responsibilities will also concern themselves with the methods a plan makes available to draw down retirement assets and whether the plan's decumulation policy fosters the goal of helping participants avoid running out of money after retirement. The marketplace offers a number of lifetime income solutions for 401(k) plans, including distribution annuities, longevity annuities (i.e., an annuity product with an income stream that begins at an age later than normal retirement, such as age 80) and group annuities. Advisors operating under the evolving standard of fiduciary conduct may take it upon themselves to determine if one of these products should be recommended to a plan sponsor either as a plan investment or distribution option.

This can be a particularly difficult area, because the DOL has made it clear that the selection of an annuity provider and annuity products are fiduciary acts governed by

ERISA. This imposes a duty to act prudently and solely in the interest of the plan's participants. The problem is that there is no clear guidance from the DOL that spells out what plan sponsors and other fiduciaries should do when selecting and monitoring the plan's annuity investments. Advisors can play a key role in helping plan sponsors adopt a prudent process for evaluating these products and their providers.

Operational Matters. A fiduciary advisor does not generally have responsibility for a plan's operational failures, the correction of which constitute a drain on assets and other resources of the plan sponsor. However, an advisor with a holistic approach to his or her duties may be expected to recommend systems and controls designed to prevent such failures from occurring. These failures can take many different forms, such as delinquent or inaccurate plan contributions, failure to provide required disclosures (e.g., failure to furnish expense information related to plan investment options or a blackout notice prior to suspension of plan investment changes) or not making minimum required distributions. These mistakes can be prevented with proper advice and advisors can provide invaluable service to their plan clients by making sure not only that they know the rules but that procedures are in place to correctly implement them.

## Toward enhanced stewardship

The extension of an advisor's fiduciary duties described above entails oversight and protection, the hallmarks of stewardship. The challenge for advisors in providing these advantages to their plan clients is understanding what the law requires. However, ERISA, securities and tax law and other laws affecting employee benefit plans are themselves in a state of continual change. Therefore, in order to meet the evolving definition of a fiduciary, advisors will also need to anticipate how the law is likely to change. Fortunately, the signs are there for those advisors willing to look.

**Jaleigh White, CPA**
Executive Vice President

Hilliard Lyons

Forty

# Knowledge Is Power

## About the Author

Jaleigh White, Executive Vice President and Director of Wealth Services at Hilliard Lyons, leads wealth services strategies. For more than 25 years she has integrated a comprehensive offering for high net worth clients and provided tax and wealth management services to business owners at Fifth Third Bank, Citizens Bank, Kemper CPA Group and Arthur Anderson. Jaleigh is a national speaker on topics involving wealth, executive benefits and succession planning.

## About the Company

Hilliard Lyons is a regional wealth management firm that focuses on the creation, preservation and distribution of their clients' wealth. With its founding in Louisville, Kentucky in 1854, the firm has a distinguished history in the American marketplace and currently operates 70 branches in 12 states.

—◊◊◊—

## Evolution from pension plans to 401(k) plans

My professional background goes back to the early days of the Employee Retirement Income Security Act (ERISA) of 1974. Today, we take for granted that individuals are responsible to plan for their own retirements. But 40 years ago, the idea of personal financial responsibility was still in its infancy.

When Congress enacted IRAs back in the mid-'70s, no one in the industry could have envisioned the advent of the 401(k) plan. At that time, we were asking, "How can a $2,000 IRA contribution help clients better prepare for retirement?"

During the '80s, I was a member of the American Institute of Certified Public Accountants (AICPA) retirement plan tax committee. We were helping the IRS with evaluating and defining the 401(k) regulations.

Looking back, it is stunning to me that 401(k) plans came into existence through an unintended consequence of a tax law change. The mutual fund companies were then able to utilize this small part of the tax code to change our country's retirement planning landscape.

It wasn't as if someone said, "Let's totally change the retirement system in this country." In a very short period, we went from defined benefit plans where the employer provides a monthly pension check, to a defined contribution system where the responsibility shifted to employees without a clear sense of the long-term implications.

It's important to remember that for many years pensions and Social Security satisfied most of people's retirement needs. A generation or two ago, financial planning mainly involved budgeting. A person's retirement resources were known — usually their pensions, some personal savings and Social Security — and that was it. All they needed to do was reach age 65 and Social Security and Medicare, in combination with employer benefits, would meet most of their basic retirement needs.

In the blink of an eye, historically speaking, all of the responsibility to make financial decisions was transferred to the individual. The trend that started with the evolution to 401(k) plans continues today as we turn responsibility over to individuals to save and to manage much of their own health care costs.

It's a huge shift of responsibility away from employers and the government providing for a person's needs, especially during retirement. Now, it's up the individual to determine what their financial security is going to look like.

## The necessity for financial education

As financial advisors, we feel a great deal of responsibility because our services impact so much more than just our client's discretionary income. In addition to planning for good investment outcomes, minimizing taxes or coordinating estate plans, today's advisor must help clients meet their basic retirement needs. One of the biggest risks to a client's successful retirement is longevity, which makes the role of financial planning even more critical.

The transformation towards personal responsibility has had a huge impact on what planning means, how it's done and the roles played by planners. Today, the best planners are also educators. Recent research confirms that clients prefer advisors who have good teaching skills like asking questions, informing and storytelling.

But if a person's first financial education is during adulthood, they are going to struggle to make decisions for themselves. Today, many well-educated people lack the financial acumen needed to arrive at the best outcomes.

Financial education at earlier ages is essential to ensure that everyone is equipped to start planning for retirement early in their careers. That's one reason I am a member of the AICPA National CPA Financial Literacy Commission where I help advance the CPA profession's leadership in a national effort to raise the financial literacy of all Americans. One of our goals is to raise the financial awareness of high school students through education so they are prepared to manage their financial affairs and can start planning for their retirement once they decide on college and career options.

The commission also encourages schools, parents and financial planners to participate in financial education. We need to make financial literacy a national priority because everyone needs a base level of financial knowledge to have a functional economy.

## Financial planning is now a team sport

For many reasons, as financial planning has changed, it has become more complex. It's no longer something a solo practitioner can do alone and expect to deliver a solid plan. I see planning now as a team sport with different types of specialists. Sometimes that's within a single firm, but it always involves the client's CPA, attorney and other advisors. Everyone who is advising a client has to participate in the planning process for it to be cohesive and achievable.

The value of drawing on a team of specialists and experts enables us to look at client issues through different lenses. A multifaceted view is extremely important in framing a meaningful plan.

At our firm, we keep adding specialists for disciplines that we never thought we would need. For example, we now have a professional who does nothing but build the Social Security benefit recommendations. He runs hundreds of scenarios for clients to determine when they should take Social Security based on their individual work history and goals.

Twenty years ago, the most common questions clients asked about Social Security were when to collect and where to go to sign up. Today, there are so many options and opportunities to maximize benefits across the full spectrum of retirement options. That is why it is necessary to incorporate subject matter expertise into the planning process.

It is also important to have specialists for health care, Medicare, executive compensation, income taxes (including state income tax), investments, insurance, risk management and debt management.

We have a dedicated team to deal with the needs of small business owners. A financial plan that doesn't incorporate what is often the business owner's largest asset has little chance of success.

An example of how assembling a diverse team made a difference for a client happened recently. Our client needed help with a large real estate purchase. The client said, "Okay, I just found the condo of my dreams in Florida for two million dollars. I want to close in thirty days and I want you to come back to me in two weeks with a strategy for the best way to pay for it."

Our advisor gathered a team of specialists and started by asking: "Help me figure this out. What's the best solution for this client?" The only possible way to arrive at the optimal answer was to gather everyone's expertise. In this case, the client recommendation included exercising stock options, harvesting gains and taking some losses while also taking on limited home equity debt.

No decision should ever take place in a vacuum. Answering a client's question without taking into account all implications and bringing all potential solutions into the discussion will yield a less-than-optimal answer.

## Financial plans aren't static

An effective financial plan needs to be regularly re-evaluated to adjust to changing client needs and an ever-changing environment. Financial planning is not a "one and done" event.

Building a functional plan requires very specific, personal knowledge about the client including information about their investment history, family dynamics, personal beliefs, goals and fears. Focusing only on the numbers does not make for a sound financial recommendation. Empathy and perceptiveness are also required to understand a client's true risk tolerance.

Understanding family dynamics and history also provides insights into how people process information and how adaptable they are likely to be. For married couples, planning has to involve both spouses. I never cease to be amazed that the initial discovery meetings our advisors have with clients are often the first time that both spouses have talked about key financial issues.

Along with information about the clients, a cogent financial plan has to provide a perspective on all aspects of their financial condition. It can't just be focused on investments. The plan has to touch on everything else that could impact them financially.

Goals need to be realistic in an effective financial plan. Planners need to challenge clients on the reality of their goals. Clients count on us to have frank conversations with them to make sure they are on an achievable path. The best advisors have "people skills" that enable them to challenge unrealistic client assumptions without coming across as confrontational.

Even the best plan will be of little use to the client if the agreed upon actions are never taken. Advisors can help their clients with execution accountability. That's actually one of the reasons I switched from public accounting to a financial institution. I wanted to be able to be much more involved in the execution of a client's plan. I kept seeing things break down in the execution of the client's plan and wanted to be in a position to help them throughout the process.

The best plans are those created in cooperation with the client, not for a client. Financial advisors should guide clients along the decision path so the client feels as if they're creating the plan for themselves, based on the advisor's guidance, input and ideas.

## Unintended consequences

As I watch the U.S. Department of Labor (DOL) wrestle with a new definition of fiduciary advice for retirement investors, it reminds me of early in my career and the ongoing challenges with transferring financial responsibility to the consumer.

Many elements of the regulations that are being discussed would require extensive new reporting requirements for firms and advisors who manage retirement assets for individuals. Transparency is critical and acting in our clients' best interests is an everyday objective at our firm. But I am concerned about the unintended consequences of some of the rules that are being considered.

The person I am most worried about in relation to some of the proposed regulations is the small investor, the person who needs our help the most. If it gets to the point where it's hard to recover expenses for the regulatory work we're required to do; the small investor will be harder to serve. I'm troubled about the potential for the proposed regulations to put more of a burden on small investors.

In my view, one way to deal with pending regulatory changes is to allow people to pay for services the way they want. Trying to dictate consumers' choices often muddies things up and takes away their ability to make the choices they want.

Any new government definition of fiduciary investment advice must acknowledge the need for more financial education for consumers. If we don't address the implications of the trend in pushing more responsibility for managing financial affairs onto the consumer, then any new fiduciary regulations will be a hollow gesture, creating more harm than good. Financial education needs to be part of our educational curriculum so consumers can be prepared to deal with the challenges they are being forced to tackle.

Make no mistake, everyone can benefit from professional advice, but it can't be advice taken blindly. To determine whether the advice they are receiving is valid and to be able to be active participants in the planning process, consumers need a solid base of knowledge.

Good, well-intended financial planners will be available to offer sound advice, but regulations could complicate how advice is offered. That prompts me to remind our colleagues and especially our clients that, even with all we have to contend with in our lives, knowledge is power.

58066085R00205

Made in the USA
Lexington, KY
01 December 2016